An Introduction to Object-Oriented Programming and C++

4000741

Richard S. Wiener

Lewis J. Pinson

University of Colorado at Colorado Springs

ADDISON-WESLEY PUBLISHING COMPANY

Reading, Massachusetts • Menlo Park, California • New York
Don Mills, Ontario • Wokingham, England • Amsterdam • Bonn
Sydney • Singapore • Tokyo • Madrid • San Juan

Sponsoring Editor: James T. DeWolf
Production Supervisor: Bette J. Aaronson
Production: Michael Bass & Associates
Manufacturing Supervisor: Hugh Crawford
Text Designer: R. Kharibian & Associates
Cover Designer: Marshall Henrichs

Library of Congress Cataloging-in-Publication Data

Wiener, Richard, 1941–
    An introduction to object-oriented programming and C++.

    Includes index.
    1. Object-oriented programming (Computer science)
2. C++ (Computer program language)   I. Pinson, Lewis J.   II. Title.
QA76.6.W526   1988   005.13′3   87-35076
ISBN 0-201-15413-7

8 9 10 DO 95949392

Preface

Object-oriented problem solving and object-oriented programming represent a way of thinking and a methodology for computer programming that are quite different from the usual approaches supported by structured programming languages. The powerful features of object-oriented languages support concepts that make computer problem solving a more human-like activity. With a language like C++, one can take advantage of the availability of increased hardware capability to provide more powerful software development tools at reduced cost.

C++ is a hybrid language that fuses object-oriented functionality with the features of a traditional and efficient structured language, C. C++ offers the programmer and problem solver object-oriented capability without loss of run-time or memory efficiency. Production quality code can be produced on ordinary hardware.

This book introduces the reader to the paradigm of object-oriented programming and to the C++ language. The book is aimed at intermediate-level programmers, software development professionals, and students learning C++ and object-oriented programming. (Programming experience in C is assumed.) The book might be used as a supplement in a modern software engineering course. It can also be used to support elective courses on object-oriented programming or the C++ language.

C++, developed at AT&T Bell Laboratories in the early 1980s and still evolving at the time of this writing (Fall 1987), is a superset of C that includes support for object-oriented programming. Specifically, the object-oriented language features of data abstraction, encapsulation, inheritance, and polymorphism are fully supported in C++. The C++ language goes further than Ada and Modula-2 in supporting object-oriented programming while retaining the high level of compactness and speed offered by the C programming language. It is speculated that C++ may replace C in the future, particularly for large programming projects and large software systems.

This book is partly organized around the major features of the object-oriented programming paradigm. Chapter 1 discusses object-oriented programming and its goals, features, strengths, and weaknesses. Chapters 2 and 3 focus on the non–object-oriented features of C++. Chapter 3 illustrates the C-like features of the C++ language and should help readers with only limited C programming experience because of the multitude of sample programs. Chapter 4 focuses on data-hiding and encapsulation in C++, Chapter 5 on inheritance, and Chapter 6 on polymorphism. Chapter 7 presents some major case studies that illustrate object-oriented programming in action.

The concepts in the book are supported throughout by many carefully constructed and fully tested programs. Our experience has indicated that well-chosen examples help clarify some of the difficult concepts associated with object-oriented programming and the advanced features of C++. In particular, the case studies allow the reader to see the benefits of object-oriented problem solving and C++ in practical applications. Some of the classes presented in the book may serve as foundation classes for programmers building their own re-usable software components in C++.

We are grateful for the help and encouragement given to us throughout this project by Jim DeWolf, Senior Computer Science Editor at Addison-Wesley. We are also thankful for the help given to us by Jim's assistant, John Thompson. Addison-Wesley also provided us with several helpful reviewers. They include: Mark Linton, Stanford University; Darell Long, University of California, San Diego; and Norm Meyrowitz, Brown University.

We thank Nathaniel Stitt of Guidelines Software for his support in supplying us with early versions of their outstanding C++ translator.

A group of software development professionals at AT&T, Westminster, Colorado gave us valuable suggestions and provided us the opportunity to class test an early version of the manuscript. We thank Bill Hopkins of AT&T for his insights and suggestions.

Erik Wiener's review of the manuscript and helpful suggestions throughout the project are greatly appreciated, as is Ellen Silge's careful copyediting.

Finally we thank Bjarne Stroustrup and his research group at AT&T Bell Labs for producing and continuing to refine an outstanding object-oriented software platform—namely, the C++ programming language.

Colorado Springs   R.S.W.
                                                                L.J.P.

Table of Contents

Table of Listings

1

Object-Oriented Programming

Some basic concepts and issues related to the new and exciting paradigm of object-oriented programming are introduced in this chapter. The reader may wish to read it quickly the first time for a general overview and then return after completing the book for a more enlightened consideration of the topics discussed here.

Object-oriented programming is a relatively new method for designing and implementing software systems. Its major goals are to improve programmer productivity by increasing software extensibility and reusability and to control the complexity and cost of software maintenance. When object-oriented programming is used, the design phase of software development is linked more closely to the implementation phase. As with many approaches to software design and implementation, the potential and promise of this method may surpass what is achievable in practice. Although great successes have been reported with object-oriented programming in isolated application areas, it is still too early to evaluate the relative success of object-oriented methodology in the general arena of software design and development. The goal of this book is to explore this exciting new approach to problem solving in software development and to present the new and important C++ language, which is well suited for illustrating object-oriented programming.

Object-oriented programming centers around several major concepts: abstract data types and classes, type hierarchies (subclasses), inheritance, and polymorphism. These basic concepts are introduced in this chapter.

Abstract data types are the centerpiece of object-oriented programming. An *abstract data type* is a model that encompasses a type and an associated set of operations. These operations are defined for and characterize the behavior of the underlying type.

In most object-oriented languages, a *class definition* describes the behavior of the underlying abstract data type by defining the interface to all the operations that can be performed on the underlying type. The class definition also specifies the implementation details or data structure of the type. Usually these implementation details are accessible only within the scope of the class. We call such a type a *private* type. When all or parts of the data type are accessible outside the scope of the class, we call such portions of the type *public*.

The operations that are defined on the type are also generally classified as either public or private. The public operations are those that are accessible outside the scope of the class. The private operations are accessible only within the scope of the class. In object-oriented parlance, the operations that are defined for a class are called *methods*. These methods are analogous to procedures and functions in non–object-oriented languages. If the public operations of a class are general enough to be applicable in many application areas, the class may form the basis for a reusable software component.

An *object* is a variable declared to be of a specific class. Such an object encapsulates state by containing a copy of all the fields of data (both private and public) that are defined in the class definition. Actions may be performed on such an object by invoking one or more of the methods defined in the class definition. The process of invoking a method is called sending a *message* to the object. Such a message typically contains parameters just as in a procedure or function call invocation in a non–object-oriented language. The invocation of a method (sending a message to an object) typically modifies the data stored in the particular object.

Each class variable or object represents an instance of the class. If several objects are defined to be of the same class, they will typically contain sets of values different from each other.

An object-oriented language is said to be *extensible* because the programmer can create new types that may be endowed with specific properties and whose behavior is characterized in a class definition. Objects from these new classes can be manipulated in much the same way as the predefined types provided in the programming language itself.

The object-oriented paradigm provides for hierarchies of types through subclasses. A *subclass* definition characterizes the behavior of a set of objects that inherit some of the characteristics of the parent class but acquire specialized characteristics not shared by the parent. The cost and complexity of software development may be lowered by allowing for the creation of subclasses.

Subclasses can lead to incremental problem solving. Instead of modifying existing software components (assuming that the source code for these components is available) or, worse, rewriting them, new subclasses are created from a set of baseline classes. Objects from these new subclasses form the understructure of the software architecture.

1.1   Object-Oriented Problem Solving

The architecture of an object-oriented software system is built around a set of classes that characterize the behavior of all the underlying data in the system. Objects from each class are manipulated by invoking the methods of the class;

that is, sending messages to these objects. These messages represent the actions that are taken on the set of objects.

Object-oriented programming focuses on the data to be manipulated rather than on the procedures that do the manipulating. The data form the basis for the software decomposition. Indeed, the main challenge of object-oriented software design is the decomposition of a software system into underlying data types or classes and subclasses and the definition of the properties of each of the basic classes and subclasses. The objects or class (subclass) variables correspond to the physical or logical entities in the domain of the actual problem.

The architectural framework that defines an object-oriented software system and forms the high-level design of the system reveals only a set of (sub)classes and their definitions and objects. The behavior of each class is characterized by the method interfaces. The implementation details of the methods are not part of the high-level design of the system.

In a typical object-oriented language, the interface to the methods defined in a class can be specified separately from the implementation details, allowing the design of the system to be separated from its implementation. This separation of a concept (class definition with method interfaces) from its implementation (the code that implements the data structure and algorithms of the class) is of fundamental importance in object-oriented programming and in achieving reusability and control of maintenance costs.

Reusability is enhanced in object-oriented programming because the concepts encapsulated in a class are provided in the method interfaces. The user needs to understand only the behavior of the class objects as specified in the method interfaces, without concern about their implementation. From the user's viewpoint, the method implementations are contained in a "black box" hidden from view.

Maintainability is enhanced in this approach because changes in the implementation of a data structure or algorithm (i.e., code within the class implementation) can be localized to the region of code that implements the class or part of the class. No fall-out effects are induced in the scope outside the class because the class interface is preserved. This interface forms the basis for "using" the class in terms of the actions that can be taken on the class objects from outside the scope of the class.

The major goals of object-oriented software development are to:

- Shorten the time and lower the cost of development by using reusable software components in the form of baseline classes and by employing incremental problem solving using subclasses.

- Lower the cost of software maintenance through the ability to localize changes to the implementation of one or more classes.

The reliability of an object-oriented system may be enhanced because of the high-level integration that is built into the initial design. The major pieces that make up the system are configured from the beginning and fitted together. Each major piece is defined by its abstract properties. High-level integration testing can be performed before many of the low-level details have been worked out or implemented. This contributes to improved reliability.

Object-oriented programming provides a useful platform for rapid prototyping. After the high-level decomposition of a system into classes and objects from these classes is completed, many of the important methods that characterize the behavior of the system can be quickly implemented with simple and inefficient code in order to see how the "pieces" of the system fit together. Later the implementation details can be perfected.

1.2   Classes, Objects, and Encapsulation

A closer look at classes and objects and their encapsulation is appropriate here.

A class description involves defining all the properties and features that characterize the behavior of any object that is an instance of that class.

The private section of a class definition usually defines the data structure(s) of the underlying data type. It also specifies the interface to the methods that are accessible only within the scope of the class. These methods are often used to support the implementation of the public methods. The private section of a class may sometimes include objects from other classes that can be manipulated only within the scope of the given class.

The public section of a class usually specifies the interface to the methods that form the basis for the reusability of the class across many application areas. These methods can be invoked from outside the scope of the class by sending messages to objects of the given class.

Encapsulation is the process by which individual software objects are defined. Encapsulation defines:

1. A clear boundary that encompasses the scope of all the object's internal software.

2. An interface that describes how the object interacts with other objects.

3. A protected internal implementation that gives the details of the functionality provided by the software object. The implementation details are not accessible outside the scope of the class that defines the object.

The concept of encapsulation is related to class descriptions; but it also provides a refinement on how the various components of a problem solution are grouped. The unit of encapsulation is the object, which has properties described by its class description. These properties are shared with other objects of the same class. Encapsulation as objects is more specific than saying that a class represents encapsulation. With this definition for encapsulation, each instance of a class is a separate encapsulation or component in a problem solution.

The following example introduces classes, objects and encapsulation. The abstraction of a binary search tree is briefly examined. (The search tree abstraction is examined in detail in Chapter 4.)

At the highest level, two objects are identified as being essential for representing binary search trees. The first of these objects is represented as instances of a class called tree. Since binary search trees consist of nodes, a second kind of object is represented by instances of a class called treenode.

The class treenode is characterized informally as follows:

- Instances of class treenode are the objects that form a binary search tree.

- Each treenode contains an object for determining the ordering relationship of data in the structure.

- A binary treenode contains objects that point to the left and right subtrees.

The methods that define the actions that can be taken on objects of class treenode include the following:

- new_node   Create a new instance of class treenode

- key   Return field of the data stored in the node that determines the ordering of the tree

- left   Return the left child node of the given node

- right   Return the right child node of the given node

Figure 1.1 depicts class treenode.

```
Class TreeNode
    private
        object ordering relation
        object left__subtree
        object right__subtree
    public
        method new__node
        method key
        method left
        method right
```

Figure 1.1
Depiction of class treenode.

Figure 1.2
Depiction of
class tree.

```
Class Tree
    private
        object root_node
    public
        method define
        method insert
        method remove
        method is_present
        method display
```

The class tree is characterized informally as follows:

- Instances of class tree are binary search trees.

- A binary search tree consists of treenodes, with one special node referred to as the root node. All access to the tree object is through its root node.

- Nodes in a binary search tree are ordered relative to some key object, with lesser key values being in the left subtree and larger key values being in the right subtree for any node.

- Insertion and deletion of nodes in a binary search tree must produce an object that is a binary search tree.

The methods that define the actions that can be taken on objects of class tree include the following:

- define   Create a new tree
- insert   Insert a new node in the tree
- remove   Remove an existing node from the tree
- is_present   Determine whether a particular node is in the tree
- display   Output an ordered set of the nodes in the tree

Figure 1.2 depicts class tree.

1.3   Subclasses—Inheritance and Polymorphism

As seen in the previous sections, the object-oriented approach to problem solving uses objects for encapsulation and defines objects to be instances of classes. The classes provide, through a class description, the properties of those instances.

In this section the concept of a class hierarchy is introduced. In such a hierarchy, some classes are subordinate to others and called subclasses or, as in C++, *derived classes*. Subclasses are considered to be special cases of the class under which they are grouped in the hierarchy. The lower levels in a class hierarchy usually represent an increased specialization, and higher levels usually represent more generalization.

In most object-oriented languages, if class P is a parent of subclass S, then an object s, of subclass S, can be used wherever an object p, of parent class P, can be used. This implies that a common set of messages (i.e., operations) can be sent to objects of class P and class S. When the same message can be sent to objects of a parent class and objects of its subclasses, this is defined as *polymorphism*.

Polymorphism allows each object to respond to a common message format in a manner appropriate to the subclass from which the object is taken. For example, a method print may be defined to output some fields of data that characterize the state of an object. Polymorphism allows the same message, print, to be sent to all objects within a class and its subclasses such that each object knows how to respond to this message, perhaps in a different way than objects from other subclasses. For example, different data fields may be output for objects from each of the different subclasses. The ability to use the same message for a similar operation on different kinds of objects is consistent with the way human beings think about solving problems. It is not natural to use different terminology for printing integers, floating point numbers, characters, strings of characters, and data records. Polymorphism is a key feature in the object-oriented paradigm for problem solving.

Different object-oriented languages provide a range of capability relating to the extent to which objects of a subclass may inherit, extend, or override the characteristics of the parent class. Some object-oriented languages support multiple inheritance, in which a subclass has more than one parent class. Chapter 5 focuses on inheritance and subclasses in C++, and Chapter 6 focuses on polymorphism.

1.4   Challenges in Object-Oriented Programming

Some of the challenges in object-oriented programming are partitioning software into classes, adding functionality to an existing software system, and constructing an appropriate hierarchy of types and subtypes.

1.4.1   Partitioning software into classes

For the beginning object-oriented programmer, modeling a process as a class may seem unnatural. For example, in writing a rollbook database program that stores, modifies, and deletes students' names and grades and prints reports of these names and grades, the typical approach would be to define a data type rollbook and then define the methods insert, delete, modify, and print as operations associated with the underlying data type rollbook.

The operations of insert, delete, and modify may be more properly associated with a process called edit than with a type called rollbook. Thus, the process edit can be declared as a class. This edit class could then be reused in other applications that require on-line interactive editing of database information. The class rollbook could contain an object of class edit to accomplish the insertion, deletion, and modification of names and grades.

1.4.2   Adding functionality to an existing software system

Each function or procedure in an object-oriented program is associated with a class. As new functions are added to an existing system, the designer or programmer must decide whether to add the particular procedure to an existing class, create a new class, or create a subclass.

The issue of reusability is a principal factor in determining where new functionality should be added to an object-oriented system. If the added functionality can be reused by objects from several existing classes, it may be reasonable to create a new class based on the function or procedure. If the implementation of the new function requires access to the internal details of an existing type, it may be reasonable to add the new function as an additional method to an existing class. If the new function represents a modification of an existing function (method) from a given class, it may be reasonable to create a subclass and add the function to this subclass as a method that overrides the similar method of the parent class.

1.4.3   Hierarchical structure of types and subtypes

One approach to creating classes and subclasses is *top-down* data type *decomposition,* in which a programmer identifies and models the major data elements in the system as classes. The top-level data components (classes) are partitioned into more specialized subclasses, and this process is continued until a hierarchical structure of classes and objects is constructed.

As an example, consider an automobile as a major class in a system. The class automobile can be partitioned into the subclasses engine, transmission, brakes, drive_train, exhaust_system, suspension, and so forth. The subclass engine, like the other subclasses, can be further partitioned into components like

Figure 1.3
Part of a class
decomposition for
an automobile.

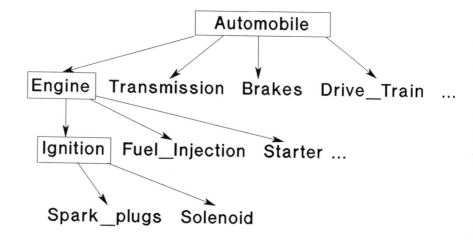

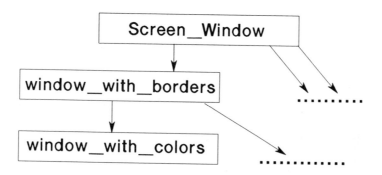

Figure 1.4
Part of a class
decomposition for
screen windows.

ignition, fuel_injection, and starter. The ignition subclass can be further partitioned into spark_plugs and solenoid. For each of the classes and subclasses, a
set of pertinent operations (methods) must be defined. Part of the class decomposition for an automobile is depicted in Figure 1.3.

Using top-down data type decomposition, the classes at the top of the hierarchy usually embody, through methods, characteristics that are common to all the
lower sections of the hierarchy.

Another approach to creating classes and subclasses is *bottom-up decomposition,* in which subclasses extend a parent class and provide greater functionality to objects of each successive subclass.

A commonly used example of bottom-up decomposition is a class screen_
window as a parent class. Such a class embodies the minimal characteristics of
all screen windows. A series of subclasses can be constructed that adds greater
functionality to the basic screen_window class, with objects of the various subclasses defining such attributes as foreground and background color, quality of
the window border, and so forth. Part of a class decomposition for screen_
window is depicted in Figure 1.4.

Exercises

1.1 Partition a software development problem of your choice into classes, subclasses, objects, and methods at the highest level of design.

1.2 Discuss an alternative decomposition of the software system of Exercise 1.1 into classes, subclasses, and objects.

1.3 What is an object in an object-oriented system?

1.4 What is a class?

1.5 What is a message?

1.6 What is a method?

1.7 Describe the principal features of object-oriented programming.

References

The reader may wish to consult the following references for general background, more specific details, or a wider overview of object-oriented programming.

Cox, Brad. *Object-Oriented Programming—An Evolutionary Approach.* Reading Mass.: Addison-Wesley, 1986.

Cox, Brad. "Message/Object Programming: An Evolutionary Change in Programming Technology," *IEEE Software,* January 1984, 50–61.

Cox, Brad, and Bill Hunt. "Objects, Icons, and Software IC's," *BYTE Magazine, 11*(8), August 1986, 161–176.

Ford, Gary, and Richard Wiener. *Modula-2—A Software Development Approach.* New York: Wiley, 1986.

Goldberg, Adele, and David Robson. *Smalltalk-80: The Language and Its Implementation.* Reading, Mass.: Addison-Wesley, 1983.

Halbert, Daniel, and Patrick O'Brien. "Using Types and Inheritance in Object-Oriented Programming," *IEEE Software,* September 1987, 71–79.

Kaehler, Ted, and Dave Patterson. *A Taste of Smalltalk.* New York: Norton, 1986.

Meyer, Bertrand. "Reusability: The Case For Object-Oriented Design," *IEEE Software,* March 1987, 50–64.

Meyer, Bertrand. "Genericity versus Inheritance," *Proceedings of ACM Conference on Object-Oriented Programming,* Portland, Ore., November 1986.

Pascoe, Geoffrey. "Elements of Object-Oriented Programming," *BYTE Magazine, 11*(8), August 1986, 136–144.

Pinson, Lewis, and Richard Wiener. *An Introduction to Object-Oriented Programming and Smalltalk.* Reading, Mass.: Addison-Wesley, 1988.

Schmucker, Kurt. "MacApp: An Application Framework," *BYTE Magazine, 11*(8), August 1986, 189–194.

Stroustrup, B. *The C++ Programming Language.* Reading, Mass.: Addison-Wesley, 1986.

Tesler, Larry. "Object Pascal Report," *Structured Language World, 9*(3), 1985.

Wiener, Richard, and Richard Sincovec. *Software Engineering with Modula-2 and ADA.* New York: Wiley, 1984.

CHAPTER

2

From C to Shining C++

This chapter offers a history of C++ and the goals of its developers. Non–object-oriented features of the language are introduced. The chapter summarizes the small differences between C++ and C and highlights the significant differences between the two languages. These significant differences involve the support for object-oriented programming.

Chapter 3 greatly expands on the discussion of new non–object-oriented features, and the remaining chapters focus on the object-oriented features of C++. In particular, Chapter 4 introduces and illustrates data-hiding and encapsulation using classes. Chapter 5 introduces and illustrates subclasses. Chapter 6 introduces and illustrates polymorphism using virtual functions. Chapter 7 presents three case studies that demonstrate object-oriented programming in C++.

2.1   The Language and Its History

C++ is based on C and is a superset of C. C++ retains C's power and flexibility to deal with the hardware–software interface and low-level system programming. The efficiency, economy, and power of expression of C are retained in C++. More importantly, however, C++ provides a platform to support object-oriented programming and high-level problem abstraction. C++ goes further than ADA in its support for object-oriented programming and is similar to Modula-2 in its simplicity and support for modularity, while retaining the cutting-edge efficiency and compactness of C.

C++ is a hybrid language. The object-oriented paradigm can be exploited fully to produce a purely object-oriented solution to a problem, or C++ can be treated as a procedural language that contains some additional constructs beyond C. In practice, C++ software reflects both the procedural programming paradigm as well as the newer object-oriented paradigm. This duality in C++ presents a special challenge to the beginning C++ programmer. Not only is there a new language to learn, but there is also a new way of problem solving and thinking.

C++ derives some inspiration from BCPL and Simula67. The notion of subclass (derived class) and virtual functions is taken from Simula. The capability to overload operators and the flexibility to include declarations close to their first point of application are reminiscent of Algol68. It is clear that C++, like other modern programming languages, represents an evolution and refinement of some of the best features of previous languages. It is closest, of course, to C.

C++ was developed by Bjarne Stroustrup at Bell Labs in the early 1980s. Dr. Stroustrup developed C++ to support the writing of some complex event-driven simulations for which considerations of efficiency precluded the use of Simula67. He credits Rick Mascitti with the name of the language.

In July 1983 C++ was first installed outside of Stroustrup's language development group. In the summer of 1987, C++ was still evolving. There is no formal language standard or language committee. Dr. Stroustrup and his colleagues at AT&T Bell Labs continue to make refinements based on their growing experience with the language. They have also made a commitment to achieving a relatively high degree of stability as the language evolves.

A key design decision and commitment on the part of AT&T has been to make C++ compatible with C. This preserves the integrity of millions of lines of perfected C code, maintains the integrity of the extensive C libraries and C tools that have been developed, and provides a tremendous incentive for a C programmer to learn C++ without having to give up that which has perhaps become sacred. For many software developers a language is like a religion, so the good news for C programmers is that they do not have to abandon their religion when converting to C++. In fact, the C language itself has been influenced by the development of C++. The draft ANSI C standard contains some key features of C++, such as function prototyping.

C++ is designed to support software development on a large scale. The increased type checking present in the language, compared to C, reduces errors in C++ software systems and provides better support for multiperson programming efforts.

The most significant aspect of the C++ language (and the focus of this book) is its support for the object-oriented paradigm described in the previous chapter. To derive significant benefit from C++ requires a modification in one's approach to problem solving. Objects and their operations must be identified. Classes and their subclasses must be constructed. Concern about implementation details must be deferred until the overall structure and interplay of objects are solidified.

Because the C language allows a programmer to attain direct control of the underlying system, many C programmers work in a strictly bottom-up manner, worrying first about low-level structures and eventually weaving them together into the high-level architecture of the system. The challenge to such programmers who migrate to C++ is to partially reverse this process. Both top-down and bottom-up development should take place together. As the need for abstract objects is identified and their interplay with other abstract objects is defined, it is appropriate to begin the initial implementation of the data structures and algorithms that are encapsulated in the abstract object. Rapid prototyping involves the quick development of an implementation for a class in order to be able to test its role in relation to other classes in the system. The perfection and refinement of the implementation of each class should be deferred until the entire system structure (the set of classes and their interrelationships) has been defined.

As with all object-oriented languages, extensibility is key. It is the challenge of the object-oriented software designer to map the entities and operations of the problem as naturally as possible to the language being used to implement the solution. In most high-level programming languages this is a difficult task because of the limited number of built-in language constructs and features. For example, in many FORTRAN software systems in which the programmer must represent a set of record structures, multiple arrays of scalar data are used to represent the set of data. The multiple arrays are tied together by a common index. So, for example, if there are five datum that characterize each record, these data would be obtained by accessing the same index location in the five arrays defined to represent the array of records.

A better solution might be to define an abstract object, data_base, that can receive messages to insert, delete, access, or display information contained within the object. The manipulation of such data_base objects can then be performed in a humanlike, natural manner. For example, if one wished to insert a new record into the data_base object, one would merely do the following:

```
data_base.insert( data )
```

The data_base is an object appropriately declared, the insert function is a method suitably defined in the class that supports data_base objects, and the data parameter is the specific information that is to be added to the data_base object. The class of objects that includes data_base is not part of the underlying language. The programmer extends the language to suit the problem by defining a new class of objects or modifying an existing class (creating a subclass). This enables a much more natural mapping from the problem space to the program space (solution space) to occur. C++, like other object-oriented languages, excels in natural extensibility. The exciting challenge is to master this capability.

2.2   How C++ Enhances C in Small Ways

Although support for object-oriented programming is the most significant difference between C and C++, the newer language enhances C in small ways, also. The novel, non–object-oriented features of C++ are the following:

- Comment delimiter to the end of a line
- Name of an enumeration is a type name
- Name of a struct or class is a type name
- A declaration within a block is a statement
- Scope qualifier operator
- Const specifier
- Anonymous unions
- Explicit type conversion
- Function prototypes
- Overloading of function names
- Default values for function parameters
- Functions with an unspecified number of parameters
- Reference parameters in functions
- The inline specifier
- The new and delete operators
- Pointers to void and functions that return void

These features are explained in the following sections.

2.2.1   Comments

C++ introduces the comment to end of line delimiter, //. The comment brackets, /* and */, from C can still be used.

2.2.2   Enumeration names

The name of an enumeration is a type name. It is not necessary in C++ to use the qualifier enum in front of the enumeration type name. This streamlines notation.

2.2.3   Struct or class names

The name of a struct or class is a type name. It is not necessary in C++ to use the qualifier struct or class in front of a struct or class name. The class construct does not exist in C.

2.2.4   Declarations within blocks

C++ allows declarations within blocks and after code statements. This allows a programmer to declare an entity closer to its first point of application. It also allows an index to be declared within a loop, as follows:

```
for ( int i = 0; i < 12; i++ )
. . .
```

2.2.5   Scope qualifier operator

The new operator :: is used to resolve name conflicts. For example, if the automatic variable vector_sum is declared within a function and there exists a global variable vector_sum, the specifier ::vector_sum allows the global variable to be accessed within the scope of the automatic variable vector_sum.

The reverse is not true. It is not possible for the automatic variable vector_sum to be accessed from outside its scope. The scope qualifier :: is also used in connection with classes.

2.2.6   The const specifier

The const specifier can be used to freeze the value of an entity within its scope. It can be used to freeze the data pointed to by a pointer variable, the value of the pointer address, or the values of both the pointer address and the data pointed to.

The parameters of a function can be declared as const to freeze the value of the parameters within the function.

2.2.7   Anonymous unions

Unions without a name can be defined anywhere a variable or field can be defined. They allow sharing of memory storage among two or more fields of the struct for economy of memory storage.

2.2.8   Explicit type conversion

The name of a predefined type or programmer-defined type can be used as a function to convert data from one type to another. Such explicit type conversion is an alternative to a cast conversion.

2.2.9   Function prototypes

C++ comes closer in style to the function interfaces of Pascal, Modula-2, and ADA by allowing a programmer to specify the name and type of each function parameter inside of the parentheses next to the function name. An example of a function prototype is the following:

```
float vector_sum( float vector[ ], int size )
{
. . .
```

The commensurate C interface would be

```
float vector_sum( vector, size )
float vector[ ], int size;
{
. . .
```

The C++ translator performs type checking to ensure that the number and type of values sent into a function when it is invoked match the number and type of the formal arguments defined for the function. A check is also made to ensure that the return type for the function matches the variable used in the expression involving the function. This desirable parameter checking is missing in most C systems.

2.2.10   Overloading of function names

C++ functions can use the same names (within the same scope) if the programmer uses the specifier overload, and each of the overloaded functions can be distinguished on the basis of the number and type of its parameters.

2.2.11   Default value for function parameters

The trailing set of parameters in a C++ function can be assigned default values. In such a case, the function can be invoked using fewer than the total number of parameters. Any trailing parameters that are missing assume their default values.

2.2.12   Functions with an unspecified number of parameters

Using the ellipsis, . . . , C++ functions can be specified with an unknown number and type of parameters. This feature can be used to suppress parameter type checking and to allow flexibility in the interface to the function.

2.2.13   Reference parameters in a function

C++ allows the formal parameters of a function to be declared as reference parameters using the ampersand operator. An example is the following:

```
void increment( int &value )
{
value++;
}
int j;
increment( j );
```

Because value is defined as a reference parameter, the address of the parameter value is assigned to the address of j when increment is invoked. The value of j that is sent in is incremented within function increment and returned to variable j outside of function increment. It is not necessary for the address of j to be explicitly passed into function increment, as in C.

Reference variables can be used in a more general way in C++. They are typically used to specify operations for programmer-created types. This is illustrated in Chapter 4.

2.2.14   The inline specifier

The specifier inline can be used to instruct the compiler to perform inline substitution of a given function at the location where the function is invoked. This saves function call overhead at the expense of potentially increased code size. For small inline functions, both space and time may be saved.

2.2.15   The new and delete operators

The operators new and delete are introduced in C++ to provide reliable programmer-controlled allocation and deallocation of storage in the heap.

2.2.16   Pointers to void and functions that return void

The type void is used in C++ to indicate that a function returns nothing. Pointer variables can be declared to point to void. Such pointers can be assigned to any other pointers that point to an arbitrary base type.

2.3   How C++ Enhances C in Large Ways

Of more concern to the beginning C++ programmer than the small enhance-ments to C are the object-oriented features of C++. These important features are the following:

- The class construct and data encapsulation
- Struct as a special case of class
- Constructors and destructors
- Private, protected, and public sections
- Objects and messages
- Friends
- Overloading of operators and function names in classes
- Derived classes
- Virtual functions
- The stream library

2.3.1   The class construct and data encapsulation

The class construct in C++ provides the basic underpinning for object-oriented programming. The class serves as the vehicle for data abstraction and data hid-ing. The set of values of an abstract object and the associated set of operations (methods) can be encapsulated in a class definition. Objects can be declared to be of a given class and messages can be sent to objects. Each object of a given class contains its own private set and public set of the data representative of the class. Chapter 4 is devoted exclusively to the important role of the class in object-oriented programming in C++.

2.3.2   Struct as a special case of a class

The struct in C++ is a special case of a class with no private or protected sec-tions. As a special type of class, a struct can contain both data (the normal case in C) and functions.

2.3.3   Constructors and destructors

Constructor and destructor methods provide guaranteed initialization of the data contained within an object declared to be of a given class. The declaration of an object activates the initialization specified in a constructor. A destructor provides for automatic deallocation of the storage associated with an object when the scope in which the object is declared is exited.

2.3.4   Private, protected, and public sections

A C++ class contains up to three sections: private, protected, and public.

The data and functions (class members) declared in the *private* section of a class are not accessible outside the class. Only the functions declared within the class have access to the private data and functions of the class.

The data and functions declared in the *protected* section of a class are not accessible outside the class except within subclasses derived from the given parent class.

The data and functions declared in the *public* section of a class are available outside the class. Normally the operations that can be performed on an abstract data type are specified in the public section of the class. It is exclusively through these functions (methods) that objects of a given class are manipulated.

2.3.5   Objects and messages

Objects form the basic fabric of object-oriented programming. Objects are manipulated by sending messages to them. Each object responds to a message by determining an appropriate action to take based on the nature of the message. The set of possible messages that can be sent to an object is specified in the class description for the object. Each possible message is given by a corresponding method in the class description.

In C++, methods are defined using function prototypes in a class definition. Messages are sent to objects (variables declared to be of a given class) using a mechanism similar to function call invocation. As an example, if obj is an object, and meth is a method with a single integer parameter, the message meth(3) is sent to the object, obj, as follows:

```
obj.meth( 3 );
```

2.3.6   Friends

Another important object-oriented feature of C++ is the friend construct. Data hiding and encapsulation imply denied access to the inner structure of the abstract objects that make up a system. Normally the private section of a class (the inner structure) is totally off-limits to any function outside the class. The construct of friend allows this opaque wall to be selectively broken. One or more outside functions or an entire outside class can be declared to be a *friend* of a given class. Such a friend can access the private data and functions of the given class.

2.3.7   Overloading of operators and function names in classes

A large set of existing operators can be given new meaning within a class definition by *overloading* operators. For example, in a rational number class the operations of +, −, *, and / can be defined for rational numbers. Thus if three objects of class rational_number are declared as

```
rational_number x, y, z;
```

the following operations are valid:

```
x = y * z;
z = x / y;
y = x - z;
y = y + z;
```

The overloading of operators allows C++ to be extended into specialized domains in a natural manner.

2.3.8   Derived classes

A hierarchy of abstractions can be established using subclasses, or derived classes. Objects of a derived class can be defined so as to inherit all the methods of the parent class or only some of the methods of the parent class. In addition, new methods not contained within the parent class are usually specified that are peculiar to the subclass. Every object of a subclass contains fields of data from the parent class as well as its own private data.

2.3.9   Virtual functions

Virtual functions are used to support *polymorphism* in C++. Polymorphism involves a tree structure of parent classes and their subclasses. Each subclass within this tree can receive one or more messages with the same name. When a message is received by an object of a class within this tree, the object determines the particular application of the message that is appropriate for an object of the given subclass. Polymorphism allows for a higher level of abstraction in software design (the designer need only worry about actions, not the implementation of the actions) and provides for easier software maintenance. Chapter 6 deals exclusively with polymorphism and virtual functions.

2.3.10   The stream library

An important library, stream, is provided with every C++ implementation. The classes cin, cout, and cerr are provided for terminal and file input and output. The operators in the cin, cout, and cerr classes can be overloaded within a programmer-defined class. This allows input and output operations to be easily extended into new domains. These classes are discussed in Chapter 4.

Exercises

2.1 Describe a C++ class. How can such a class be used to model an abstract data type? (You may wish to review the discussion of data types in Chapter 1 before answering this question.)

2.2 Describe the purpose of a constructor in C++.

2.3 Describe the purpose of a destructor in C++.

2.4 Describe the difference between the private and public sections of a C++ class.

2.5 What is a friend in a C++ context?

2.6 What is meant by the overloading of operators?

2.7 Describe three contexts in which the overloading of operators might be useful.

3

Getting Up to Speed with C++

This chapter introduces the non–object-oriented new features of C++. It serves as a transition to the last four chapters that focus on the object-oriented features of this powerful language. The advanced features of C++, such as operator overloading, classes, derived classes, and virtual functions, are presented in Chapters 4, 5, 6, and 7.

This book assumes that the reader has some familiarity with C++'s substrate language, C. The programs and program segments included in this chapter are chosen to introduce C++'s new but non–object-oriented features and to review some important features of C. It has been our experience that studying carefully chosen examples is an effective way to quickly get "up to speed" with a new language.

3.1   Comments

Comments in C++, as in any other high-level language, are for the human reader only. Sections of a program marked as comments are treated like white space by the compiler.

The careful use of comments can lower the cost of maintenance and lead to more reliable software. Comments should never be used as a substitute for self-documenting software containing sensible and descriptive names for program identifiers. Comment maintenance is challenging and requires a strong commitment on the part of the programmer. No generalized tools exist for assisting in comment maintenance. Whenever a section of code is modified, it is imperative that the comments embedded in the section of code also be suitably modified.

The symbols // are used in C++ to indicate a comment to the end of a line. The older C-like comment delimiters, /* and */, can also be used to bracket a comment. The latter style is more appropriate for bracketing a multiline comment, the former for a single line comment.

3.2 Constants, Types, and Declarations

Most entities named by identifiers must be declared before they are used in C++, as in C. Such entities include constants, types, variables, and functions.

Listing 3.1 presents an assorted set of declarations.

The first declaration is of a constant, size, whose value is set at 100. The constant specifier is new in C++ and is part of the proposed new C standard. Once declared, the value of a constant cannot be changed within its scope of definition.

The next declaration is of an array with a capacity of size floating point numbers. Memory is statically allocated for this array, and the initial values of the array are set to 0.0.

The static array, title, is initialized to the string, "First program in Chapter 3." Memory allocation for this string (28 bytes) is performed at compile time.

Within the main function, two external declarations (not definitions) allow the compiler to accept references to the functions square and input_values to be defined later in the file. The first function, square, is assigned a default value for its second parameter. If only one value is passed to this function (as is actually the case in this program), the value $n = 100$ is used for the second parameter. Default parameters are an important improvement of C++ over C.

Function prototyping, in which the parameters of a function are specified within the parameter definition section of the function, is a new feature in C++ and will be incorporated in the draft ANSI standard for C. Such function prototyping allows the compiler to perform strong type checking to ensure that the user sends the correct number and type of parameters to each function. In older versions of C, the compiler would tolerate serious interface problems in passing data to functions. Using function prototyping, this common source of errors can be minimized. The C++ programmer can use the older style of C functions and bypass strong type checking if this is desired or if older C modules must be linked to a newer C++ software system.

Function square is invoked using only the first parameter in the statement

```
printf( ''\nThe sum of the square of values = %f'',
    square( data ) );
```

The correct value is returned because all the values in the global array data are initialized to zero at the point of declaration.

The reader should note that the variable i, of type int, is declared inside of the for loop, right at its point of application. This is not permissible in C.

Listing 3.1
Assorted
Declarations
in C++

```
#include <stdio.h>
const int size = 100;
float data[ size ];
char title[ ] = ''First program in Chapter 3'';
```

Listing 3.1
(continued)

```
main( )
{
    extern float square( float *value, int n = size );
    extern void input_values( float *scores, int n );

    int num_values;
    printf( "%s", title );
    printf( "\n\nHow many values must be squared: " );
    scanf( "%d", &num_values );
    input_values( data, num_values );
    printf( "\nThe sum of the square of values = %f",
            square( data ) );
}

float square( float value[ ], int n )
{
    float sum = 0.0;

    for ( int i = 0; i < n; i++ )
        sum += value[ i ] * value[ i ];
    return sum;
}

void input_values( float scores[ ], int n )
{
    for ( int i = 0; i < n; i++ )
    {
        printf( "\nEnter score %d : ", i + 1 );
        scanf( "%f", &scores[ i ] );
    }
}
```

Output for Listing 3.1 is given as:

```
First program in Chapter 3
How many values must be squared: 5
Enter score 1 : -1
Enter score 2 : -2
Enter score 3 : -3
Enter score 4 : -4
Enter score 5 : 5
The sum of the square of values = 55.000000
```

Declarations such as

```
extern float square( float value[ ], int n = 100 );
extern void input_values( float scores[ ], int n );
```

make reference to entities that are defined elsewhere (in this case, later in the program file). Declarations such as

```
const int size = 100;
float data[ size ];
char title[ ] = "First program in Chapter 3";
```

define the entities' size, data, and title. Memory is allocated at the point of declaration, and initial values are assigned in the case of all three of the above definitions.

There can be only one definition of each identifier in a C++ program. There is no limit on the number of times such an identifier can be declared. The C++ compiler (translator) ensures that all the declarations of the same entity are identical. If not, an error message is given and the translation process is halted.

Listing 3.2 introduces additional declarations. The code segment shown is part of the shell of a traffic control simulation program.

The declaration

```
typedef enum { red, green, amber } traffic_light_color;
```

introduces the user-defined type identifier traffic_light_color. Any variables declared to be of this new type can have one of the values from the value set: red, green, and amber. The type identifier traffic_light_color can be used alone without the qualifier enum attached to it.

The declaration

```
struct intersection
{
    traffic_light_color traffic_light;
    int number_cars_queued;
    int cumulative_number_cars;
};
```

introduces another user-defined type identifier, intersection. This type is a structure that contains a field, traffic_light, of type traffic_light_color (without an enum specifier); a field, number_cars_queued, of type int; and a field, cumulative_number_cars, of type int. The type identifier, intersection, is used without the qualifier struct that is required in C.

The definition (declaration)

```
intersection network[ 50 ];
```

allocates memory storage for an array of 50 intersections.

The output statement

```
cout << ''The light at the 2nd intersection is '' <<
        network[ 1 ].traffic_light;
```

produces one of the values 0, 1, or 2 depending on whether the structure field traffic_light has the value red, green, or amber. The stream operator, <<, could be overloaded to output the values red, green, or amber if the user so desires. This is shown in Listing 3.3. The reader is urged to consult Chapter 4 for details about operator overloading and the stream library.

Listing 3.2
Examples of
Additional C++
Declarations

```
#include <stream.h>
enum { red, green, amber } traffic_light_color;
struct intersection
{
    traffic_light_color traffic_light;
    int number_cars_queued;
    int cumulative_number_cars;
};

intersection network[ 50 ];

main()
{
    // . . .
    cout << ''The light at the 2nd intersection is '' <<
        network[ 1 ].traffic_light;
}
```

Listing 3.3
A Preview
of Operator
Overloading

```
#include <stream.h>
typedef enum { red, green, amber } traffic_light_color;
struct intersection
{
    traffic_light_color traffic_light;
    int number_cars_queued;
    int cumulative_number_cars;
    friend ostream& operator << ( ostream &s,
                                  intersection &light
                                );
};

ostream& operator << ( ostream &s,
                       intersection &light )
{
    switch ( light.traffic_light )
    {
        case red : return ( s << ''red'' );
        case green : return ( s << ''green'' );
        case amber : return ( s << ''yellow'' );
    }
}

intersection network[ 50 ];

main()
{
    network[ 1 ].traffic_light = amber;
    cout << ''\nThe light at the 2nd intersection is '' <<
        network[ 1 ];
}
```

The output of Listing 3.3 is:

```
The light at the 2nd intersection is yellow
```

In Listing 3.3, the struct, intersection, contains the interface to a function that overloads the stream operator, <<. In C++ the struct is a special case of a new construct, the class. The struct, like a class, encapsulates both data and functions (values and operations). The next chapter is devoted to this most powerful construct in C++. Indeed, the struct and class constructs are at the center of object-oriented programming in C++. Further discussion of operator overloading and the stream operators is deferred to Chapter 4.

All C++ declarations introduce an identifier name into a scope or subset of the program text. Identifiers declared in functions have a scope from the point of declaration to the end of the function block. Global identifiers, declared outside of a function, have a scope from the point of declaration to the end of the file in which the declaration exists.

If a local identifier uses the same name as a global identifier, the global identifier is hidden within the region of program text given by the scope of the local identifier. C++ provides a mechanism for accessing the global identifier within this local scope. The scope operator, ::, can be used. This is illustrated in Listing 3.4.

The output of this program is

```
The local value of ch = e
The global value of ch = A
```

The reader should take note of the return type, void, declared for function hide_identifier. The void type means "returns nothing" and is part of the draft ANSI C standard. The void type has been implemented in some recent C compilers.

A pointer of any type is assignment-compatible with type void. Thus the statement

```
void *ptr;
```

implies that ptr is a pointer of an unknown type.

Listing 3.4
The Scope
Operator, ::

```
#include <stdio.h>
char ch = 'D';
void hide_identifier()
{
   int local_ident_1, local_ident_2;
   char ch;

   ch = 'e';
   printf( "\nThe local value of ch = %c", ch );
   // . . .
   ::ch = 'A';
}
main()
{
   hide_identifier();
   printf( "\n\nThe global value of ch = %c", ch );
}
```

An identifier that is local to a function cannot be accessed outside of the function.

In C, the name lvalue is introduced to refer to any variable or expression that can be on the left side of an assignment statement. In C++, an object (in a non–object-oriented context) is defined as a region of storage and an lvalue as an expression that refers to an object. Because of the different meaning attached to objects in an object-oriented context, we use the term *program variable* rather than the term *object*.

In C++, a *program variable* is created (memory allocated) at its point of definition and is destroyed (memory deallocated) when its name is no longer within its scope of the program text. Program variables declared outside of a function are created and initialized once and live for the full duration of the program. Program variables declared with the storage specifier, static, do the same. All static and global variables are automatically initialized to the value zero unless the programmer provides an alternative value at the point of declaration.

The two new C++ operators new and delete allow a programmer to directly control the lifetime of a variable. Program variables can be created and destroyed at will. Along with this power comes responsibility. It is easy for a novice to forget to deallocate what has been allocated. Any program variable created with the new function must be deallocated with the delete function, as illustrated in Listing 3.5.

The function create_string declares and defines two local variables, num_chars of type int, and name, a pointer to type char. The reader should note that the second declaration for name occurs in the middle of the function body. This is illegal in C, in which all variable declarations must precede the body of code that implements the function. C++ allows variable declarations anywhere within the body of a function. Good software development practice suggests that identifiers be declared as close to their first point of application as possible.

The statement

```
char *name = new char[ num_chars + 1 ];
```

declares name as a pointer to type char and allocates num_chars + 1 bytes at the address name. This address is returned by function name. The C programmer should recognize this as similar to the C statement

```
char name = ( char * ) malloc( num_chars + 1 );
```

The last line of function create_string is

```
delete name;
```

If the program in Listing 3.5 were to omit this statement, the memory that was dynamically allocated using the new function would not be returned to the central memory pool (in the heap part of memory) and would be lost to the pro-

Listing 3.5
The Functions New
and Delete

```
#include <stdio.h>
void create_string()
{
   int num_chars;

   printf( "\nHow many characters in your first name: " );
   scanf( "%d", &num_chars );

   char *name = new char[ num_chars + 1 ];

   printf( "\nEnter your first name: " );
   scanf( "%s", name );
   printf( "\n\nYour first name, %s, is very nice.", name );
   delete name;
}

main()
{
   create_string();
   // . . .
}
```

grammer. Although in many small applications this loss might go unnoticed, it is nevertheless poor programming practice to fail to clean up all dynamic storage in the heap. In some large applications such poor programming could result in the failure of the system.

The new operator stores information concerning the size of a dynamic entity so that the delete operator does not require the programmer to explicitly indicate the size of the structure to be deallocated.

The delete operator can have a numerical argument. An example is delete [500] vector. The numerical argument affects the number of elements for which destructors are called.

C++ retains the same predefined types as C. These include:

- char
- int
- short int (short)
- long int (long)
- float
- double
- unsigned char
- unsigned short int
- unsigned int
- unsigned long int

If the type identifier int is not present in a type declaration and no other type is present, the type int is assumed by the compiler.

As in C, a C++ programmer can take advantage of the underlying hardware by choosing variables of the appropriate type for a particular machine.

3.3   C++ Operators

C++ retains all of C's rich and useful set of operators. It is very important for C and C++ programmers to know the precedence of these operators. Although many C programmers learn operator precedence informally by practice, it is im-

TABLE 3.1   Operators for Type Integer

Arithmetic operators

+	unary plus, addition
−	unary minus, subtraction
*	multiplication
/	division
%	remainder
x=	modify and replace, where x can be +, −, *, /, or %
++	increment
−−	decrement

Logical operators

&&	and
||	or
!	negate
==	equal
!=	not equal
>	greater than
>=	greater than or equal
<	less than
<=	less than or equal

Bitwise operators

&	and
|	or
^	exclusive or
~	negation
>>	right shift
<<	left shift
x=	modify and replace, where x can be &, |, ^, >>, or <<

TABLE 3.2 Operators for Type Float

Arithmetic operators

+	unary plus, addition
−	unary minus, subtraction
*	multiplication
/	division
x=	modify and replace, where x can be +, −, *, /, or %
++	increment
−−	decrement

Logical operators

&&	and
||	or
!	negate
==	equal
!=	not equal
>	greater than
>=	greater than or equal
<	less than
<=	less than or equal

portant to be able to formally reference the precedence hierarchy when needed. Table 3.1 presents C++'s operators for integer types, and Table 3.2 presents the operators for floating point types. Table 3.3 presents the entire operator precedence hierarchy. We assume that the reader is familiar with these operators from C.

3.4 Pass-by-Reference

Consider a C function, increment, that adds one to an integer parameter and returns the value through the same parameter. Listing 3.6 presents such a C function, which illustrates a *pass-by-reference* solution.

The address of i must be sent to function increment. The function increment adds one at the address of the parameter value and returns the new value to the main function.

Listing 3.6
C Solution to Pass-by-Reference

```
#include <stdio.h>

main()
{
    extern void increment();
```

Listing 3.6
(continued)

```
    int i = 7;

    increment( &i );
    printf( ''The value of i = %d'', i );
}

void increment( value )
int *value;
{
    ( *value )++;
}
```

Listing 3.7 presents the C++ solution to the same problem.

The symbol & is used in front of the pass-by-reference parameter. This instructs the compiler to pass the address of the parameter into the function rather

TABLE 3.3   C++ Operator Precedence Hierarchy

[]	Array subscripting
( )	Function invocation
.	Structure field selection
->	Structure field selection using indirection
++, --	Postfix/prefix increment and decrement. Postfix has higher precedence if both occur in the same expression
sizeof	Size of a variable or type (in bytes)
(cast)	Cast to a type
~	Bitwise negation
!	Logical NOT
-	Unary minus
&	Address of
*	Dereference operator (indirection)
*, /, %	Multiply, divide, remainder. Equal precedence
+, -	Addition, subtraction. Equal precedence
<<, >>	Left shift, right shift. Equal precedence
<, >, <=, >=	Inequality testing. Equal precedence
==, !=	Test for equality, inequality. Equal precedence
&	Bitwise AND
^	Bitwise exclusive OR
|	Bitwise OR
&&	Logical AND
||	Logical OR
? :	Conditional operator
=, +=, -=, *=, /=, <<=, >>=, &=, ^=, |=	Assign and replace. Equal precedence
,	Comma operator for sequential evaluation of expressions

than making a copy of the function as is normally the case. The function, increment, is invoked without sending in the address of the variable, as shown in Listing 3.7.

Listing 3.7
The C++ Solution
to Pass-by-
Reference

```
#include <stdio.h>
main( )
{
    extern void increment( int &value );
    int i = 7;

    increment( i );
    printf( "The value of i = %d", i );
}
void increment( int &value )
{
    value++;
}
```

As another example of pass-by-reference, consider the function swap given in Listing 3.8.

Listing 3.8
Swapping
Numbers Using
Pass-by-Reference

```
#include <stdio.h>
main( )
{
    extern void swap( int &a, int &b );
    int i = 7,
        j = -3;

    swap( i, j );
    printf( "The value of i = %d j = %d", i, j );
}
void swap( int &a, int &b )
{
    int temp = b;
    b = a, a = temp;
}
```

3.5   Pointers

To master C or C++ means to master pointers. C++ handles pointers in a manner similar to C's approach. Because of the tremendous importance of C++ pointers, this section reviews the highlights of pointer variable usage.

Figure 3.1
Pointer to
an integer.

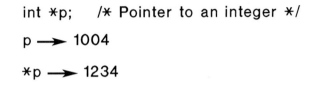

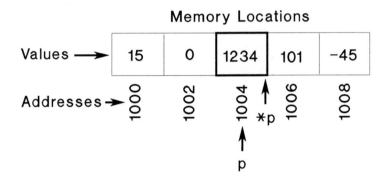

A *pointer* is a memory address. Its value indicates where an entity is stored, not what is stored.

The operator symbol * is used to denote a "pointer to." For example, consider the following declaration:

```
int *int_ptr
```

This declaration reads, "int_ptr is a pointer to an integer." The value int_ptr is an address. The value *int_ptr is an integer stored at the address. Here, the * operator is used as a dereference symbol and *int_ptr reads, "the value at the address int_ptr."

Figure 3.1 illustrates the difference between a pointer and the value it is pointing to.

A common and serious hazard in using C or C++ pointers is the failure to initialize such pointers before they are used. Pointers declared outside a function or declared as static inside a function are automatically initialized to zero, like all global variables in C++. The address 0 cannot be assigned by the memory allocation function new and can therefore serve as a unique sentinel for terminating dynamic structures.

Pointers declared inside a function (automatic variables) are not initialized to any address. If an assignment is attempted for such an uninitialized pointer, a critical part of the computer's memory, such as the location where the operating system resides, may be overwritten, causing a major failure. Most often, a program "hangs" (freezes in its execution) when an uninitialized pointer is used.

Apart from the issue of initializing pointers is the issue of allocating memory space for pointer variables. Consider the following code segment:

```
float *x, *y;
*x = 12.4;
*y = 15.2;
```

The declaration float *x, *y causes the compiler to set aside storage for two pointers, not storage for the data pointed to (floating point numbers). The assignments *x = 12.4 and *y = 15.2 are bound to overwrite the memory locations to which x and y point. The proper way to accomplish these assignments is given as follows:

```
x = new float[ 1 ];
y = new float[ 1 ];
*x = 12.4;
*y = 15.2;
```

Memory is allocated for two floating point numbers. The memory allocation function new assigns appropriate addresses for x and y.

There are three ways to assign a meaningful initial value to a pointer variable:

- Declare the pointer outside any function or with the static designator. Its initial value is the null memory address, 0. Memory must still be allocated for such pointers before they can be used.

- Assign the pointer to another pointer that has been properly initialized.

- Use the memory allocation function new.

In addition to the problem of uninitialized pointers, there are several other potential hazards in using pointer variables.

The problem of aliasing is illustrated below:

```
int *x = new int[ 1 ];
int *y = new int[ 1 ];
*x = 26;
*y = 32;
y = x;
*x = 97;
```

The assignment of x to y means that x and y point to the same memory location. As a side effect, the statement *x = 97 assigns the value 97 to the location pointed to by y. This side effect may not always be desirable. Furthermore, the value *x = 26 is lost forever. Storage for an integer remains locked up in the heap with the value 26, and the programmer can never again purposefully access this value. This "dangling" memory problem, if abused, can cause a premature heap overflow failure in a large software system.

Figure 3.2 presents an example of aliasing and dangling memory similar to the example just described.

Figure 3.2
Aliasing and
dangling memory
addresses.

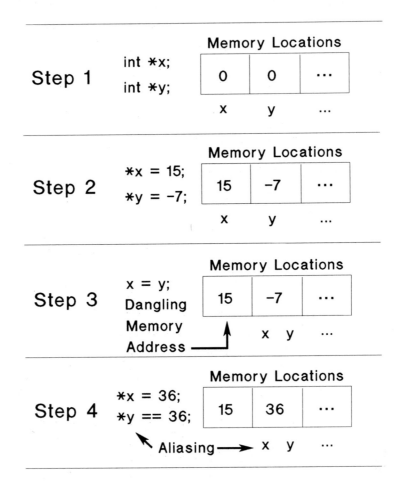

Pointers in C and C++ are intimately associated with arrays. The reader should recall that in the C language the name of an array is actually a pointer to the address of the data at the first index location. Pointers can be added, subtracted, and compared for equality and inequality.

Pointer arithmetic is performed in terms of the underlying base type of the pointer. Thus ptr + 6 means to add six memory units of the base type to the address ptr. If ptr were declared as

```
int *ptr;
```

and an int type requires 2 bytes of storage, then ptr + 6 would mean add 12 bytes to the address of ptr.

It is essential that the programmer distinguish between a pointer (an address) and the value that the pointer points to (some data).

Several C++ programs that use pointers will be useful in reviewing this important language component. Listing 3.9 presents a program that highlights the relationship between pointers and arrays.

The declaration

```
float *data = new float[ size ];
```

allocates space at address data for size floating point numbers. The function new returns the address of data.

The declaration

```
float *end_ptr = data + size - 1;
```

assigns the variable end_ptr to the address of the last element of the array data. The address arithmetic, data + size − 1, is performed in units of the array's underlying base type, float. Thus on a machine that represents a floating point number in 8 bytes, the actual address of data + 1 is offset from the address of data by 8 bytes.

The for loop assigns a series of values to the data array.

The function print_array takes data as its first parameter and the address of the last index location in the array as its last parameter. The while loop,

```
while ( value != end_of_array )
   printf( "\n%f", *value++ );
```

uses the C idiom *value++ to dereference and output the floating point number at address value and to increment the address (not the value stored at the address) value.

Listing 3.9
Pointer and Arrays

```
#include <stdio.h>
main()
{
   extern void print_array( float *value, float
                             *end_of_array );
   const int size = 1000;

   float *data = new float[ size ];
   float *end_ptr = data + size;

   for ( int i = 0; i < size; i++ )
      data[ i ] = 3 * i + 12;
   print_array( data, end_ptr );
}

void print_array( float *value, float *end_of_array )
{
   while ( value != end_of_array )
      printf( "\n%f", *value++ );
}
```

```
#include <stdio.h>

main()
{
    int *data = new int[ 50 ];

    for ( int index = 0; index < 50; index++ )
        data[ index ] = 10 * index;
    printf( "\n ++*data = %d", ++*data );
    printf( "\n *++data = %d", *++data );
}
```

Listing 3.10 illustrates some additional idioms that one must understand to read and write C++ code.

An array, data, is declared with a capacity of 50 integers. The for loop loads the array with integer values.

The statement

```
printf( "\n ++*data = %d", ++*data );
```

does the following: The value stored in data (the first index location of the array) is incremented by 1 (incremented from 0 to 1).

The statement

```
printf( "\n *++data = %d", *++data );
```

does the following: The address of data is incremented to the second index location in the array, and the value at that address is dereferenced. Thus the output of Listing 3.10 is

```
++*data = 1
*++data = 10
```

Listing 3.11 presents the celebrated quicksort algorithm in function quick_sort. This algorithm, developed by C. A. R. Hoare, has become popular for sorting arrays of data because it is very fast and does its work in place. That is, there is no auxiliary storage required.

The key element in quick_sort is function partition. This function forces all the elements to the left of a pivot index position to be smaller than the pivot element and all of the elements to the right of the pivot index position to be larger than the pivot element. Pointers are used extensively.

The interface to function quick_sort,

```
void quick_sort( float *low_ptr, float *high_ptr );
```

takes two pointers, low_ptr and high_ptr, as input parameters. The first of these pointers is the address of the lowest index position in the array, and the second is the address of the highest index position.

The main program loads the array data using the code

```
for ( int i = 0; i < size; i++ )
    *( data + i ) = sin( i ) / ( 2.4 + sqrt( i ) );
```

The function sin(i) / (2.4 + sqrt(i)) is used to quickly generate a series of floating point values to be sorted. The left side of the statement,

```
*( data + i )
```

is used in place of data[i].

The declaration

```
float pivot = *( low_ptr + ( high_ptr - low_ptr ) / 2 );
```

in function partition is used to assign the floating point variable, pivot, the value stored in the middle index position of the array.

Recursion is used in function quick_sort as follows:

```
if ( low_ptr < high_ptr )
{
    pivot_ptr = partition( low_ptr, high_ptr );
    quick_sort( low_ptr, pivot_ptr - 1 );
    quick_sort( pivot_ptr, high_ptr );
}
```

Finally, it is noted that two pass-by-reference parameters are used in function swap.

Listing 3.11 contains additional comments that explain the purpose of some of the code.

Listing 3.11
Quicksort Program
to Illustrate
Pointers

```
// Quicksort—An algorithm developed by C. A. R. Hoare

#include <stdio.h>
#include <math.h>

const int size = 12800;

float *data;

main()
{
    extern void quick_sort( float *low_ptr, float *high_ptr );
    extern void display_data( float *data );

    data = new float[ size ];
    for ( int i = 0; i < size; i++ )
        *( data + i ) = sin( i ) / ( 2.4 + sqrt( i ) );

    quick_sort( data, data + size - 1 );
    display_data( data );
}
```

Listing 3.11
(continued)

```
void quick_sort( float *low_ptr, float *high_ptr )
{
  float *pivot_ptr;
  extern float *partition( float *low_ptr, float *high_ptr );

  if ( low_ptr < high_ptr )
  {
    pivot_ptr = partition( low_ptr, high_ptr );
    quick_sort( low_ptr, pivot_ptr - 1 );
    quick_sort( pivot_ptr, high_ptr );
  }
}
float *partition( float *low_ptr, float *high_ptr )
{

  void swap( float &value1, float &value2 );

  float pivot = *( low_ptr + ( high_ptr - low_ptr ) / 2 );

  /*
    Upon termination of this loop, the value of all the array
    elements to the left of pivot will be less than the value
    of the pivot element, and the value of all the elements
    to the right of pivot will be greater than the value of
    the pivot element.
  */
  while ( low_ptr <= high_ptr )
  {
    // Find a value in the lower part of the array greater
    // than pivot

    while ( *low_ptr < pivot )
      low_ptr++;
    // Find a value in the upper part of the array less
    // than pivot

    while ( *high_ptr > pivot )
      high_ptr --;
    if ( low_ptr <= high_ptr )
      swap( *low_ptr++, *high_ptr --);
  }
  return low_ptr;
}
void swap( float &value1, float &value2 )
{
  float temp = value1;

  value1 = value2, value2 = temp;
}
void display_data( float *data )
{
  for ( int i = 0; i < size; i++ )
    printf( ''\n%f'', data[ i ] );
}
```

Listing 3.12 provides another example that illustrates C++ pointers, arrays, and pass-by-reference.

The function enter_list has two reference parameters that both output data to the main function. The first parameter, grades, is the address of an array of integers. The second parameter, size, is the number of integers in the array. The main program invokes function enter_list and prints out all the values input into the scores array.

The function enter_list declares a pointer variable, next_grade, to point to type int and initializes this variable by assigning it to the starting address of the array of integers.

The for loop,

```
size = 0;
for ( ; scanf( "%d", next_grade ), *next_grade != -1;
    ( size )++, next_grade++ )
printf( "\nEnter next grade ( -1 to quit ): " );
```

uses the stdio library function scanf within the for loop to get the next_grade and compare the value of next_grade to -1. If the value of next_grade is not -1, size is incremented and the address of next_grade is incremented to point to the next index location. Here, C++'s (C's) economy of expression and power of operators are evident.

It should be noted that function enter_list does not protect the user against entering more grades than the capacity of the array equal to 100.

Listing 3.12
Another Example
of Pointers and
Arrays

```
#include <stdio.h>
int scores[ 100 ];
main( )
{
    extern void enter_list( int *grades, int &size );
    int size;

    enter_list( scores, size );
    for ( int index = 0; index < size; index++ )
      printf( "\nscores[ %d ] = %d", index, scores[ index ] );
}

void enter_list( int *grades, int &size )
{
    // This procedure prompts the user for a series of
    // grades. It outputs this information in the array
    // grades.

    int *next_grade = grades; // Starting address of input
                              // array

    printf( "\nEnter next grade ( -1 to quit ): " );
    size = 0;
    for ( ; scanf( "%d", next_grade ), *next_grade != -1;
        ( size )++, next_grade++ )
      printf( "\nEnter next grade ( -1 to quit ): " );
}
```

3.6   The Const Specifier

We have seen earlier in this chapter that the const specifier can be used in declaring an identifier whose value cannot change during program execution. Thus it would be illegal to do the following:

```
const float x = 14.7;
. . .
x = 19;
```

The const specifier freezes the value of the identifier within its scope.

Structured variables such as arrays can be declared as const, as shown below:

```
const float data[] = {1.1, 2.2, 3.3, 4.4, 5.5};
const int unity_vector[] = {1, 1, 1, 1, 1, 1, 1};
```

It would be illegal to alter any of the values of the arrays data or unity_vector. The const specifier may improve the readability of a program by allowing a descriptive name to be used in place of a less-descriptive literal.

The const specifier can also be used in connection with function parameters. Consider the following function:

```
void print_value( const int value )
{
   printf( ''\n\n%d'', value );
}
```

It would be illegal for the body of the function print_value to reassign the parameter a new value. Some compilers can perform better code optimization with functions that have const parameters.

When the specifier const is used with pointers, the data stored at the pointer is a constant, not the pointer address itself. This is illustrated in Listing 3.13.

The pointer constant name is initialized in Listing 3.13 with the value "Richard". It would be illegal to write

```
name[ 0 ] = 'C';
```

because the value of the pointer constant is frozen. It is perfectly legal to assign the pointer to another address and with another value such as name = "Lewis".

Listing 3.13
Pointer Constants

```
#include <stdio.h>

main()
{
   const char *name = ''Richard'';
```

Listing 3.13
(continued)

```
        printf( "\n%s", name );
        name = "Lewis";
        printf( "\n%s", name );
    }
```

If one wishes to freeze the value of the pointer address itself rather than the value being pointed to, this can be accomplished as follows:

```
char *const name = "Richard";
name[ 0 ] = 'C'; // Legal
name = "Lewis"; // Illegal
```

One can freeze both the address and the value pointed to by using the construction

```
const char *const name = "Richard";
```

3.7 Enumeration Types

Listing 3.2 introduced the enumeration type

```
typedef enum { red, green, amber } traffic_light_color;
```

The C++ translator associates the constant red with the integer constant 0, the constant green with the value 1, and the constant amber with the value 2. The identifier traffic_light_color can be used alone, without the enum specifier, in declaring variables to be of type traffic_light_color. Consider the declaration, traffic_light_color light;
It would be legal to write

```
if ( light == 1 )
    printf( "\nThe value of light is green" );
```

It would be much more descriptive to write

```
if ( light == green )
    printf( "\nThe value of light is green" );
```

Values other than 0, 1, and 2 can be associated with the enumeration literals red, green, and amber. It is legal to define the enumeration type traffic_light_ color as follows:

```
typedef enum { red = 34,
               green = 17,
               amber = 21 } traffic_light_color;
```

3.8   Anonymous Unions

Anonymous unions are unions without a name. This structure is illustrated in the following:

```
struct data_rec
{
   char *last_name;
   char *first_name;
   int id_number;
   union
   {
      float annual_salary;
      float hourly_wage;
   }
};
```

All members of a union require only as much memory storage as the largest member. For the structure given above, storage for only one floating point entity is required. The union members annual_salary and hourly_wage are stored at the same memory address. Each instance of a data_rec can only store one of these members.

One can access a member of an anonymous union as in the following:

```
data_rec my_record;
printf( "My annual salary = %f", my_record.annual_salary );
```

3.9   Explicit Type Conversion

In C++, the name of a type can be used in the same way as a function to accomplish type conversion, as an alternative to type casting as done in C. For example, the conversion from an integer to float can be done as

```
int i = 10;
float r = float( i );
```

rather than as

```
int i = 10;
float r = ( float ) i;
```

Listing 3.14 illustrates explicit type conversion. A struct, example, is defined with field y of type int and field z of type float. On the particular machine and C++ translator used, this struct requires exactly six bytes of storage. A type, example_ptr, is defined as a pointer to type example. A static array of 6 bytes, str, is defined and initialized to "ABCDEF".

First, the 6-byte str is converted to a pointer to type example using the cast conversion:

```
my_example = ( example * ) str;
```

Next, the 6-byte str is converted to info (a pointer to type example) using the explicit type conversion:

```
my_info = example_ptr( str );
```

Both conversions are risky because they are so machine and implementation dependent. The type conversion causes the system to reinterpret the bit pattern originally defined as a string into an integer and a floating point number.

It is recommended that whenever type conversion is used, the code be clearly marked with a hazard warning and localized with other potentially non-portable code.

Listing 3.14
Example of Explicit
Type Conversion

```
#include <stdio.h>

struct example
{
   int y;
   float z;
};
typedef example* example_ptr;

char str[ 6 ] = "ABCDEF";

main( )
{
   example *my_example;
   example *my_info;

   my_example = ( example * ) str;
   printf( "\nmy_example -> y = %d", my_example -> y );
   printf( "\nmy_example -> z = %f", my_example -> z );
   my_info = example_ptr( str );
   printf( "\nmy_info -> y = %d", my_info -> y );
   printf( "\nmy_info -> z = %f", my_info -> z );
}
```

3.10   Functions

This section introduces and discusses those features of functions that are new in C++. We do not present a complete tutorial on C functions.

3.10.1   Function prototypes

Function prototypes were introduced in Section 3.2 and are used in almost all of the listings of this chapter. Listing 3.15 compares the newer function prototyping with the older C-like function declaration.

The function function_2 uses the older C function declaration. C++ translators may not accept this older style of function declaration (some translators may require that a compiler switch be set in order to promote upward compatibility between C code and C++ code).

Listing 3.15
Comparing
Function
Prototyping to the
Older C Function
Declaration

```
#include <stdio.h>
void function_1( int a, int b )
{
    printf( ''\na = %d. b = %d'', a, b );
}
void function_2( c, d )
int c, d;
{
    printf( ''\nc = %d. d = %d'', c, d );
}
main()
{
    int i = 4,
        j = 5;
    function_1( i, j );
    function_2( i, j );
}
```

3.10.2   Inline functions

A function declaration can be prefaced with the specifier inline. Thus function function_1 could be declared as

```
inline void function_1( int a, int b )
{
    printf( ''\na = %d. b = %d'', a, b );
}
```

The inline specifier forces the C++ compiler to substitute the body of code for function_1 inline at the location where the function invocation occurs. Although this may increase execution speed because function call overhead is eliminated, there may be a severe penalty in code size, particularly if the function involves many lines of code and is invoked many times in the program. We advise caution in the use of the inline specifier.

3.10.3 Default arguments

One or more arguments in a C++ function can be specified as having default values. Whenever this is done, the arguments with default values must be given as the last (trailing) set of arguments in the function.

For example,

```
void default_function1( int first,
                        float second = 12.5,
                        char third = 'c',
                        char *fourth = ''default'' );
```

is legal, whereas

```
void default_function2( int first = 3,
                        float second,
                        char third = 'c',
                        char *fourth = ''default'' );
```

is illegal.

The function default_function1 can be invoked by sending in one value, two values, three values, or four values. The compiler supplies the missing values using the default values if fewer than four parameters are sent in.

3.10.4 Overloading function names

C++ allows function names to be overloaded. That is, the same identifier name can be used in the same scope of both functions. In order to do this, the specifier overload must be given before the overloaded functions are declared. The compiler determines the function to be used based on the number and type of parameters that are used in the function invocation.

Listing 3.16 illustrates the overloading of functions and default arguments in functions.

The declaration overload print instructs the compiler to allow function print to be defined three times. Without this declaration, the compiler would not allow the overloading of this function name.

The main function contains an extern reference to function display (defined later in the file). The default value, "default", is given in this first declaration rather than in the actual function definition.

The output of Listing 3.16 is

```
Parameter 1 default
Parameter 1 on display
The value of the integer = 7
The value of the string = Hello
123456789
```

Listing 3.16
Function Name
Overloading and
Default Arguments

```
// Overloading functions and default arguments

#include <stdio.h>

overload print;
extern void print( int i );
extern void print( char* str );
extern void print( int* a );

int data[ 9 ] = { 1, 2, 3, 4, 5, 6, 7, 8, 9 };

main( )
{
   void display( const char* name1,
                 const char* name2 = ''default'' );

   display( ''Parameter 1'' );
   display( ''Parameter 1'', ''on display'' );
   print( 7 );
   print( ''Hello'' );
   print( data );
}

void display( const char* name1, const char* name2 )
{
   printf( ''\n%s %s'', name1, name2 );
}

void print( int i )
{
   printf( ''\nThe value of the integer = %d'', i );
}

void print( char* str )
{
   printf( ''\nThe value of the string = %s'', str );
}

void print( int* a )
{
   printf( ''\n'' );
   for ( int i = 0; i < 9; i++ )
     printf( ''%d'', a[ i ] );
}
```

3.10.5 Functions with an unspecified number of arguments

C++ allows functions to be declared with an unspecified number of arguments. Ellipsis marks are used to indicate this, as follows:

```
return_type function_name( . . . )
```

The function printf, from library stdio, is declared as

```
int printf( char* . . . );
```

Calls to printf must have at least one argument, namely a string. Beyond this, the additional arguments are unspecified both in type and in number.

Argument checking is turned off when a function is declared to have an unspecified number of arguments. We therefore recommend against using this capability unless it is absolutely necessary.

Library stdarg.h contains a set of macros for accessing unspecified arguments. The reader is urged to study the macros in this library interface.

3.10.6 Pointers to functions and generics

Functions can be passed as parameters to other functions in C++, as they can in C. Actually a pointer to a function is sent as a parameter to another function. Pointers to functions are briefly reviewed here because of their importance in both C and C++ programming.

It is sometimes useful to control the flow of logic in a menu-driven C or C++ application by defining an array that contains function pointers. Each element in the array points to a function that implements a menu item. Listing 3.17 shows a simple prototype program that uses an array of functions to control the menu-driven application.

The declaration

```
typedef void ( * menu_fcn )();
```

defines a pointer to a function, menu_fcn, that returns void and has no parameters. The declaration

```
menu_fcn command[ 4 ];
```

defines an array of four such functions.

Function assign_functions actually loads the array of command functions by assigning the four function pointers to command[0], . . . , command[3].

For the purposes of this illustrative example, each of the four functions prints out a message.

Listing 3.17

An Array of
Function Pointers
Used to Control
a Menu-Driven
Application

```c
#include <stdio.h>

typedef void ( *menu_fcn )( );

menu_fcn command[ 4 ];

main( )
{
  extern void assign_functions( );
  extern void function_1( );
  extern void function_2( );
  extern void function_3( );
  extern void function_4( );

  int choice;

  assign_functions( );
  do
    {
      printf( "\nMenu item 1 --> " );
      printf( "\nMenu item 2 --> " );
      printf( "\nMenu item 3 --> " );
      printf( "\nMenu item 4 --> " );
      printf( "\nMenu item 5 (Exit program) --> " );
      printf( "\n\nEnter your choice: " );
      scanf( "%d", &choice );
      if ( choice >= 1 && choice <= 4 )
        command[ choice - 1 ]( );
    }
  while ( choice != 5 );
}

void function_1( )
{
  printf( "\nActivated menu item 1.\n" );
}

void function_2( )
{
  printf( "\nActivated menu item 2.\n" );
}

void function_3( )
{
  printf( "\nActivated menu item 3.\n" );
}

void function_4( )
{
  printf( "\nActivated menu item 4.\n" );
}

void assign_functions( )
{
  command[ 0 ] = function_1;
  command[ 1 ] = function_2;
  command[ 2 ] = function_3;
  command[ 3 ] = function_4;
}
```

Function parameters are useful in writing generic functions, as illustrated
by the generic sorting function in Listing 3.18. A similar example appears in

Stroustrup's *Programming in C++* and serves well to illustrate generics. Normally one would encapsulate a sorting function in a more general class using the methods of Chapter 4. Here we focus on the issue of parameter passing using function pointers.

Sorting any set of objects requires that we specify an ordering relation that allows us to compare any two objects. A generic sorting function must be able to order any arbitrary set of data sent in as input. The user must specify the ordering relationship for the particular data by defining an ordering function. A pointer to this function must be passed into the sorting function as part of the input data to the sorting function.

In Listing 3.18, the type definition,

```
typedef int ( *compare )( void*, void* );
```

specifies type compare as a pointer to a function that returns type int and has two parameters, each of type pointer to void (void can be substituted for a pointer to any type).

The particular type of data that is to be sorted in Listing 3.18 is given by the struct name_type. The initial values of an array of name_type my_records are specified globally. The same generic sorting function, sort, first sorts by name and then by id_number. The important point is that the same sort function is used in both cases. Indeed, this sort function could be used to sort any type of data for which an ordering function can be specified and sent in as a parameter.

Functions cmp1 and cmp2 are given as

```
int cmp1( void* p, void* q ) // Compare records by name
{
   return strcmp( rec_type( p ) -> name,
                  rec_type( q ) -> name );
}
int cmp2( void* p, void* q ) // Compare id_numbers
{
   return ( rec_type( p ) ->
     id_number - rec_type( q ) -> id_number );
}
```

Explicit type conversion is used in cmp1 and cmp2 to allow a p and q to be compared in terms of the underlying base type. The value 1 is returned if datum p is larger than datum q.

The generic function sort takes as its first parameter a pointer to type char. Type char represents the smallest storage unit in C++. The second parameter, n, represents the number of entities to be sorted. The third parameter, elemsize, represents the number of bytes of each entity to be sorted. The fourth parameter, cmp, is a pointer to the particular ordering function that specifies how to compare two objects from the set to be sorted.

A simple, but inefficient, bubble-sort algorithm is used in function sort. The elements are compared two at a time, each time performing an interchange if the first element is smaller than the second element. The key block of code in function sort is given as

```
if ( ( *cmp )( bj, bj1 ) < 0 )
    // swap b[ j ] and b[ j - 1 ]
    // Do a byte by byte interchange
    for ( int k = 0; k < elemsize; k++ )
    {
        char temp = bj[ k ];
        bj[ k ] = bj1[ k ];
        bj1[ k ] = temp;
    }
```

The externally defined function cmp is used to compare two elements, given the starting address of the two elements. If an interchange is required, the for loop performs a byte-by-byte interchange by knowing the number of bytes at each address bj, and bj1 (elemsize).

The output of the program is

```
Apple      5
Grapefruit      4
Lemon      1
Lime       2
Orange     7
Pear       3
Plum       0

Plum       0
Lemon      1
Lime       2
Pear       3
Grapefruit      4
Apple      5
Orange     7
```

Listing 3.18
Generic Sorting
Using Function
Parameters

```
// Generic sorting in C++

#include <string.h>
#include <stream.h>

typedef int ( *compare )( void*, void* );

struct name_type
{
    char* name;
    int id_number;
};

typedef name_type* rec_type;

name_type my_records[] = { ''Apple'', 5,
                           ''Orange'', 7,
                           ''Pear'', 3,
                           ''Grapefruit'', 4,
                           ''Lemon'', 1,
                           ''Plum'', 0,
                           ''Lime'', 2 };
```

```
main( )
{
   extern int cmp1( void* p, void* q );
   // Compare records by name

   extern int cmp2( void* p, void* q );
   // Compare records by id_number

   extern void sort( char* base, unsigned n, int elemsize,
                     compare cmp );

   extern void print( rec_type r, int n );
   sort( ( char* ) my_records, 7, sizeof( name_type ),
         cmp1 );
   print( my_records, 7 );
   sort( ( char* ) my_records, 7, sizeof( name_type ),
         cmp2 );
   print( my_records, 7 );
}

void sort( char* base, unsigned n, int elemsize,
           compare cmp )
// Bubble sort algorithm
{
   for ( int i = 0; i < n - 1; i++ )
     for ( int j = n - 1; i < j; j -- )
       {
         char* bj = base + j * elemsize;   // b[ j ]
         char* bj1 = bj - elemsize;        // b[ j - 1 ]
         if ( ( *cmp )( bj, bj1 ) < 0 )
           // swap b[ j ] and b[ j - 1 ]
           // Do a byte-by-byte interchange
           for ( int k = 0; k < elemsize; k++ )
             {
               char temp = bj[ k ];
               bj[ k ] = bj1[ k ];
               bj1[ k ] = temp;
             }
       }
}

void print( rec_type r, int n )
{
   cout << ''\n\n'';
   for ( int i = 0; i < n; i++ )
     cout << r[ i ].name << ''\t'' << r[ i ].id_number << ''\n'';
}

int cmp1( void* p, void* q ) // Compare records by name
{
   return strcmp( rec_type( p ) -> name,
                  rec_type( q ) -> name );
}

int cmp2( void* p, void* q ) // Compare id_numbers
{
   return ( rec_type( p ) ->
     id_number - rec_type( q ) -> id_number );
}
```

3.11   Files and the Physical Organization of C++ Systems

C++, like C, provides the software developer tremendous flexibility in organizing a software system. The range of possibilities goes from the extreme of having one main program file that contains everything to the other extreme of having a separate file for each function in the system.

Common sense and experience suggest that a C++ software system be partitioned into logically homogeneous files, each file containing a series of related units. In Chapter 4, when data abstraction, abstract objects, and classes are introduced along with encapsulation, it is argued that separate implementation and header files should be provided for each class. One useful physical organization of a C++ software system is illustrated in Figure 3.3.

A header file includes the interface to a class or the interface to a set of related functions and data declarations that should be available outside the file in which the definitions are supplied. We illustrate this practice in the major case studies presented in Chapters 4, 5, 6, and 7.

The static specifier should be used in front of any function that the programmer wishes to hide within a given file. This specifier makes the function invisible to the linker, so that the function cannot be invoked any place other than within

Figure 3.3
Representation
of one possible
physical organization
of a C++ software
system.

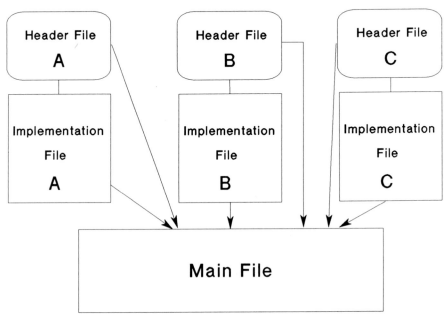

the file in which it is defined. The class construct, which is the main focus of Chapter 4, provides a much better vehicle for function and data hiding.

In some applications, a header file can be used as a mini user's guide. The purpose of each function can be explained in comments, and typical usage can be illustrated. Since a header file is often all that is available to a programmer (the source code for the implementation file is not supplied), it is a natural place for the user to seek help in understanding how to use the functions declared in this file. The header file should provide this help.

Exercises

3.1 Discuss the advantages of using const declarations in C++. Show two examples in which declarations might be useful.

3.2 Show the interface to four C++ functions of your choice using function prototypes.

3.3 Show two examples of the use of the scope operator ::.

3.4 Using the functions new and delete, create a set of C++ functions for constructing dynamic strings. Memory for a dynamic string is allocated on demand, or "on the fly." When a substring is deleted from a dynamic string, memory for the original string is deallocated before memory is allocated for a new string. (You should include functions for appending two strings to produce a third string, inserting a substring into a given position within a dynamic string, and deleting a substring from a given position within a dynamic string.)

3.5 Using the pass-by-reference operator, write a C++ function that prompts a user to enter his or her social security number and returns this information as a parameter of the function.

3.6 Discuss the standard techniques for initializing a pointer variable.

3.7 Discuss the statement

```
printf( ''\n *++data = %d'', *++data );
```

3.8 What is the output of the following program?

```
#include <stdio.h>
main()
{
   int *data = new int[ 12 ];
```

```
        for ( int index = 0; index < 12; index++ )
          data[ index ] = 10 * index;
        printf( ''\n ++*data = %d'', ++*data );
        printf( ''\n *++data = %d'', *++data );
    }
```

3.9   Perform a line-by-line explanation of the following quicksort code:

```
// Quicksort - An algorithm developed by C. A. R. Hoare
#include <stdio.h>
#include <math.h>

const int size = 12800;

float *data;

main()
{
    extern void quick_sort( float *low_ptr, float *high_ptr );
    extern void display_data( float *data );

    data = new float[ size ];
    for ( int i = 0; i < size; i++ )
      *( data + i ) = sin( i ) / ( 2.4 + sqrt( i ) );

    quick_sort( data, data + size - 1 );
    display_data( data );
}

void quick_sort( float *low_ptr, float *high_ptr )
{
    float *pivot_ptr;
    extern float *partition( float *low_ptr, float *high_ptr );

    if ( low_ptr < high_ptr )
    {
      pivot_ptr = partition( low_ptr, high_ptr );
      quick_sort( low_ptr, pivot_ptr - 1 );
      quick_sort( pivot_ptr, high_ptr );
    }
}

float *partition( float *low_ptr, float *high_ptr )
{

void swap( float &value1, float &value2 );

float pivot = *( low_ptr + ( high_ptr - low_ptr ) / 2 );

/*
   Upon termination of this loop, the value of all the array
   elements to the left of pivot will be less than the value
   of the pivot element, and the value of all the elements to
   the right of pivot will be greater than the value of the
   pivot element.
*/

while ( low_ptr <= high_ptr )
{
    // Find a value in the lower part of the array greater
    // than pivot
```

```
    while ( *low_ptr < pivot )
      low_ptr++;
    // Find a value in the upper part of the array less
    // than pivot
    while ( *high_ptr > pivot )
      high_ptr --;
    if ( low_ptr <= high_ptr )
      swap( *low_ptr++, *high_ptr --);
    }
    return low_ptr;
}
void swap( float &value1, float &value2 )
{
    float temp = value1;
    value1 = value2, value2 = temp;
}
void display_data( float *data )
{
    for ( int i = 0; i < size; i++ )
      printf( "\n%f", data[ i ] );
}
```

3.10 What is the output of the following program? Explain each line of code.

```
#include <stdio.h>
main( )
{
    const char *name = "C++ is an interesting language.";
    printf( "\n%s", name );
}
```

3.11 Write and explain three anonymous unions.

3.12 Write and explain the function interfaces to four C++ functions that use default arguments.

3.13 Redo Listing 3.18 and write a generic quicksort function. See Exercise 3.9.

4

Data Encapsulation and Data Hiding Using Classes

4.1 Procedural Languages, Data Abstraction, Encapsulation, and Data Hiding

Encapsulation and data hiding are the centerpieces of the object-oriented paradigm. Indeed, encapsulation is the foundation upon which object-oriented problem solving and programming are built.

In non–object-oriented procedural languages such as FORTRAN, C, and Pascal, data structures are the centerpiece of problem solving. The architecture of an entire software system is centered around one or more key data structures. Operations are performed on data passed to procedures and functions. In fact, the data processing industry draws its name from this data-structure–based paradigm of problem solving and programming. For the several generations of programmers and software developers who have cut their teeth on procedural languages, the notion of sending data to procedures and functions is as natural as breathing.

Procedure-oriented languages, structured programming, and the data-structure–problem solving paradigm have led to modest improvements in software efficiency and reliability, particularly for small- to moderate-size software systems. Books such as Niklaus Wirth's *Algorithms + Data Structures = Programs* have had a profound and useful influence on the software development process. But as software systems have grown in size and complexity, it has become more and more apparent that the data-structure paradigm itself must be reevaluated. Stress cracks have formed in many large software systems because of the enormous load imposed by program and problem complexity.

The major defect of the data-structure–problem solving paradigm is the scope and visibility that the key data structures have with respect to the surrounding software system. The implementation of many important procedures and functions (subprograms) in such systems is critically dependent on the key data structures. If any changes are made to one or more of these key data structures, the fall-out effects on the software system may be pervasive. Many procedures and functions have to be rewritten. In some cases, the entire structure of the software system collapses because of a change in several key data structures. The deleterious effects of this basic defect in the data-structure paradigm become more and more evident as the size and complexity of the software system increase.

Encapsulation and data hiding bind data and procedures tightly together and limit the scope and visibility of the procedures and functions that can manipulate the data to a highly localized region of code in the software system. Indeed, the data and related procedures and functions become inseparable. A new entity, an *object,* is defined. An object has its own data and its own procedures. The object has sole access to and assumes full responsibility for manipulating its private data using its private procedures and functions. The user can manipulate the object through a precisely specified set of *methods,* which are activated by passing messages to an object. Objects assume control of the system and pass messages to other objects. The architecture of an object-oriented software system is not dependent on an object's internal structure but only on the methods that define the operations that can be performed on the object's internal data.

The notion of an abstract data type has gained currency in recent years, though its evolution can be traced back some 25 years. An *abstract data type* is a software model that specifies an allowable set of values for data and a set of allowable operations that can be performed on the data. In procedural languages such as C and Pascal, abstract data types are implemented by defining global data structures and an assorted set of functions or procedures that define and implement the operations on the central data structure.

In more recent years, procedural languages such as Modula-2 and Ada have provided a more elegant and useful implementation of abstract data types. These languages have provided the programmer a vehicle to separate the definition of an abstract data type from its implementation using two physically separate compilation units or modules. In the definition module, the name of the abstract data type is given and the interface to the operations that can be performed on the underlying data are specified. In the implementation module, the actual code bodies that implement the algorithms used to manipulate the underlying data are provided. An opaque shield shrouds the internal structure of the underlying data and prohibits the programmer from accessing the internal structure of the underlying data except in the implementation module itself. Only the procedures and functions that are specified in the definition module can be used to access the underlying data.

The separation of definition from implementation for an abstract data type represents a giant step forward in software technology. The binding of underlying data with an associated set of procedures and functions that can be used to manipulate the data is called *encapsulation;* the inaccessiblity of the internal structure of the underlying data is called *data hiding.* Using encapsulation and data hiding in either Modula-2 or Ada allows a software engineer to avoid many of the maintenance problems discussed earlier in connection with the data-structure–problem solving paradigm. If the structure of an underlying data type is modified, only the localized region of code given by the implementation module must be changed. The rest of the software system remains intact because it is connected to the underlying data only through the procedure and function interfaces specified in the definition module.

Although Modula-2 and Ada offer significant advances in software engineering technology, they are still procedural languages rather than object-oriented languages. They are fundamentally based on the notion that one passes data to procedures rather than messages to objects. Because they offer us encapsulation and data hiding they represent a transition to truly object-oriented languages, in which the object not the function or procedure represents the centerpiece of problem solving. Perhaps it is fair to characterize both Modula-2 and Ada as quasi-objective languages. Only when the emphasis is not on sending data to functions but rather on sending messages to objects do we have a truly object-oriented language.

4.2   An Introduction to Classes in C++

The class construct is the vehicle used in C++ for encapsulation and data hiding. Objects are defined in terms of classes. A class description defines the characteristics of all objects declared to be of the given class. The class construct also provides the basic unit of reusability in C++. It binds an underlying data type with a set of public and private methods (functions) that allow the underlying data type to be manipulated by passing messages to the object. (Chapter 5 discusses the class construct as a unit of reusability in connection with inheritance.)

Figure 4.1 depicts the private and public sections of a class. The public section is shown as transparent because its data and member functions are accessible outside the scope of the class. The private section is caged because its data and member functions are inaccessible outside the scope of the class.

A class is generally constructed as follows:

```
class class_name_identifier
{
  private:
    data and methods – members
    // The data and methods cannot be accessed directly

  protected:
    data and methods – members
    // The data and methods cannot be accessed except
    // by derived classes. See Chapter 5.
```

Figure 4.1
Class
decomposition.

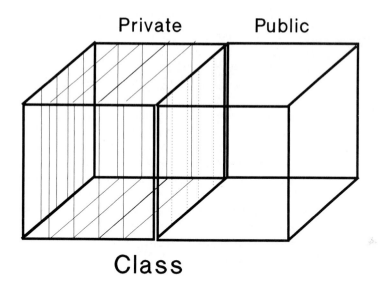

```
      public:
         data and methods – members
         // The data and methods can be accessed directly
   };
```

A discussion of protected class members is deferred until the next chapter since such members are related to derived classes and inheritance.

The construction of a class and class objects can be illustrated with a simple example. Let us consider the concept of a counter abstract data type (ADT). The value set for our counter ADT includes the nonnegative integers from 0 to 65535. The allowable operations (methods) for our counter ADT are increment, decrement, and value. We also desire that each instance of class counter—that is an object of class counter—be automatically initialized to value 0 when the object is declared.

Listing 4.1 presents a definition and implementation of class counter. The counter class has a data member value, of type unsigned int, in its private section. Each object declared to be of class counter contains its own private copy of value. This internal data can be accessed only through the methods declared in the public section of class counter—namely, increment, decrement, and access_value. Only the implementation sections of methods increment, decrement, and value can access the internal structure of the private data, in this case value.

For this simple class, the implementation bodies of methods increment, decrement, and access_value are given in the class definition. Whenever a method implementation is given in a class definition, the C++ compiler implements the function in-line, trading off increased execution speed against more object code. There is no function call overhead associated with invoking in-line methods.

The first method, counter, takes the name of the class and is called a *constructor*. The body of code of a class constructor is executed when an object is declared to be of the given class. In the case of the counter class, the private data, value, of each class object is initialized to 0 by mere declaration of the class object.

Listing 4.1
Class Counter

```
// This code defines the class called counter
// File count.h
class counter
{
  private:
    unsigned int value;

  public:
    counter(){value = 0;};  // A constructor

    void increment(){if ( value < 65535 ) value++;};

    void decrement(){if ( value > 0 ) value--;};

    unsigned int access_value(){return value;}
}; // Note that a class definition must end with a semicolon
```

Listing 4.2 presents a short test program that uses the counter class. Two objects, c1 and c2, are declared to be of class counter using the code

```
counter c1;  // Automatically initialized
counter c2;  // Automatically initialized
```

Because of the constructor given in the counter class definition, objects c1 and c2 are initialized with private data of value equal to 0.

In the first for loop, the message increment is sent to each of the objects c1 and c2. In addition, the message access_value( ) is sent to the object c1.

As is evident from Listing 4.2, messages are sent to objects in C++ by using the object name followed by a dot followed by the method name. A method can have one or more parameters, which must be supplied with the message sent to the object.

Listing 4.2
Test Program That
Uses the Counter
Class

```
// Test program that uses class counter
// File countst.cpp
#include <stdio.h>
#include "count.h"

main()
{
  counter c1;  // Automatically initialized
  counter c2;  // Automatically initialized
```

```
for ( int i = 1; i <= 15; i++ ) // Notice the declaration of int i
{
    c1.increment( );
    printf( ''\nc1 = %u'', c1.access_value( ) );
    c2.increment( );
}
printf( ''\nAfter the loop the value of c2 = %u'',
        c2.access_value( ) );
for ( i = 1; i <= 5; i++ )
    c2.decrement( );
printf( ''\nThe final value of c2 = %u'', c2.access_value( )
);
printf( ''\nThe final value of c1 = %u'', c1.access_value( )
);
}
```

The output of the program of Listing 4.2 is

```
c1 = 1
c1 = 2
c1 = 3
c1 = 4
c1 = 5
c1 = 6
c1 = 7
c1 = 8
c1 = 9
c1 = 10
c1 = 11
c1 = 12
c1 = 13
c1 = 14
c1 = 15
After the loop the value of c2 = 15
The final value of c2 = 10
The final value of c1 = 15
```

At first glance the idea of sending a message through a method name to an object may appear to be a superficial variation on sending data to a procedure. But it is not. Each object carries its own private data and a set of public and private methods bound to this underlying data. When a message is sent to an object, the object determines how the underlying data is to be manipulated.

Suppose the test program in Listing 4.2 were to attempt to access the internal structure of the object c1 by adding the following line to the program at the end of the program:

```
printf( ''\nObject c1 has value = %u'', c1.value );
```

This access attempt is illegal. The private section of any class is accessible only in the implementation section for each method of the given class. For the particular C++ translator used in testing the program of Listing 4.2, the presence of the above offending line of code is trapped by the translator, which emits the following error message:

```
''countst.cpp'', line 25: error: value is private
```

The error is trapped at compilation time, which is desirable. The C++ translator in essence is telling the programmer, "These data are off limits." The programmer is thus forced to manipulate the underlying counter data through the methods available in the class counter. Consistency of usage is ensured for all objects of class counter.

By encapsulating the concept of a counter in class counter, the programmer is prohibited from accidentally mixing a variable (object) of class counter with a variable of some other integer class. For example, the expression

```
weight = 100 + c1
```

is illegal if c1 is an object of class counter. If c1 were simply declared as an integral type, such an error would go undetected by the compiler and might cause a serious program error.

Instead of implementing each method of class counter in-line, as in Listing 4.1, we might wish to separate the implementation from the definition and use a separate file for implementing class counter. Such a decomposition is shown in Listing 4.3. The dotted line in Listing 4.3 indicates the separation between the definition file and the implementation file.

The strange-looking syntax

```
counter::counter( ) { value = 0; }
```

means that the constructor counter( ) comes from class counter. The syntax

```
void counter::increment( ) { if ( value < 65535 ) value++; };
```

means that the method increment( ) also comes from class counter.

In general, if a class method is not implemented in the class definition, the class name must be prepended to the method name and separated from the method name by a double colon.

For the decomposition given in Listing 4.3, the file count.cpp must be compiled separately from the file countst.cpp. The linker must be invoked so as to link the object file resulting from the compilation of countst.cpp to the object file resulting from the compilation of count.cpp.

Even with a class as simple as the counter class we can make an observation about software maintenance. If the internal structure of class counter were changed in the future, the only section of code in the software system that would have to be modified would be the file count.cpp. Since the rest of the software system communicates with objects of class counter by sending these objects messages, the messages would not have to be changed. Only the implementation of the methods would require modification in response to a change in the

internal structure of the underlying data of this class. Such localized maintenance is very desirable because it protects the integrity of the software system;
the architecture of the software system based on passing messages between objects remains intact.

Listing 4.3
Decomposition of
Class Counter
into a Definition
Section and an
Implementation
Section

```
// This code defines the class called counter
// File count.h
class counter
{
  private:
    unsigned int value;

  public:
    counter( );

    void increment( );

    void decrement( );
    unsigned int access_value( );
};
```

```
// Implementation of class counter
// File count.cpp
#include ''count.h''
counter::counter( ) { value = 0; }
void counter::increment( ) { if ( value < 65535 ) value++; };
void counter::decrement( ) { if ( value > 0 ) value--; };
unsigned int counter::access_value( ) { return value; }
```

As another alternative to the decomposition shown in Listing 4.3, we may
wish to implement each method of class counter in a separate file. This decomposition is shown in Listing 4.4. The advantage of such a decomposition is that
it makes possible linkage to only the methods actually used, thus saving code.
The disadvantage of this fine level of decomposition is that it is more difficult to
manage the complexity of many independent library files (modules). In most
cases we suggest that all or most of the class methods be implemented in the
same file.

Listing 4.4
A Finer
Decomposition of
Class Counter

```
// Partial implementation of class counter
// File count1.cpp
#include ''count.h''
counter::counter( ) { value = 0; }
```

```
// Partial implementation of class counter
// File count2.cpp
```

Listing 4.4
(continued)

```
#include ''count.h''
void counter::increment(){if ( value < 65535 ) value++;};
```

```
// Partial implementation of class counter
// File count3.cpp
#include ''count.h''
void counter::decrement(){if ( value > 0 ) value--;};
```

```
// Partial implementation of class counter
// File count4.cpp
#include ''count.h''
unsigned int counter::access_value(){return value;}
```

To summarize some of the observations from the class counter example:

■ A class can have three sections: private, protected, and public.

■ The private section of a class is inaccessible outside the section(s) of the software system in which the methods are implemented. An exception can be made using the friend construct, to be described later in this chapter.

■ The name of a class followed by a double colon must be used in front of the method name whenever the method is implemented outside of the class definition.

■ A constructor is a method that has the same name as its class and is used to initialize the private data of an object, when the object is declared.

■ A message is sent to an object by using the name of the object followed by a dot and the name of the method (with its parameters).

■ The implementation of class methods can be performed in a single file separate from the file that contains the class definition. Each method or group of methods can be implemented in a separate file apart from files containing the other method implementations.

■ In most cases it is suggested that all methods be implemented in the same file to reduce the complexity of library management.

A structure (struct) in C++ is a class with all data and methods automatically public. Thus a C++ struct can contain methods and not just data as is the case in C.

Let us consider one final, and undesirable, implementation of the counter ADT in Listing 4.5. Because counter is defined as a struct counter rather than as a class counter, the data member value is public. Thus the main function, included in this file, can and does access the internal structure of this underlying data type. This is exactly what we wish to avoid when we encapsulate an abstract data type.

Listing 4.5
Implementation
of Counter ADT
Using a Struct
Instead of a Class
Definition

```
#include <stdio.h>
struct counter
{
   unsigned int value;
   counter(){value = 0;}; // A constructor
   void increment(){if ( value < 65535 ) value++;};
   void decrement(){if ( value > 0 ) value--;};
   unsigned int access_value(){ return value; }
};
main()
{
   counter c1; // Automatically initialized
   counter c2; // Automatically initialized
   for ( int i = 1; i <= 15; i++ ) // Notice the declaration of int i
   {
      c1.value++;
      printf( "\nc1 = %u", c1.value );
      c2.value++;
   }
   printf( "\nAfter the loop the value of c2 = %u",
           c2.value );
   for ( i = 1; i <= 5; i++ )
      c2.value--;
   printf( "\nThe final value of c2 = %u", c2.value );
   printf( "\nThe final value of c1 = %u", c1.value );
}
```

4.3 Self-Reference in Classes

C++ classes can contain objects from other classes, pointers to objects from other classes, or pointers to objects of their own class (*self-reference*).

In the implementation of a member function (method belonging to a particular class), method names can be used without explicit reference to an object.

The reserved word *this* is defined as a pointer to the object that sent a message invoking a particular method. The pointer this can thus be used as a self-reference. It is normally used when implementing methods that manipulate pointers directly. Listing 4.6 illustrates the use of the self-reference pointer this with a "dog" tutorial.

The class dog contains private data that includes a pointer to a character string, name, and two pointers to objects of class dog. The class dog has three public methods: dog_name( ), which returns a pointer to a character string containing the private data, name; create_tail(char* name_of_tail), which allocates storage for the private data tail and assigns the new dog object a tail name; and get_name_of_tail( ), which looks into the private tail data for a given dog object and returns the name of the tail. A constructor is specified in the definition of class dog.

Let us examine the implementation of each of the methods. The constructor contains the following code:

```
name = new char[ strlen( dog_name ) + 1 ];
strcpy( name, dog_name );
tail = body = 0;
```

The first line of code allocates strlen(dog_name) + 1 bytes in the heap and returns the address, name. Each object of class dog has its own private pointer, name. The second line of code copies the string dog_name to the address name. The third line of code assigns the addresses of tail and body to nil (0).

The method dog_name( ) returns the address of the private data, name.

The method create_tail(char* name_of_tail) contains the following code:

```
tail = new dog( name_of_tail );
tail -> body = this;
```

The first line of code uses the memory allocation function new to create a new instance of a dog with the name name_of_tail. The constructor function, described above, is automatically activated by this line of code. The second line of code assigns the private data body, a pointer to an object of class dog, to the memory address of the object that sent the message create_tail. The tail is thus linked back to the dog that created it.

Finally, the method get_name_of_tail( ) uses the following line of code:

```
return this -> tail -> dog_name( );
```

This line of code could be written

```
return tail -> dog_name( );
```

Self-reference is totally optional and in fact would ordinarily not be used. As indicated earlier, class members can be referenced within the implementation of a method without using an object name. More meaningful illustrations of the self-reference pointer this are presented in later examples in this chapter.

Listing 4.6
About Dogs,
Their Tails, and
Self-Reference

```
// About dogs and their tails - A tutorial tale

#include <stdio.h>
#include <string.h>

class dog
{
   private:
      dog* body;
      char* name;
      dog *tail;
```

```
      public:
        dog( char* dog_name );
        char* dog_name();

        void create_tail( char* name_of_tail );

        char* get_name_of_tail();
};

dog::dog( char* dog_name )
{
    name = new char[ strlen( dog_name ) + 1 ];
    strcpy( name, dog_name );
    tail = body = 0;
}

char* dog::dog_name()
{
    return name;
}

void dog::create_tail( char* name_of_tail )
{
    tail = new dog( name_of_tail );
    tail -> body = this;
}

char* dog::get_name_of_tail()
{
    return this -> tail -> dog_name();
}

main()
{
    dog sheep_dog( ''Rover'' );

    sheep_dog.create_tail( ''Furry'' );

    printf( ''\nThe name of the dog is %s'',
            sheep_dog.dog_name() );
    printf( ''\nThe type of tail is %s'',
            sheep_dog.get_name_of_tail() );
}
```

4.4   Constructors and Destructors

Constructors are methods with the same name as the class in which they are defined that provide for the automatic initialization of objects at their point of declaration. *Destructors,* indicated by the tilde symbol, ~, in front of the class name, are methods that provide for the automatic deallocation of the storage occupied by an object when the block containing the object is exited. This is particularly important when an object contains storage in the heap. Such storage can only be explicitly deallocated by the programmer using the delete function unless automatic deallocation using a destructor is provided.

The use of constructors and destructors is illustrated by building a C++ class that defines and implements an integer stack abstract data type. The C++ implementation of the stack ADT is contrasted with a comparable implementation in Modula-2. By comparing the C++ implementation that uses constructors with a Modula-2 implementation without constructors (they are not available in Modula-2), the purpose and value of constructors will be more apparent.

4.4.1   Stack abstract data type implemented as a C++ class

In implementing a stack abstract data type as a C++ class, we define our integer stack ADT as containing the allowable set of values from -32787 to 32767. The operations that can be performed are push and pop. The push operation is used to add a new integer to the stack. The pop operation removes an integer from the stack. The stack follows the first-in-last-out queue discipline.

The definition and implementation of a class stack are shown in Listing 4.7. This class encapsulates the concept of an integer stack abstract data type. It hides the representation of the stack from all outside users.

The private section contains the private data top and bottom. Each of these datum are pointers to type int.

The constructor, stack( ), assigns the private pointers top and bottom initially to the same address and allocates storage in the heap for 100 integers. This simple implementation of a stack is defective because it limits the number of integers that can be stored to a fixed value. The abstraction of a stack imposes no such upper limit on the number of objects that can be stored. We shall live with this restriction for now.

The code for the in-line implementation of method push is

```
if ( ( top – bottom ) < 100 )
  *top++ = c;
```

After checking that the capacity of the stack has not been exceeded, the integer c is assigned to the address top, and then this address is incremented.

The code for the in-line implementation of method pop is

```
if (--top >= bottom )
  return *top;
```

After checking to see that there still exists at least one element on the stack and after decrementing the address top, the integer stored at address top is returned.

Finally, the destructor, ~stack( ), deallocates the storage at memory address bottom and deallocates the storage for an object of class stack when the block containing the object is exited.

Listing 4.7
Interface and
Implementation
of Integer Stack

```
// Interface and implementation of integer stack
// File stack.h
#include <stdio.h>
#include <string.h>
class stack
{
  private:
    int *top;

    int *bottom;

  public:
    stack()
    {
      top = bottom = new int[ 100 ];
    }

    void push( int c )
    {
      if ( ( top - bottom ) < 100 )
        *top++ = c;
    }

    int pop()
    {
      if (--top >= bottom )
        return *top;
    }

    -stack()
    {
      delete bottom;
    }
};
```

Listing 4.8 presents a simple test program that uses the class stack to reverse the characters of a name. It must be remembered that in C++, as in C, characters are implemented as integers so that a stack of integers can be used to store characters.

Function reverse_name(char* name) declares an automatic object, s, of class stack. The private pointers top and bottom of the object s are automatically initialized, and storage for the stack data is automatically allocated.

In the first for loop, the message push(name[i]) is sent to object s. In the second for loop, the message pop( ) is sent to the object s. The effect is to load the reverse sequence of characters into the string reverse. The address of this string is returned to the main function in the printf statement.

Upon exit of function reverse_name, the storage in the heap for the object s is automatically deallocated because of the destructor -stack( ).

A typical run of this program produces

```
Enter your name: Richard
Your name backwards is drahciR
```

Listing 4.8
Test Program That
Uses Class Stack

```cpp
// Test program that uses class stack
// File stacktst.cpp
#include "stack.h"
char* reverse_name( char* name )
{
    stack s;
    char* reverse;

    for ( int i = 0; i < strlen( name ); i++ )
        s.push( name[ i ] );
    reverse = new char[ strlen( name ) + 1 ];
    for ( i = 0; i < strlen( name ); i++ )
        reverse[ i ] = s.pop();
    reverse[ strlen( name ) ] = '\0';
    return reverse;
}

main()
{
    char your_name[ 20 ];
    char name_backwards[ 20 ];

    printf( "\nEnter your name: " );
    scanf( "%s", your_name );
    printf( "\nYour name backwards is %s",
            reverse_name( your_name ) );
}
```

4.4.2   Stack abstract data type implemented in Modula-2

As we see how the stack abstract data type is implemented in Modula-2, we can compare this implementation with that in C++. The reader who is not interested in a comparison of Modula-2 opaque types with C++ classes is urged to skip or skim over this section.

Listing 4.9 shows a Modula-2 DEFINITION MODULE that specifies an opaque type stack.

The opaque type stack is defined without any representational details. The interfaces to three procedures, push, pop, and define, are given. Each of these procedures has a first parameter of type stack. In a procedural language such as Modula-2, data is passed to procedures rather than procedures being passed to data. We must inform each procedure which stack we wish to manipulate with the first parameter.

The procedure define, not included in the class definition for stack in Listing 4.7, must be manually invoked by the Modula-2 programmer using this abstraction. There is no mechanism for automatically initializing a stack by mere virtue of its declaration as in C++. Although this may seem trivial to the reader, the inability to automatically initialize opaque variables is a shortcoming of the Modula-2 language, which requires the programmer to assume this burden.

Listing 4.9
DEFINITION
MODULE for Stack
ADT in Modula-2

```
DEFINITION MODULE stack;
   EXPORT QUALIFIED
      (* type *) stack,
      (* proc *) push, pop, define;
TYPE stack;
PROCEDURE define
         ( VAR s : stack );
PROCEDURE push
         ( s : stack ;
           c : CHAR );
PROCEDURE pop
         ( s : stack ) : CHAR;
END stack.
```

Listing 4.10 shows the Modula-2 IMPLEMENTATION MODULE that includes the body of each procedure.

The Modula-2 stack is implemented as a pointer to an array of 100 characters. In procedure define, memory storage is allocated to hold 100 characters and the integer index top is initialized to 0. Procedures push and pop work in a manner similar to their C++ counterparts.

Listing 4.10
IMPLEMENTATION
MODULE for Stack
ADT in Modula-2

```
IMPLEMENTATION MODULE stack;
   FROM Storage IMPORT ALLOCATE;
   VAR
      top : INTEGER;
TYPE stack = POINTER TO ARRAY[ 0 . . 99 ] OF CHAR;
PROCEDURE define
         ( VAR s : stack );
BEGIN
   NEW( s );
   top := 0;
END define;
PROCEDURE push
         ( s : stack;
           c : CHAR );
BEGIN
   IF top <= 100
   THEN
      s^[ top ] := c;
      INC( top );
   END;
END push;
PROCEDURE pop
         ( s : stack ) : CHAR;
```

Listing 4.10
(continued)

```
BEGIN
    IF top > 0
    THEN
        DEC( top );
        RETURN s^[ top ];
    END;
END pop;
END stack.
```

Listing 4.11 presents the counterpart of the C++ test program given in Listing 4.8. In addition to being considerably longer than the C++ test program, some key differences between the C++ and Modula-2 implementation of the integer stack ADT are the following:

- The storage in the heap for the variable stack that is defined as a local variable in procedure reversename is not deallocated upon the exit of this procedure. Another procedure, deallocatestack, would have to be defined and exported from the definition module stack and manually invoked by the user before exiting from procedure reversename.

- If the programmer forgets to invoke procedure define in procedure reversename, the system crashes because of an attempt to write data to an uninitialized pointer. In contrast, the C++ class stack, because of its constructor, provides automatic initialization and storage allocation by virtue of declaring an object, s, to be of class stack.

- In the two FOR loops in the main section of the program, data is sent to procedures push and pop rather than messages sent to the object s. This major difference between a procedural approach to problem solving and an object-oriented approach will become clearer as more examples are presented.

It is not the mission of this book to discuss the syntax and semantics of the Modula-2 language, so we refer the reader to the books, *Modula-2—A Software Development Approach* by Ford and Wiener (Wiley, 1986), *Modula-2 Wizard—A Programmer's Reference* by Wiener (Wiley, 1987), or *A First Course in Computer Science Using Modula-2* by Pinson, Sincovec, and Wiener (Wiley, 1987) for detailed descriptions of Modula-2 and its role in software development.

Listing 4.11
Modula-2 Test
Program That
Uses the Stack
ADT

```
MODULE stacktst;

    FROM stack IMPORT
        (* type *) stack,
        (* proc *) push, pop, define;

    FROM Strings IMPORT
        (* proc *) Length;

    FROM termio IMPORT
        (* proc *) writestring, readstring, writeln;
```

```
TYPE nametype = ARRAY[ 0..19 ] OF CHAR;
PROCEDURE reversename
          ( name              : nametype;
            VAR backwards : nametype );
VAR
     s          : stack;
     i          : INTEGER;
BEGIN
   define( s );
   FOR i := 0 TO Length( name ) - 1 DO
     push( s, name[ i ] );
   END;
   FOR i := 0 TO Length( name ) - 1 DO
     backwards[ i ] := pop( s );
   END;
   backwards[ Length( name ) ] := 0C;
END reversename;
VAR
     yourname, namebackwards : nametype;
BEGIN (* Main program *)
   writestring( ''Enter your name: '' );
   readstring( yourname );
   reversename( yourname, namebackwards );
   writeln;
   writeln;
   writestring( ''Your name backwards is '' );
   writestring( namebackwards );
END stacktst.
```

4.5   Class Objects as Members

The nesting of class objects within class definitions is common and useful. As we consider class objects as members in C++, the issue of initializing objects internal to a class must be addressed. Let us consider the example given in Listing 4.12.

Class inner_class specifies a constructor that takes a single parameter and a method, write( ), that outputs the value of the private datum, x.

Class outer_class includes two internal objects as part of its private data, x and r. The constructor for class outer_class takes a single parameter, z. Suppose we wish to assign the values 20 and −36 to the internal objects x and r, respectively. The internal objects x and r are initialized by the constructor for class outer_class as follows:

```
outer_class::outer_class( int z ) : x( 20 ), r( -36 )
{
   y = z;
}
```

Constructors are listed after a colon, separated by commas. The constructors for the internal objects can be listed in any order. The constructors for the internal objects are executed before the constructor for the class containing the internal objects.

The reader should note the implementation of methods write_inner_x( ) and write_inner_r( ), given as

```
void write_inner_x(){x.inner_class::write();}
void write_inner_r(){r.inner_class::write();}
```

The name of class inner_class is used as a member name qualifier in front of message write so that the compiler knows which method write to use (both class inner_class and class outer_class have a method write).

When a class containing internal objects is deallocated because of its destructor, the body of the destructor code for the object containing internal objects is executed before the destructor code for the internal objects.

Listing 4.12
Initializing Objects
Internal to a Class

```
// Program to illustrate class members that are objects
#include <stdio.h>
class inner_class
{
  private:
    int x;

  public:
    inner_class( int z ){x = z;}
    void write(){printf( "\n%d", x );}
};
class outer_class
{
  private:
    int y;
    inner_class x;
    inner_class r;
  public:
    outer_class( int z );
    void write(){printf( "\n%d", y );}
    void write_inner_x(){x.inner_class::write();}
    void write_inner_r(){r.inner_class::write();}
};
outer_class::outer_class( int z ) : x( 20 ), r( -36 )
{
  y = z;
}

main()
{
  outer_class object( -12 );
```

```
        object.write_inner_x();
        object.write_inner_r();
        object.write();
}
```

4.6   Vectors of Objects

To declare a *vector of objects* of a class with a constructor, that class must have a constructor that can be called without an argument list. Even default arguments cannot be used.

Consider the code in Listing 4.13. A class point is defined with two private data, x1 and x2, which represent the coordinates of a point in a plane. A constructor,

```
point( int x, int y ) { x1 = x; x2 = y; }
```

allows the user to set the coordinates of a point when it is declared.

In the main program, a point with coordinates 3, 4 is declared and the x and y coordinates printed out.

The last line of code declares a vector, more_data, of 20 points. This statement is illegal because the class point has a constructor. One might consider fixing this vector problem by removing the constructor from class point. This solution is unacceptable because the user must be able to initialize the coordinates of a point when a point object is declared. A better solution is given in Listing 4.14. A private method, init, takes two parameters x and y. Two constructors are provided. The first is the same as the constructor in Listing 4.13. The second calls the private method init and sets x1 and x2 to 0.

The output of the program in Listing 4.13 is:

```
The y coordinate = 4
The x coordinate of index 18 = 0
```

Listing 4.13
Vectors of Objects
with an Error

```
// Vectors of objects

#include <stdio.h>

class point
{
    private:
        int x1, x2;

    public:
        point( int x, int y ) { x1 = x; x2 = y; }
        int x_cord() { return x1; }
        int y_cord() { return x2; }
};
```

Listing 4.13
(continued)

```
main()
{
  point data( 3, 4 );
  printf( "\nx coordinate = %d", data.x_cord() );
  printf( "\ny coordinate = %d", data.y_cord() );
  point more_data[ 20 ]; // This statement is illegal
}
```

Listing 4.14
Vector of Objects
Without an Error

```
// Vectors of objects
#include <stdio.h>
class point
{
  private:
    int x1, x2;
    void init( int x, int y )
    {
      x1 = x;
      x2 = y;
    }
  public:
    point( int x, int y ) { x1 = x; x2 = y; }

    point() { init( 0, 0 ); }

    int x_cord() { return x1; }

    int y_cord() { return x2; }
};

main()
{
  point data( 3, 4 );
  printf( "\nThe y coordinate = %d", data.y_cord() );

  point more_data[ 20 ];
  printf( "\nThe x coordinate of index 18 = %d",
          more_data[ 18 ].x_cord() );
}
```

4.7   Friends

The friend construct is a useful adjunct to encapsulation and data hiding, but one that should be used with caution. Some benefits of encapsulation and data hiding—namely, the localization of maintenance if changes are made to the representation of the underlying data type and consistency of usage for a class of objects throughout the software system—have already been discussed. A possible drawback of encapsulation and data hiding using classes is that they tightly bind a data type to a set of methods and force the user to manipulate the underlying data type using the methods specified for the underlying type. That is, only a prescribed set of messages can be sent to an object of the given class.

The private data and methods of a class are available only within the class definition and also within the implementation of the methods, which might be in different files. This limited availability imposes an enormous responsibility on the software designer to ensure that each class has sufficient methods to provide manipulation of the underlying data for all situations that might be encountered.

Data hiding has the potential for increasing computational overhead. The case of one object sending a message to another object is common. If the message being sent is not implemented in-line, as is often the case for complex method implementations, then function call overhead must be expended. This computational overhead may be acceptable if it happens infrequently but may become intolerable if it happens often. If a method is implemented in-line, no function call overhead is incurred when the method is invoked.

C++ provides the software developer a by-pass that allows selected outside classes or functions to access the private data of the class. For example, if object a (class A) frequently sends a particular message to object b (class B), and the method implementation is not in-line, it may be wise to declare the particular method in class B to be a *friend* of class A. This will allow the method in class B to directly access the private data of class A and by-pass the function call overhead that would otherwise be required.

When a class declares either another class or a specific function to be a friend, this is equivalent to boring a peephole into the opaque shield that shrouds the private section of the class. If too many such peepholes are bored, the benefits of data hiding may be severely compromised. Thus it is recommended that the friend construct be used with great restraint.

Figure 4.2 illustrates a class A and its friend class B. The declaration of friends is illustrated by declaring function int method_a(float z), the entire class B, and method char* strange( ) from class C to be friends of class A.

```
class A
{
   friend int method_a( float z );
   friend class B;
   friend char* C::strange( );

   . . .
};
```

A friend declaration can be placed into either the private or public section of a class—it makes no difference.

Figure 4.2
Friends.

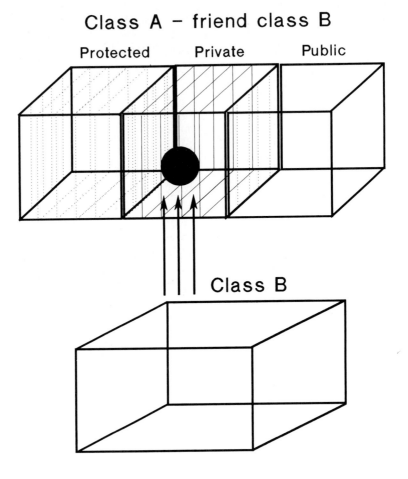

4.8   Static Members of a Class

As already mentioned, each object of a given class has its own copy of all the data defined by the class. There are times when it is desirable for all the objects of a particular class to share a datum or to share data. If a class member is declared as *static,* there will be only one copy of the class member shared by all objects of the class.

Figure 4.3 depicts four objects of the same class, ABCD, that each have their own copy of char ch but share a single integer, s.

Figure 4.3
Static variables.

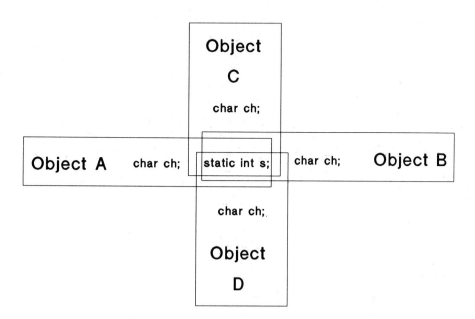

4.9 Overloading of Operators

The capacity to overload operators enhances the extensibility of the C++ language. A major goal of object-oriented programming is to create code that naturally represents the problem space; that is, the code should map easily to the entities in the problem space. With the advent of high-level languages, it has become easier to accomplish this goal. C++ is an extensible language because as new classes are defined, their objects are endowed with properties that are not part of the base language. For example, the complex number class that is supplied with most C++ implementations allows a programmer to define and manipulate complex numbers as if they were predefined in the language. The operations that one would normally wish to use in manipulating complex numbers include addition, subtraction, multiplication, and division. One could, of

TABLE 4.1   C++ Operators That Can Be Overloaded

+	−	*	/	%	^	&	|	~	!
=	<	>	+=	−=	*=	/=	%=	^=	&=
|=	<<	>>	>>=	<<=	==	!=	<=	>=	&&
||	++	−−	[]	()	new	delete			

course, define methods with the names add, sub, mult, and div. Then if z1 and z2 were declared as objects from class complex, addition would be performed as follows:

```
z1.add( z2 ) or z2.add( z1 ).
```

That is, the message add with parameter z2 would be sent to object z1, or the message add with parameter z1 would be sent to object z2. This is much more cumbersome than the simple operation

```
z1 + z2
```

Performing the addition of two objects both from class complex, like z1 and z2 above, requires the *overloading* of the + operator. That is, the + operator must be redefined as a method of class complex. Once this is done, then the addition of two complex objects, such as z1 and z2, can be represented in a natural way. The language will have been extended so naturally that a beginning C++ programmer might think that complex numbers are predefined in the language.

Operator overloading in general allows a large set of operators, given in Table 4.1, to be redefined as methods within a class. The goal is to provide language extensibility in a natural way.

A programmer should be careful in choosing the appropriate operator from the wide choice given in Table 4.1 when defining an operator method for a class. If the '+' operator is overloaded to mean multiply for a numerical class such as complex, the compiler will be none the worse for this—but the human reader will!

4.9.1   Binary and unary operators

Binary and unary operators differ slightly in the classes and functions within which their methods can be defined. A binary operator, such as +, −, *, or /, can be defined by either a method within a class taking one argument or a friend function taking two arguments. A hidden argument, this, is always present for operator functions defined as class methods. Therefore only operators with zero or one parameters can be defined as methods within a class. Operators with two parameters must be defined as functions with the friend qualifier.

A unary operator, such as $++$, can be defined by either a method within a class taking no arguments or a friend function taking one argument.

Consider a binary operator, B. The expression

```
operand_1 B operand_2
```

can be interpreted as either operand_1.operatorB (operand_2) or operatorB (operand_1, operand_2).

Consider a unary operator, U. The expression

```
operandU
```

or

```
Uoperand
```

can be interpreted as either operand.operatorU( ) or operatorU(operand).

When the operators $++$ or $--$ are overloaded, it is not possible to distinguish prefix from postfix application.

An overloaded operator function must either be a method within a class or have at least one object as an argument, except for new and delete. This restriction ensures that a programmer cannot redefine an expression that does not involve a user-defined object.

If an overloaded operator might have a predefined type as its first parameter, the operator cannot be a method within a class but must be a friend function. Consider an overloaded binary operator, B, such as '+'. The operation

```
z + 27
```

can be interpreted as z.operator+(27)—that is, send the message '+' with parameter 27 to the object z.

What about, 27 + z? Clearly the expression

```
27.operator+( z )
```

does not make sense since 27 is not a user-defined object.

4.9.2   Some examples of operator overloading

In this section two examples of operator overloading are presented.

We first reconsider the simple counter class, presented in Section 4.2 and Listing 4.1. One defect of this class definition is that it defines the methods increment and decrement rather than the more natural ++ and −−. Let us see how we can overload the unary operators ++ and −− to produce a more natural counter class. In addition, we replace the method access_value with the overloaded operator ().

Listings 4.15, 4.16, and 4.17 present the interface, implementation, and test program for an improved class counter that overloads the operators ++, −−, and ().

In the counter class definition given in Listing 4.15, the operators ++, −−, and () are specified as overloaded operators using the code

```
void operator ++ ();
void operator −− ();
unsigned int operator () ();
```

The reserved word operator followed by the overloaded symbol is used to redefine the operator symbol. The third operator, ( ), is being used to mean "the value of."

Listing 4.16 examines one of the three operator implementations; namely, the '+' operator. The code is given as

```
void counter::operator ++ ()
{
   if ( value < 65535 )
     value++;
}
```

The syntax is the same as for any class method except that the reserved word operator is used in front of the symbol ++.

In Listing 4.17, the for loop,

```
for ( int i = 0; i < 12; i++ )
{
   my_great_counter++;
   printf( "'\nmy_great_counter = %d'', my_great_counter() );
}
```

is much more natural because of the overloaded operator ++. Compare the code of this main test program with the code in Listing 4.2.

Listing 4.15
Interface to Class
Counter with
Overloaded
Operators

```
// Interface to improved counter class with overloaded
// operators.
// File count.h

#include <stdio.h>

class counter
{
    private:
        unsigned int value;

    public:
        counter() { value = 0; }

        void operator ++ ( );

        void operator -- ( );

        unsigned int operator ( ) ( );
};
```

Listing 4.16
Implementation of
Class Counter with
Overloaded
Operators

```
// Implementation of improved counter class
// File count.cpp
#include "count.h"

void counter::operator ++ ( )
{
    if ( value < 65535 )
        value++;
}

void counter:: operator -- ( )
{
    if ( value > 0 )
        value--;
}

unsigned int counter::operator ( ) ( )
{
    return value;
}
```

Listing 4.17
Test Program That
Uses Improved
Class Counter

```
// Test program that uses improved counter class
// File countst.cpp
#include "count.h"

main()
{
    counter my_great_counter;
    for ( int i = 0; i < 12; i++ )
    {
        my_great_counter++;
        printf( "\nmy_great_counter = %d", my_great_counter() );
    }
    my_great_counter--;
    my_great_counter--;
    printf( "\nmy_great_counter = %d", my_great_counter() );
}
```

TABLE 4.2 Operations Defined for Rational Number Class

Operator	Used to:
assign	Assign a given numerator and denominator to a rational number.
=	Assign one rational number to another.
x=	Perform the arithmetic operation, x on the rational number with the value given by the right side of the expression. x can be either +, −, *, or /.
==	Compare two rational numbers for equality.
!=	Compare two rational numbers for inequality.
+	Add two rational numbers.
−	Subtract two rational numbers.
*	Multiply two rational numbers.
/	Divide two rational numbers.
real	Convert a rational number to a float format.
<<	Overload the output stream operator.

The second example of operator overloading is much more extensive. We define a class called rational_number. The reader may recall that a rational number is defined as any number that can be represented as a ratio of whole numbers. The numbers 2/3, 117/257, and −12/36 are all rational numbers. The number square root of 2 is irrational.

Since rational numbers are not predefined in C++, we must effectively extend the language by creating a rational number class.

The rational number abstract data type is characterized by the following set of values:

`Value set: ratio of any two long integers.`

The operations listed in Table 4.2 are defined for the rational number abstract data type.

The rational_number class will employ each of the method names given in Table 4.2.

The interface to class rational_number is given in Listing 4.18. The operators (member functions) specified in the listing correspond exactly to the operation names given in Table 4.2. The overloading of operator symbols allows the user to manipulate rational numbers as if they had been predefined in the language.

The private section of the rational number class contains a method, void simplify(rational_number &num), that takes an object, num, by reference. Its purpose is to reduce to a common denominator any rational number argument sent into it. For example, if the rational number −12/36 was sent into method simplify, the output would be −1/3.

The constructor method allows the user to specify the numerator and denominator of a rational number at the point of declaration. If no such parameters are sent in, the default values of numerator = 0 and denominator = 0 are used.

The reader should note that friend functions are used for the operations +, −, *, /, ==, !=, real, and <<. With the exception of function real, which has one parameter, the other friend functions each have two parameters and thus cannot be implemented as member functions. The function real could be implemented as a member function.

Listing 4.18
Interface to
Rational Number
Class

```
// The interface to the class rational_number
// File rational_number.h
#include <stream.h>
class rational_number
{
   private:
     void simplify( rational_number &num );

     long numerator, denominator;
   public:
     rational_number( long num = 0, long den = 1 )
     {
        numerator = num;
        denominator = den;
        simplify( *this );
     }

     void assign( long num, long den )
     // Used to assign a rational number a given numerator
     // and denominator.
     // Usage:
     // rational_number number;
     // number.assign( 12, 18 );
     {
        numerator = num;
        denominator = den;
        simplify( *this );
     }

     rational_number operator = ( rational_number &num )
     /* The argument is taken in as a reference parameter to
        avoid making a copy of it (saving memory space).
     */
     // Assignment operator
     // Usage:
     // rational_number num1, num2;
     // num2 = num1; This means num2.operator = ( num1 );
     {
        numerator = num.numerator;
        denominator = num.denominator;
        simplify( *this );
        return ( *this );
     }
```

Listing 4.18
(continued)

```
rational_number operator = ( long whole_number )
// Assignment operator
// Usage:
// rational_number num;
// num = 1456;
{
   numerator = whole_number;
   denominator = 1;
   return ( *this );
}

rational_number operator += ( rational_number &num )
// Operator addition
// Usage:
// rational_number num1, num2;
// num2 += num1;
{
   long old_denom = denominator;
   long old_num = numerator;
   long d = num.denominator;
   long n = num.numerator;
   denominator *= d;
   numerator = old_num * d + old_denom * n;
   simplify( *this );
   return ( *this );
}

rational_number operator -= ( rational_number &num )
// Operator subtraction
// Usage:
// rational_number num1, num2;
// num2 -= num1;
{
   long old_denom = denominator;
   long old_num = numerator;
   long d = num.denominator;
   long n = num.numerator;
   denominator *= d;
   numerator = old_num * d - old_denom * n;
   simplify( *this );
   return ( *this );
}

rational_number operator *= ( rational_number &num )
// Operator multiplication
// Usage:
// rational_number num1, num2;
// num2 *= num1;
{
   numerator *= num.numerator;
   denominator *= num.denominator;
   simplify( *this );
   return *this;
}

rational_number operator /= ( rational_number &num )
// Operator division
// Usage:
// rational_number num1, num2;
```

```
// num2 /= num1;
// If the denominator is zero, no operation is
// performed.
{
   if ( num.numerator != 0 )
   {
     numerator *= num.denominator;
     denominator *= num.numerator;
     simplify ( *this );
     return *this;
   }
}

friend rational_number
     operator + ( rational_number &num1,
                  rational_number &num2 );
// Operator addition
// Usage:
// rational_number num1, num2, num3;
// num3 = num1 + num2;
// This means num3 = operator + ( num1, num2 );

friend rational_number
     operator - ( rational_number &num1,
                  rational_number &num2 );
// Operator subtraction
// Usage:
// rational_number num1, num2, num3;
// num3 = num1 - num2;

friend rational_number
     operator * rational_number &num1,
                rational_number &num2 );
// Operator multiplication
// Usage:
// rational_number num1, num2, num3;
// num3 = num1 * num2;

friend rational_number
     operator / ( rational_number &num1,
                  rational_number &num2 );
// Operator division
// Usage:
// rational_number num1, num2, num3;
// num3 = num1 / num2;

friend int operator == ( rational_number &num1,
                         rational_number &num2 );
// Operator equality
// Usage:
// rational_number num1, num2;
// if ( num1 == num2 ) . . .

friend int operator != ( rational_number &num1,
                         rational_number &num2 );
// Operator inequality
// Usage;
// rational_number num1, num2;
// if ( num1 != num2 ) . . .
```

Listing 4.18
(continued)

```
friend double real( rational_number &num );
// Conversion from rational_number to real
// Usage:
// rational_number num1; double r;
// r = real( num1 );

friend ostream& operator << ( ostream &s,
                              rational_number &num );
// Output stream overloading
// Usage:
// rational_number num;
// cout << num;
};
```

Listing 4.19 presents the implementation of class rational_number.

Let us examine the private method simplify. The following code segment determines the greatest common divisor between the numerator and the denominator. This is a middle-ending loop that terminates if gcd equals 0, or if the numerator and the denominator can both be divided evenly by the gcd.

```
gcd = ( abs( number.numerator ) >
        abs( number.denominator ) ?
        abs( number.denominator ) :
        abs( number.numerator ) );
if ( gcd == 0 ) return;
do
{
   if ( gcd == 1 ) break;
   if ( ( number.numerator % gcd == 0 ) &&
        ( number.denominator % gcd == 0 ) ) break;
   else gcd--;
}
while ( 1 ); // Simulates infinite loop
```

Following this segment of code, the function simplify attaches the correct sign to the numerator after dividing both the numerator and denominator by the gcd. This is done with the code segment

```
number.numerator /= gcd;
number.denominator /= gcd;
// Attach correct sign to the numerator
if ( number.numerator < 0 && number.denominator < 0 )
{
   number.numerator = - number.numerator;
   number.denominator = - number.denominator;
}
else if ( number.numerator < 0 ||
          number.denominator < 0 )
{
   number.numerator = - abs( number.numerator );
   number.denominator = abs( number.denominator );
}
```

Because the parameter number is passed in as a reference parameter, the simplified rational number is passed back to the object that sent the message simplify.

The implementation of the + operation is more complex than the implementation of the * operation. Let us examine each of these. The code for the + implementation is

```
rational_number
        operator + ( rational_number &num1,
                     rational_number &num2 )
{
   long nresult, dresult;

   dresult = num1.denominator * num2.denominator;
   nresult = num1.numerator * num2.denominator +
             num1.denominator * num2.numerator;
   return rational_number( nresult, dresult );
}
```

The parameters num1 and num2 are reference parameters only to save stack space. Copies of each of these parameters are not made on the system stack because of the & designator. The initial value of the denominator, dresult, is given as the product of the two denominators. The initial value of the numerator, nresult, is given as the sum of products of the first numerator multiplied by the second denominator and the first denominator multiplied by the second numerator, as required algebraically. The constructor rational_number is used to return a copy of the required rational number object. The constructor also simplifies the rational number with initial numerator nresult and initial denominator dresult before returning the number.

The code for the implementation of the * operation is

```
rational_number
        operator * ( rational_number &num1,
                     rational_number &num2 )
{
   long nresult, dresult;

   nresult = num1.numerator * num2.numerator;
   dresult = num1.denominator * num2.denominator;
   return rational_number( nresult, dresult );
}
```

Algebraically, the operations for the multiply operator are much simpler than for the addition operator. The initial value of the numerator, nresult, is given as the product of the two numerators. Likewise, the initial value of the denominator is given as the product of the two denominators. Finally, a copy of the rational number formed using the constructor rational_number is returned in simplified form.

The stream operator, <<, is discussed in the next section. The code that overloads this stream operator to permit the natural output of rational numbers is given as

```
ostream& operator << ( ostream &s, rational_number &num )
{
   if ( num.denominator != 1 )
      return ( s << num.numerator <<
                  ''/ '' << num.denominator );
   else
      return ( s << num.numerator );
}
```

Only if the denominator is not equal to 1 is the rational number output as numerator/denominator; otherwise only the numerator is output.

Listing 4.19
Implementation of
the Rational
Number Class

```
// Implementation of class rational
// File rational.cpp
#include ''rational.h''
#include <stdlib.h>
void rational_number::simplify( rational_number &number )
// Returns the rational_number number in simplest form
// i.e. 2 / 3 = simplify( 20 / 30 )
{
   extern int abs( int );

   int gcd;
   if ( number.numerator == 0 )
   {
      number.denominator = 1;
      return;
   }
   gcd = ( abs( number.numerator ) >
           abs( number.denominator ) ?
           abs( number.denominator ) :
           abs( number.numerator ) );
   if ( gcd == 0 ) return;
   do
   {
      if ( gcd == 1 ) break;
      if ( ( number.numerator % gcd == 0 ) &&
         ( number.denominator % gcd == 0 ) ) break;
      else gcd--;
   }
   while ( 1 ); // Simulates infinite loop
   number.numerator /= gcd;
   number.denominator /= gcd;
   // Attach correct sign to the numerator
   if ( number.numerator < 0 && number.denominator < 0 )
   {
      number.numerator = - number.numerator;
      number.denominator = - number.denominator;
   }
```

```
      else if ( number.numerator < 0 ||
             number.denominator < 0 )
      {
        number.numerator = - abs( number.numerator );
        number.denominator = abs( number.denominator );
      }
}

ostream& operator << ( ostream &s, rational_number &num )
{
    if ( num.denominator != 1 )
      return ( s << num.numerator <<
             '' / '' << num.denominator );
    else
      return ( s << num.numerator );
}

rational_number
        operator + ( rational_number &num1,
                    rational_number &num2 )
{
    long nresult, dresult;
    dresult = num1.denominator * num2.denominator;
    nresult = num1.numerator * num2.denominator +
            num1.denominator * num2.numerator;
    return rational_number( nresult, dresult );
}

rational_number operator - ( rational_number &num1,
                            rational_number &num2 )
{
    long nresult, dresult;

    dresult = num1.denominator * num2.denominator;
    nresult = num1.numerator * num2.denominator -
            num1.denominator * num2.numerator;
    return rational_number( nresult, dresult );
}

rational_number
        operator * ( rational_number &num1,
                    rational_number &num2 )
{
    long nresult, dresult;

    nresult = num1.numerator * num2.numerator;
    dresult = num1.denominator * num2.denominator;
    return rational_number( nresult, dresult );
}

rational_number operator / ( rational_number &num1,
                            rational_number &num2 )
{
    long nresult, dresult;

    if ( ( num2.numerator != 0 ) )
    {
      nresult = num1.numerator * num2.denominator;
      dresult = num1.denominator * num2.numerator;
      return rational_number( nresult, dresult );
    }
}
```

```
int operator == ( rational_number &num1,
                  rational_number &num2 )
{
   return ( float ) num1.numerator /
          ( float ) num1.denominator ==
          ( float ) num2.numerator /
          ( float ) num2.denominator;
}
int operator != ( rational_number &num1,
                  rational_number &num2 )
{
   return ( float ) num1.numerator /
          ( float ) num1.denominator !=
          ( float ) num2.numerator /
          ( float ) num2.denominator;
}

double real( rational_number &num )
{
   return ( double ) num.numerator /
          ( double ) num.denominator;
}
```

A test program that uses the rational number class is shown in Listing 4.20.
The code is self-explanatory. Most of the rational operations are exercised.

```
// Test program for class rational
// Must link to rational.obj
// File ratntst.cpp

#include "rational.h"
#include <stream.h>

main()
{
   rational_number a( 4, 5 );
   rational_number b( -10, 6 );
   cout << "\na = " << a;
   cout << "\nb = " << b;

   a *= b;
   cout << "\n( a *= b ) = " << a;

   a = b;
   cout << "\nAfter a = b, a = " << a << " b = " << b;

   a += b;
   cout << "\n( a += b ) = " << a;

   a -= b;
   cout << "\n( a -= b ) = " << a;

   a = b;
   a -= a;
   cout << "\na = b; a -= a; a = " << a;

   rational_number c( 15 );
   a += c;
   cout << "\n( a += 15 ) = " << a;
```

```
    a = 1234567;
    cout << "\n( a = 1234567; a = " << a;

    long d = 4;
    a = d;
    cout << "\n( a = long d = 4; a = " << a;

    a += ( b = 5 );
    cout << "\n( a += ( b = 5 ); ) = " << a;

    rational_number j( 4, 5 );
    rational_number k( 5, 4 );

    rational_number l = j + k;
    cout << "\n" << j << " + " << k << " = " << l;

    l = l + l;
    cout << "\n( l + l ) = " << l;

    l = l + k;
    cout << "\nk = 5/4; ( l = l + k ) = " << l;

    rational_number e, f, g, h, i, m;
    e = 17;
    f = 15;
    g = e / f;
    cout << "\n" << e << " / " << f << " = " << g;

    h = g;
    i = 1;
    m = i * h;
    cout << "\n" << h << " * " << i << " = " << m;

    if ( g == m )
      cout << "\nThe value of " << g << " equals that of "
           << m;
    else
      cout << "\nThe value of " << g <<
              " doesn't equal that of " << m;

    double r = real( g );
    cout << "\nThe real value of " << g << " = " << r;
    rational_number number;
    number.assign( 12, 15 );
    cout << "\nassign( 12, 15 ); number = " << number;
}
```

4.9.3   The <stream.h> library

C++, like C, includes no predefined functions for input or output. Input and output are handled through external libraries such as stdio or streams. This section discusses the stream library. Although we digress here from our general discussion of the overloading of operators, we indulge in this aside because of the great importance of the overloaded stream operators and input/output. The reader is referred to Chapter 8 of Stroustrup's book, *The C++ Programming Language,* for more details concerning the stream library.

The stream library input and output operations are concerned with converting typed objects such as integers, and reals to sequences of characters and vice versa.

The class ostream is defined in the stream library. The operator $<<$ ("put to") is overloaded to handle output of all the predefined types. It can also be overloaded to handle the output of user-defined types such as rational number in Listing 4.19.

A greatly simplified version of class ostream is the following:

```
class ostream
{
  // . . .
  public:
    ostream& operator << ( char * ch );
    ostream& operator << ( int i );
    ostream& operator << ( long l );
    ostream& operator << ( double r );

    . . .
};
```

The stream library defines the standard streams cout (for output that can be redirected), cin (for input that can be redirected), and cerr (for terminal output).

The operation

```
cout << i;
```

can be interpreted as

```
cout.operator<<( i );
```

The operation

```
cout << i << j;
```

can be interpreted as

```
( cout.operator<<( i ) ).operator<<( j );
```

Listing 4.21 illustrates the $<<$ operator and the standard output stream, cout. The output of this program is

```
r1 * r2 = -734.37
ch = 65
i = -560
The value of d is 1.234568
```

Listing 4.21
The Stream <<
Operator

```
// First illustration of the stream << operator
#include <stream.h>
main()
{
    float r1 = -27.3;
    float r2 = 26.9;
    char ch = 'A';
    int i = -560;
    double d = 1.23456789123;
    cout << ''\nr1 * r2 = '' << r1 * r2;
    cout << ''\nch = '' << ch;
    cout << ''\ni = '' << i;
    cout << ''\nThe value of d is '' << d;
}
```

Note that the character ch is output as an integer. If the character value of ch is desired, the statement

```
cout << ''\nch = '' << chr( ch );
```

should be used.

In general, if formatted output is desired, it can be achieved through the functions given in Table 4.3.

For C++ programmers who like the power and flexibility of the C output function printf, printf can be used directly from library stdio.h as we have been doing, or the function form can be used. This function is specified as

```
char* form( char* format . . . );
```

If the line

```
cout << form( ''Output is %.0f\ni = %d'', r1, i );
```

was added to Listing 4.21, the output would be

```
Output is -27
i = -560
```

TABLE 4.3 Functions for Formatted Output

char* oct(long, int = 0)	Octal representation
char* dec(long, int = 0)	Decimal representation
char* hex(long, int = 0)	Hexadecimal representation
char* chr(int, int = 0)	Character representation
char* str(char*, int = 0)	String representation

Because we assume that the reader has used the C function printf we will not explain all the formatting options of function form. (The reader is directed to any C book for details if our assumption is incorrect.) The function form works just like printf. We must confess a preference for the printf function for most output; therefore printf will be used in most of our later applications rather than stream functions.

Let us reexamine the overloaded stream operator $<<$ given in Listing 4.19 in connection with class rational_number. This code is

```
ostream& operator << ( ostream &s, rational_number &num )
{
  if ( num.denominator != 1 )
    return ( s << num.numerator <<
             '' / '' << num.denominator );
  else
    return ( s << num.numerator );
}
```

The first parameter, &s, binds a stream object such as cout or cerr to the operator $<<$. The second parameter is an object of class rational_number, num. The function returns the address of the output stream.

The body of code that implements the overloaded operator $<<$ uses the $<<$ operator on predefined data such as num.numerator and num.denominator.

A strong argument in favor of using the $<<$ from library stream is consistency of usage for both predefined and programmer-defined output. Streams can be connected to user-created files. The class ostream has the following constructors:

```
class ostream
{
  // . . .
  ostream( streambuf *s );      // Binds to stream buffer
  ostream( int fd );            // Binds to file buffer
  ostream( int size, char* p ); // Binds to vector
  . . .
}
```

The constructors associate a buffer with a stream. The class streambuf manages a buffer. The class filebuf is derived from class streambuf and manages a user-defined file. (We refer the user to Stroustrup's book for details.) A user always has the option of using the standard C library stdio.h or any other input output library from C for managing file input and output.

File input is similar to file output. The standard file cin is defined in the stream library as an object from class istream. The input operator $>>$ ("get from") can be used to obtain input for some predefined types.

A simplified version of class istream is given as

```
class istream
{
  // . . .
  public:
    istream& operator >> ( char * ); // String
    istream& operator >> ( char & ); // Character
    istream& operator >> ( int & );  // Integer
    istream& operator >> ( long & ); // Long
    istream& operator >> ( float & );
    istream& operator >> ( double & );
    . . .
}
```

A short example that illustrates the use of the >> operator and stream cin is given in Listing 4.22.

The following results are produced by running this program:

```
Enter an integer: -14

The integer input is -14

Enter a real: -34.6

The real number input is -34.599998

Enter a string: Hello

The string input is Hello
```

Listing 4.22
The Operator >>
from Stream Cin

```
#include <stream.h>

main()
{
  int i;
  float r;
  char str[ 80 ];

  cout << ''\nEnter an integer: '';
  cin >> i;
  cout << ''\nThe integer input is '' << i;

  cout << ''\n\nEnter a real: '';
  cin >> r;
  cout << ''\nThe real number input is '' << r;
  cout << ''\n\nEnter a string: '';
  cin >> str;
  cout << ''\nThe string input is '' << str;
}
```

The streams istream and ostream have a state associated with them. Error handling is performed by testing the state of these streams after input or output operations are performed. The states defined for these streams are given by

```
enum stream_state { _good, _eof, _fail, _bad );
```

Attempting an input operation to a stream that is not in state_good results in a null operation. Stroustrup (*The C++ Programming Language,* p. 238) indicates that "the difference between the states_fail and_bad is subtle and only really interesting to implementors of input operations. In the state_fail, it is assumed that the stream is uncorrupted and that no characters have been lost. In the state_bad, all bets are off."

The stream operator >> can be overloaded for programmer-created objects such as rational numbers. Consider the code segment given in Listing 4.23 that defines >> for rational numbers. The input format that is assumed is

```
numerator / denominator
```

The following code can be added to the test program given in Listing 4.20.

```
rational_number r;
cout << "Enter a rational number: ";
cin >> r;
cout << "\n\nThe rational number entered is " << r;
```

Listing 4.23
Overloaded >>
Operator for Class
Rational_Number

```
istream& operator >> ( istream &s, rational_number &num )
{
    long n, d;
    char ch;

    s >> n;
    s >> ch;
    if ( ch != '/' )
        s.clear( _bad ); // Set stream state to bad
    s >> d;
    num = rational_number( n, d );
    return s;
}
```

4.10   Some Baseline Classes

A central challenge in object-oriented program design is the decomposition of a problem into a set of objects and associated classes. Some classes must be designed specifically for a given problem. Other baseline classes should be available in software libraries for reuse in many applications. Included in this latter category are classes for stacks, queues, lists, and trees. Objects from these baseline classes are required in many application areas. Other baseline classes might include graphics, database management, natural language processing, numerical methods, and so forth.

A common characteristic of objects from classes stack, queue, list, and tree is that the operations that can be performed on the underlying data are independent of the base type of entity stored in each object. For example, a stack stores entities in such a way as to ensure that the last item to be stored is the first item to be available. The first item to be stored is the last item that is available. The nature of the entities stored on the stack does not affect the operations that can be performed on objects of class stack. We refer to such a stack class as a *generic* stack. Chapter 5 shows how generic classes can be used as the basis for deriving data-specific classes such as lists of integers or trees of a particular data structure. There it is shown how generic stacks and queues can be derived from generic lists.

Because of the fundamental importance of generic lists and trees, and to provide more examples of encapsulation and data hiding, the definition and implementation (encapsulation) of generic lists and trees are examined.

4.10.1   Generic lists

A generic list, like any other abstract data type, is characterized by the set of values and the set of operations that can be performed on objects of class list.

The set of values cannot be specified if the list is to be generic. This value set is established when a data-specific list is derived from the generic list. This derivation is shown in Chapter 5.

A minimum set of operations that define the list are

- insert   Add to the front of the list
- append   Add to the back of the list
- get   Remove an item from the front of the list
- clear   Remove all items from the list

Not included in the minimal list class are operations that allow two lists to be concatenated, or merged; the presence or absence of an element to be determined; and many other such operations. The goal here is to demonstrate how generic classes can be constructed.

The interface to the generic list is given in Listing 4.24.

A class node is defined with private data next, a pointer to the next node in the singly linked list, and contents, a pointer to the smallest unit of storage, char. Normally one might be tempted to associate the class member contents with a character string. In this case, the private member contents must be interpreted as the starting address of an array of bytes. The storage for this array is allocated dynamically in the implementation section of class node.

Since objects of class node will need to access the private data of class node, class list is declared to be a friend of class node.

Class list has a private section with head, a pointer to the first node in the list, and size, the number of bytes associated with the contents in each node.

The constructor for class list initializes the private datum head to 0 and assigns size to the value sent in as a parameter.

Public methods insert and append both take a single parameter, a, given as a pointer to type char. This address represents the starting address of the information to be stored at address contents.

Listing 4.24
Interface to
Generic List
Class

```
// This code defines a class for a singly linked list.
// File list.h.
#include <stdio.h>
class node
{
   friend class list;

   private:
      node* next;
      char* contents; // contents dynamically allocated
};
class list
{
   private:
      node* head; // Head of list
      int size; // Number of bytes for contents
   public:
      list( int s ) { head = 0; size = s; }
      void insert( char* a ); // Add to the front of the list.
      void append( char* a ); // Add to the back of the list.
      char* get();            // Remove the head of the list.
      void clear();           // Remove all the nodes in list.
      ~list() { clear(); }
};
```

Listing 4.25 presents the implementation of class list.

In the implementation of method insert an automatic object, temp, is declared as a pointer to class node. The space for temp is allocated on the heap using the memory allocation function new. The contents field of object temp is allocated by declaring size bytes in function new.

The for loop,

```
for ( int i = 0; i < size; i++ )
   temp -> contents[ i ] = a[ i ];
```

performs a byte-by-byte transfer of data from address a to address temp -> contents.

If the pointer head is nonzero, implying that the element being inserted is not the first element in the list, the code

```
temp -> next = head;
head = temp;
```

assigns the next field of private datum head to the old head and resets the new head to equal temp. If the pointer head is zero, implying that the element being inserted is the first element in the list, the code

```
temp -> next = 0;
head = temp;
```

assigns the next field of temp to 0 and assigns head to temp.

The code for append is more complex because the element to be inserted is at the end of the list. The list must be traversed before making the insertion.

If head is not zero (the insertion is not the first in the list), the following code is used:

```
previous = head;
current = head -> next;
while ( current != 0 )
{
   previous = current;
   current = current -> next;
}
newnode = new node;
newnode -> contents = new char[ size ];
newnode -> next = 0;
for ( int i = 0; i < size; i++ )
   newnode -> contents[ i ] = a[ i ];
previous -> next = newnode;
```

The list is traversed by replacing previous with current and current with current $->$ next until current $= 0$.

Then the pointer to node, newnode, is allocated, along with storage for its contents. The for loop performs a byte-by-byte assignment of the data to contents, as with method insert. Finally, the pointer previous is linked to the pointer newnode.

If the pointer head is zero (the insertion is the first in the list), the following code is used:

```
head = new node;
head -> contents = new char[ size ];
head -> next = 0;
for ( int i = 0; i < size; i++ )
   head -> contents[ i ] = a[ i ];
```

Storage for head and its contents are allocated. The data at address a is transferred byte-by-byte to head $->$ contents.

Finally, let us examine the code for method clear, given as

```
node* l = head;
if ( l == 0 ) return;
do
{
    node* l1 = l;
    l = l -> next;
    delete l1;
} while ( l != 0 );
```

The list is traversed starting at address head, deleting the storage for the contents at each node and then deleting the storage for each node until the end of the list is reached.

The reader is urged to walk through the code for method get( ).

Listing 4.25
Implementation
of Class List

```
// Implementation of class list
// File list.cpp

#include ''list.h''

void list::insert( char* a )
{
    node* temp;
    temp = new node;

    temp -> contents = new char[ size ];
    for ( int i = 0; i < size; i++ )
        temp -> contents[ i ] = a[ i ];
    if ( head )
    {
        temp -> next = head;
        head = temp;
    }
    else
    {
        temp -> next = 0;
        head = temp;
    }
}

void list::append( char* a )
{
    node *previous, *current, *newnode;

    if ( head )
    {
        previous = head;
        current = head -> next;
        while ( current != 0 )
        {
            previous = current;
            current = current -> next;
        }
```

```
        newnode = new node;
        newnode -> contents = new char[ size ];
        newnode -> next = 0;
        for ( int i = 0; i < size; i++ )
          newnode -> contents[ i ] = a[ i ];
        previous -> next = newnode;
      }
    else
      {
        head = new node;
        head -> contents = new char[ size ];
        head -> next = 0;
        for ( int i = 0; i < size; i++ )
          head -> contents[ i ] = a[ i ];
      }
}
char* list::get()
{
    if ( head == 0 )
      printf( "Error --> get() from empty list" );
    else
      {
        char* r;
        r = new char[ size ];
        node* f = head;
        for ( int i = 0; i < size; i++ )
          r[ i ] = f -> contents[ i ];
        head = head -> next;
        return r;
      }
}
void list::clear()
{
    node* l = head;
    if ( l == 0 ) return;
    do
      {
        node* ll = l;
        l = l -> next;
        delete ll -> contents;
        delete ll;
      } while ( l != 0 );
}
```

Listing 4.26 presents a test program that uses class list. The output of this program is

```
3.500000
2.500000
1.500000
6.000000
```

It is important that the address of r be coerced to be a pointer to type char in the messages insert and append, in order to match the interface specified in the list definition given in Listing 4.24.

Since the message get( ) returns a pointer to type char, it is necessary to coerce the pointer to be a pointer to type float in the loop

```
for ( int i = 0; i < 4; i++ )
{
    r = ( float * ) my_list.get();
    printf( "\n%f", *r );
}
```

Listing 4.26
Test Program That
Uses Class List

```
// A test program that uses class list
// File listst.cpp
#include "list.h"
main()
{
    list my_list( sizeof( float ) );

    float *r;

    *r = 1.5;
    my_list.insert( ( char * ) r );

    *r = 2.5;
    my_list.insert( ( char * ) r );

    *r = 3.5;
    my_list.insert( ( char * ) r );

    *r = 6.0;
    my_list.append( ( char * ) r );

    for ( int i = 0; i < 4; i++ )
    {
        r = ( float * ) my_list.get();
        printf( "\n%f", *r );
    }
}
```

4.10.2   A generic search table implemented as a binary search tree

A search table is a widely used and important data abstraction. Its importance derives from its multiplicity of applications. It is central in database applications and word processing and is used in compiler construction, operating system design, graphics, and numerical methods as well as in other application areas. Indeed, any application that requires storing, accessing, and quickly retrieving objects is a natural candidate for the search table abstraction.

A search table can be implemented in a variety of ways. The simplest implementation is an array of elements. Moving up the ladder of complexity, a list abstraction can be used to implement a search table. Moving still further up the ladder of complexity, one can implement a search table with a binary tree. This is the data structure that will be used in this section.

The above discussion about search_table implementation is typically the major concern and focus in early computer science data structure courses. Unfortunately, this preoccupation, while it may serve to strengthen the beginning student's programming skills, may distract the future software engineer from important questions such as:

- What can one do with objects of class search_table?
- What are the basic properties of such search_table objects?
- What are the messages that one can send to search_table objects?

The issue of learning efficient implementations, while ultimately very important, is really useful only if one understands what can be done with search_table objects in the first place.

The following sections focus on the construction of a search_table abstraction. In later chapters several important applications of search tables are presented.

The architecture of an object-oriented system is based on a framework of objects and message passing. We must pay close attention to the issue of developing reliable, robust, and efficient classes of objects.

The basic operations of the simple search_table abstraction that we construct are

- Insertion of an entity into the table
- Removal of an entity from the table
- Determining the presence of a particular entity in the table
- The display of all the entities in the table

We wish our search_table to be generic. That is, we wish to be able to insert, remove, and display any type of entity. This will allow us to manipulate objects of any arbitrary type using the same basic set of messages.

In this implementation, the search table is restricted to homogeneous but arbitrary elements. In Chapter 6, when polymorphism is discussed, this constraint is removed and a search_table abstraction is constructed that allows for heterogeneous elements in the same table.

It is interesting to contrast the encapsulation of a simple search_table abstraction in a powerful and modern procedural language such as Modula-2 with the encapsulation of the same search_table abstraction in a powerful and modern object-oriented language—namely, C++. We therefore make a brief presentation (interface only) of a Modula-2 encapsulation in the next section, followed by a detailed presentation of a C++ encapsulation of the search_table abstraction.

4.10.2-1 Modula-2 Encapsulation of Search_Table Abstraction
Listing 4.27 presents the Modula-2 interface to a simple search_table. The reader who is not interested in comparing a Modula-2 encapsulation with a C++ encapsulation may wish to skim or skip over this section.

The reader interested in the Modula-2 implementation (IMPLEMENTATION MODULE) and a detailed discussion of the Modula-2 code may wish to consult *Data Structures Using Modula-2* by Sincovec and Wiener (Wiley, 1986).

A basic issue that must be addressed whenever a generic class or module is developed is: What information must the user (consumer) of the data type need to supply in order for the implementation to work? Specifically in connection with a binary tree implementation of a search_table abstraction, this question becomes: How can insertions or deletions (which require that two entities be compared for equality and inequality) be performed on a tree without a priori knowledge of the type of entities that will be stored in the structure? The answer is that the user must have a vehicle for defining the meaning of equality and inequality for any two entities to be inserted or removed from the search table and for transmitting this information to the search table.

The method that is actually used to accomplish this definition and transmission is quite similar in the Modula-2 and C++ encapsulations. In both cases, the user passes functions into the search table using function parameter passing.

In the Modula-2 encapsulation, this is done when procedure define is invoked. Procedure define is given as follows:

```
PROCEDURE define
  ( VAR t     : table          (* out *) );
    equal     : equaltype      (* in *);
    lessthan  : lessthantype   (* in *) );
```

This procedure must be invoked in the user's program before any of the other procedures. If not, a serious uninitialized pointer error will occur. Procedure define returns a pointer to a search table. Thus many search table variables can be defined in the same software system.

The parameters equal and lessthan are procedure types, with the templates given at the top of the definition module, as shown below.

```
TYPE equaltype    = PROCEDURE( elementtype, elementtype ) :
                    BOOLEAN;

TYPE lessthantype = PROCEDURE( elementtype, elementtype ) :
                    BOOLEAN;
```

Any procedure that takes two elementtypes as its two parameters and returns a BOOLEAN qualifies for either an equaltype or a lessthantype procedure. It is the user's responsibility to ensure that the particular procedures that are passed into define do what they are supposed to do. The algorithms in the implementation module assume that procedure equal compares two entities for equality and procedure lessthan compares the first entity with the second and returns true if the first is smaller, otherwise returning false.

Procedure processnodes also requires the user to send in a procedure for displaying the data record that comprises each node of the binary search tree used to implement the search table abstraction. The author of the search_table abstraction cannot make any assumptions about the format or set of entities that are to be displayed. For example, in a database application, each entity in the search table may consist of a record with many fields of data. The decision about how to display each record must rest with the user of the abstraction, not with the designer of the abstraction.

The reader should note that the Modula-2 definition module provides no clue about the representational details of the data structure used to implement the search table. Here data hiding is taken quite literally. The opaque type declaration

```
TYPE table;
```

ensures that the representational details of table are inaccessible outside the IMPLEMENTATION MODULE. Modula-2 provides no selected peepholes through a friend mechanism, so data hiding is strictly enforced, which many software developers consider desirable.

Because Modula-2 is a procedural language, data is sent to functions for processing. Each procedure whose interface is given in Listing 4.27 has a first parameter of type table. These procedures provide the basic set of operations that are essential in any abstract data encapsulation. Missing, as mentioned earlier in connection with the Modula-2 stack implementation, is automatic initialization or deallocation of constructors or destructors. The user must assume full responsibility for invoking the appropriate procedures.

Listing 4.27
Modula-2 Interface
to Search_Table
Abstraction

```
DEFINITION MODULE searchtable;
(* The interface to the ADT searchtable *)
  FROM elements IMPORT
    (* type *) elementtype;
  EXPORT QUALIFIED
    (* type *) table,
    (* proc *) define,
    (* proc *) remove,
    (* proc *) insert,
    (* proc *) processnodes,
    (* proc *) ispresent;
  TYPE table;
  TYPE equaltype    = PROCEDURE( elementtype, elementtype ) :
                        BOOLEAN;
  TYPE lessthantype = PROCEDURE( elementtype, elementtype ) :
                        BOOLEAN;
  TYPE displaytype  = PROCEDURE( VAR elementtype );
  PROCEDURE define
    ( VAR t      : table         (* out *) );
      equal      : equaltype     (* in   *);
      lessthan   : lessthantype  (* in   *) );
  (* This procedure must be used before any other procedure *)
```

Listing 4.27
(continued)

```
PROCEDURE remove
  ( VAR t    : table        (* in/out *);
    item     : elementtype (* in *);
(* Removes the item from table t, if it is present. *)

PROCEDURE insert
  ( VAR t    : table        (* in/out *);
    item     : elementtype (* in *);
(* Inserts the item into table t. *)

PROCEDURE processnodes
  ( t             : table        (* in *);
    displayproc : displaytype (* in *) );
(* Displays the item elements of the table in order. *)

PROCEDURE ispresent
  ( t         : table        (* in *);
    item      : elementtype (* in *) : BOOLEAN;
(* Returns true if item is present in table otherwise false. *)

END searchtable.
```

4.10.2-2   C++ Encapsulation of Search_Table Abstraction

A class search_table is defined for the C++ encapsulation of the abstract data type search table. The interface to this class is shown in Listing 4.28.

Before defining any classes, the global type definitions for the functions lessthan, equal, and visittype are provided. These are similar to the three procedure type templates given at the top of the Modula-2 DEFINITION MODULE. As an example, the definition

```
typedef int ( *lessthan )( char*, char* );
```

specifies that lessthan is a pointer to a type of function that returns an integer and has two parameters, each the address of a character. Here, as in Section 4.10.1, the address of a character is used as a least common denominator—a pointer to the smallest memory unit for generic purposes.

A class node that declares class search_table a friend (i.e., provides class search_table with total access to the private section of class node) is specified. The private section of this class contains pointers to the left and right child of the node as well as a pointer to type char. This pointer will be the starting address of the actual data stored in each object of class search_table.

Next class search_table is specified. The private section of this class is given as follows:

```
private:
  node* root; // Root node of search_table
  int size; // Number of bytes for contents
  lessthan lt; // lt is a pointer to a function
  equaltype eq; // eq is a pointer to a function
  visittype visit; // visit is a pointer to a function
```

The datum root is an object that points to class node. The datum size stores the number of bytes for the data stored in each node object. The datum lt is a pointer to a function of type lessthan, eq is a pointer to a function of type equal, and visit is a pointer to a function of type visittype. The user must transmit these functions to the object using the constructor, which is given as:

```
search_table( int s, lessthan l, equal e, visit v )
{
   root = 0;
   size = s;
   lt = l;
   eq = e;
   visit = v;
}
```

The user must send in functions l, e, and v as parameters in the constructor method. The pointers to these functions are stored as part of the private data of each object. The methods process_nodes and clear are discussed in the next section in connection with implementation. The methods insert, remove, and is_present all take a pointer to type char as their sole parameter. This provides the generic capability for each of these methods; that is, the messages insert, remove, and is_present can be sent to any types of objects.

Listing 4.28
C++ Interface
to Search_Table
Abstraction

```
// Interface to search_table
// File search.h
typedef int ( *lessthan )( char*, char* );
typedef int ( *equal )( char*, char* );
typedef void ( *visit )( char* );
class node
{
   friend class search_table;
   private:
     node *left, *right;
     char* contents;
};
class search_table
{
   private:
     node* root;        // Root node of search_table
     int size;          // Number of bytes for contents
     lessthan lt;       // lt is a pointer to a function
     equal eq;          // eq is a pointer to a function
     visittype visit;   // visit is a pointer to a function
```

Listing 4.28
(continued)

```
public:
    search_table( int s, lessthan l, equal e, visittype v )
    {
        root = 0;
        size = s;
        lt = l;
        eq = e;
        visit = v;
    }
    void insert( char* a );
    void remove( char* a );
    int is_present( char* a );
    // Call process_nodes without any parameters
    void process_nodes( node* n = 0, int first = 1 );
    // Call clear without any parameters
    void clear( node* n = 0, int first = 1 );
    ~search_table( ) { clear( ); }
};
```

Listing 4.29 presents the implementation of the search_table class, which we shall examine in part. A detailed discussion of binary search trees is presented in Sincovec and Wiener's book.

Let us examine the code for method process_nodes. This message is sent to a search_table object when all the data contained within the object needs to be displayed.

Two parameters, node* n and int first, are shown even though no parameters should be sent in with the message. Recall that the interface to this method, given in Listing 4.28, is

```
void process_nodes( node* n = 0, int first = 1 );
```

The two parameters have default values of 0 and 1, respectively. The default value of first = 1 is used to inform the method process_nodes that a first call rather than a recursive call is being made. Each object to which the message process_nodes is sent contains its own datum root, a pointer to the root node of the binary tree used to represent the search table. Only when first = 1 is the pointer current set equal to root. Otherwise, current is assigned to n.

The C++ implementation should be contrasted with the Modula-2 schema in which the tree root pointers are generally global to the program. A tighter binding exists in the encapsulation of an abstract data type in an object-oriented language such as C++. No global pointers are available that specify the starting addresses of a structure. Each object has its own private data that include a root pointer.

The remainder of method process_nodes is a standard in-order tree traversal that uses the function visit that was input to the search_table by the programmer using this abstraction.

Looking at the implementation of method insert, we see that local pointers parent and current are declared as pointers to class node. They are used to traverse the binary search tree. Such trees have the property that the data of each node are larger than the data of all the left descendants and smaller than the data of all the right descendants. No duplicate data are allowed in the tree.

Starting at the root node (top of the tree), the first while loop compares the item (with address a) being inserted with the data in each node using the function eq, sent in by the user. If the item being inserted is smaller than the data in a given node, the traversal moves down to the left; otherwise it moves down to the right. If a matchup occurs, item a is not inserted in the tree.

Following the while loop, memory is allocated for a new node and for the data to be stored in it. Depending on whether the new node is a root node (first data to be inserted) or is to the left or right of the parent leaf node, a byte-by-byte transfer of the data at address a is performed, inserting this data at the memory address contents within the new node.

Listing 4.29
Implementation
of Search_Table
Class

```cpp
// Implementation of search_table class
// File search.cpp
#include "search.h"
void search_table::process_nodes( node* n, int first )
{
    node* current;

    if ( first )
    {
        current = root;
        first = 0;
    }
    else
        current = n;
    if ( current != 0 )
    {
        process_nodes( current -> left, first );
        ( *visit )( current -> contents );
        process_nodes( current -> right, first );
    }
}
void search_table::insert( char* a )
{
    node *parent,
         *current;
    int found = 0;

    parent = 0;
    current = root;
    while ( current && !found )
    {
        if ( ( *eq )( current -> contents, a ) )
            found = 1;
        else
        {
            parent = current;
```

Listing 4.29
(continued)

```
            if ( ( *lt )( a, current -> contents ) )
               current = current -> left;
            else
               current = current -> right;
      }
}
if ( !found )
{
   if ( !parent )
   {
      // First node in search_table
      root = new node;
      root -> left = root -> right = 0;
      // Allocate space for the contents
      root -> contents = new char[ size ];
      // Do a byte-by-byte transfer of data
      for ( int i = 0; i < size; i++ )
         root -> contents[ i ] = a[ i ];
   }
   else
   {
      if ( ( *lt )( a, parent -> contents ) )
      {
         // Add new node to the left of parent
         node* new_node = new node;

         // Allocate space for the contents
         new_node -> contents = new char[ size ];
         // Do a byte-by-byte transfer of data
         for ( int i = 0; i < size; i++ )
            new_node -> contents[ i ] = a[ i ];
         new_node -> left = new_node -> right = 0;
         parent -> left = new_node;
      }
      else
      {
         // Add new node to the right of parent
         node* new_node = new node;
         // Allocate space for the contents
         new_node -> contents = new char[ size ];
         // Do a byte-by-byte transfer of data
         for ( int i = 0; i < size; i++ )
            new_node -> contents[ i ] = a[ i ];
         new_node -> left = new_node -> right = 0;
         parent -> right = new_node;
      }
   }
}

int search_table::is_present( char* a )
{
   node *parent,
        *current;
   int found = 0;

   parent = 0;
   current = root;
   while ( current && !found )
   {
```

```
      if ( ( *eq )( current -> contents, a ) )
        found = 1;
      else
      {
        parent = current;
        if ( ( *lt )( a, current -> contents ) )
          current = current -> left;
        else
          current = current -> right;
      }
    }
    return found;
}
void search_table::clear( node* n, int first )
{
    node* current;

    if ( first )
    {
      current = root;
      first = 0;
      root = 0;
    }
    else
      current = n;
    if ( current != 0 )
    {
      clear( current -> left, first );
      clear( current -> right, first );
      delete current -> contents;
      delete current;
    }
}
void search_table::remove( char* a )
{
    node *previous,
         *present,
         *replace,
         *s,
         *parent;
    int found = 0;

    previous = 0;
    present = root;
    while ( present && ! found )
    {
      if ( ( *eq )( a, present -> contents ) )
        found = 1;
      else
      {
        previous = present;
        if ( ( *lt )( a, present -> contents ) )
          present = present -> left;
        else
          present = present -> right;
      }
    }
```

Listing 4.29
(continued)

```
if ( found )
{
    if ( present -> left == 0 )
        replace = present -> right;
    else
        if ( present -> right == 0 )
            replace = present -> left;
        else
        {
            parent = present;
            replace = present -> right;
            s = replace -> left;
            while ( s != 0 )
            {
                parent = replace;
                replace = s;
                s = replace -> left;
            }
            if ( parent != present )
            {
                parent -> left = replace -> right;
                replace -> right = present -> right;
            }
            replace -> left = present -> left;
        }
    if ( previous == 0 )
        root = replace;
    else
        if ( present == previous -> left )
            previous -> left = replace;
        else
            previous -> right = replace;
    delete present -> contents;
    delete present;
}
}
```

Listing 4.30 presents a test program that uses the search_table abstraction.
A record structure given by

```
struct info
{
    char lastname[ 20 ], firstname[ 20 ];
    int age;
};
```

is used as the basic information set to be inserted in the search table. Three
tables are built, each using a different set of functions for equality and inequality
testing.

The first table is declared as

```
search_table table1( sizeof( info ), less_than_lastname,
                     equal_lastname, display );
```

The last_name field of the structure is used as a key in building the table. Therefore, the output display of the data will be in alphabetical order according to the last_name fields.

The second table is declared as

```
search_table table2( sizeof( info ), less_than_firstname,
                     equal_firstname, display );
```

Here the first_name field of the structure is used as a key. The output display of the data will be in alphabetical order according to the first_name fields.

The third table is declared as

```
search_table table3( sizeof( info ), less_than_age,
                     equal_age, display );
```

The age field is used as a key for this search table. The output display will be in numerical order according to the age fields.

The reader should note the type cast of each structure sent in as a parameter in methods insert and remove to a pointer to type char. This satisfies the requirements of the method interfaces given in Listing 4.28.

The output of the test program in Listing 4.30 is

```
Berlin, Irving 96
Jones, Mary 26
Kansas, Wichita 123
Smith, Avery 16
Zachary, Richard 46

Smith, Avery 16
Berlin, Irving 96
Jones, Mary 26
Zachary, Richard 46
Kansas, Wichita 123

Smith, Avery 16
Jones, Mary 26
Zachary, Richard 46
Berlin, Irving 96
Kansas, Wichita 123

Kansas, Wichita 123 present in table 3.

Kansas, Wichita 124 not present in table 3.

Kansas, Wichita 124

Berlin, Irving 96
Kansas, Wichita 123
Smith, Avery 16
Zachary, Richard 46

Berlin, Irving 96
Kansas, Wichita 123
Zachary, Richard 46
```

Listing 4.29
(continued)

```
Berlin, Irving 96
Kansas, Wichita 123
Zachary, Richard 46
```

Listing 4.30
Test Program
That Uses Objects
of Class
Search_Table

```
// Test program for the generic search_tree class
// File name is treetst.cpp

#include <string.h>
#include <stdio.h>
#include "search.h"

struct info
{
   char lastname[ 20 ], firstname[ 20 ];
   int age;
};
int equal_lastname( char* n1, char* n2 )
// Keys on lastname
{
   info *info1, *info2;

   info1 = ( info * ) n1;
   info2 = ( info * ) n2;
   return ( strcmp( info1 -> lastname,
            info2 -> lastname ) == 0 );
}
int equal_firstname( char* n1, char* n2 )
// Keys on firstname
{
   info *info1, *info2;

   info1 = ( info * ) n1;
   info2 = ( info * ) n2;
   return ( strcmp( info1 -> firstname, info2 -> firstname ) == 0 );
}
int equal_age( char* n1, char* n2 )
// Keys on age
{
   info *info1, *info2;

   info1 = ( info * ) n1;
   info2 = ( info * ) n2;
   return ( info1 -> age == info2 -> age );
}
int less_than_lastname( char* n1, char* n2 )
// Keys on lastname
{
   info *info1, *info2;
   info1 = ( info * ) n1;
   info2 = ( info * ) n2;
   return ( strcmp( info1 -> lastname, info2 -> lastname ) < 0 );
}
int less_than_firstname( char* n1, char* n2 )
// Keys on firstname
{
   info *info1, *info2;
```

```
        info1 = ( info * ) n1;
        info2 = ( info * ) n2;
        return ( strcmp( info1 -> firstname, info2 -> firstname ) < 0 );
}

int less_than_age( char* n1, char* n2 )
// Keys on age
{
        info *info1, *info2;

        info1 = ( info * ) n1;
        info2 = ( info * ) n2;
        return ( info1 -> age < info2 -> age );
}
void display( char* n )
{
        info *info1;

        info1 = ( info * ) n;
        printf( ''\n%s, %s %d'', info1 -> lastname, info1 -> firstname,
                        info1 -> age );
}

main()
{
        search_table table1( sizeof( info ), less_than_lastname,
                                equal_lastname, display );

        info my_info;

        strcpy( my_info.lastname, ''Jones'' );
        strcpy( my_info.firstname, ''Mary'' );
        my_info.age = 26;
        table1.insert( (char * ) &my_info );
        strcpy( my_info.lastname, ''Zachary'' );
        strcpy( my_info.firstname, ''Richard'' );
        my_info.age = 46;
        table1.insert( (char * ) &my_info );
        strcpy( my_info.lastname, ''Smith'' );
        strcpy( my_info.firstname, ''Avery'' );
        my_info.age = 16;
        table1.insert( (char * ) &my_info );
        strcpy( my_info.lastname, ''Berlin'' );
        strcpy( my_info.firstname, ''Irving'' );
        my_info.age = 96;
        table1.insert( (char * ) &my_info );
        strcpy( my_info.lastname, ''Kansas'' );
        strcpy( my_info.firstname, ''Wichita'' );
        my_info.age = 123;
        table1.insert( (char * ) &my_info );
        table1.insert( (char * ) &my_info );
        table1.process_nodes();

        search_table table2( sizeof( info ), less_than_firstname,
                                equal_firstname, display );

        printf( ''\n'' );
        strcpy( my_info.lastname, ''Jones'' );
        strcpy( my_info.firstname, ''Mary'' );
        my_info.age = 26;
        table2.insert( (char * ) &my_info );
```

Listing 4.30
(continued)

```
strcpy( my_info.lastname, "Zachary" );
strcpy( my_info.firstname, "Richard" );
my_info.age = 46;
table2.insert( (char *) &my_info );
strcpy( my_info.lastname, "Smith" );
strcpy( my_info.firstname, "Avery" );
my_info.age = 16;
table2.insert( (char *) &my_info );
strcpy( my_info.lastname, "Berlin" );
strcpy( my_info.firstname, "Irving" );
my_info.age = 96;
table2.insert( (char *) &my_info );
strcpy( my_info.lastname, "Kansas" );
strcpy( my_info.firstname, "Wichita" );
my_info.age = 123;
table2.insert( (char *) &my_info );
table2.process_nodes();

search_table table3( sizeof( info ), less_than_age,
                     equal_age, display );

printf( "\n" );
strcpy( my_info.lastname, "Jones" );
strcpy( my_info.firstname, "Mary" );
my_info.age = 26;
table3.insert( (char *) &my_info );
strcpy( my_info.lastname, "Zachary" );
strcpy( my_info.firstname, "Richard" );
my_info.age = 46;
table3.insert( (char *) &my_info );
strcpy( my_info.lastname, "Smith" );
strcpy( my_info.firstname, "Avery" );
my_info.age = 16;
table3.insert( (char *) &my_info );
strcpy( my_info.lastname, "Berlin" );
strcpy( my_info.firstname, "Irving" );
my_info.age = 96;
table3.insert( (char *) &my_info );
strcpy( my_info.lastname, "Kansas" );
strcpy( my_info.firstname, "Wichita" );
my_info.age = 123;
table3.insert( (char *) &my_info );
table3.process_nodes();

if ( table3.is_present( (char*) &my_info ) )
  printf( "\n\nKansas, Wichita 123 present in table 3." );
else
  printf( "\n\nKansas, Wichita 123 not present in table 3." );
strcpy( my_info.lastname, "Kansas" );
strcpy( my_info.firstname, "Wichita" );
my_info.age = 124;
if ( table3.is_present( (char*) &my_info ) )
  printf( "\n\nKansas, Wichita 123 present in table 3." );
else
  printf( "\n\nKansas, Wichita 124 not present in table 3." );
table3.clear();
table3.insert( (char *) &my_info );
printf( "\n" );
table3.process_nodes();
```

```
strcpy( my_info.lastname, "Jones" );
strcpy( my_info.firstname, "Mary" );
my_info.age = 26;
table1.remove( ( char * ) &my_info );
printf( "\n" );
table1.process_nodes();
strcpy( my_info.lastname, "Smith" );
strcpy( my_info.firstname, "Avery" );
my_info.age = 16;
printf( "\n" );
table1.remove( ( char * ) &my_info );
table1.process_nodes();
table1.remove( ( char * ) &my_info );
printf( "\n" );
table1.process_nodes();
}
```

Exercises

4.1   Discuss how data hiding can be accomplished in C++.

4.2   Write a dynamic string class. Describe, using comments, the role of each method in the class.

4.3   Discuss the difference between a C++ struct and class. Be specific.

4.4   Discuss the use of the reserved word this. Show three examples that illustrate its use.

4.5   Construct two meaningful C++ classes A and B in which an object of class B is contained in class A.

4.6   Modify the following code for class stack and use a different implementation.

```
#include <stdio.h>
#include <string.h>
class stack
{
  private:
    int *top;

    int *bottom;
  public:
    stack()
    {
      top = bottom = new int[ 100 ];
    }

    void push( int c )
    {
```

```
        if ( ( top - bottom ) < 100 )
          *top++ = c;
      }
      int pop()
      {
        if ( --top >= bottom )
          return *top;
      }
      ~stack()
      {
        delete bottom;
      }
  };
```

4.7   Explain the following program in detail and show its output.

```
#include <stdio.h>
class inner_class
{
  private:
    int x;
  public:
    inner_class( int z ) { x = z; }
    void write() { printf( ''\n%d'', x ); }
};
class outer_class
{
  private:
    int y;
    inner_class x;
    inner_class r;
  public:
    outer_class( int z );
    void write() { printf( ''\n%d'', y ); }
    void write_inner_x() { x.inner_class::write(); }
    void write_inner_r() { r.inner_class::write(); }
};
outer_class::outer_class( int z ) : x( 20 ), r( -36 )
{
  y = z;
}
main()
{
  outer_class object( -12 );
  object.write_inner_x();
  object.write_inner_r();
  object.write();
}
```

4.8   Correct the error in the following program:

```
#include <stdio.h>
class point
{
   private:
      int x1, x2;
   public:
      point( int x, int y ) { x1 = x; x2 = y; }

      int x_cord() { return x1; }
      int y_cord() { return x2; }
};
main()
{
   point data( 9, 10 );

   printf( ''\nx coordinate = %d'', data.x_cord() );
   printf( ''\ny coordinate = %d'', data.y_cord() );

   point more_data[ 20 ];
}
```

4.9   Rewrite the dynamic string class of Exercise 4.2 using overloaded operators. Develop a simple test program that exercises each overloaded operator.

4.10 Implement the generic list baseline class in a different manner. (See Listing 4.24.) Run the test program of Listing 4.26 using the new implementation of generic list.

CHAPTER

5

Inheritance and Derived Classes

In Chapter 4 we have seen that the class construct provides the logical unit of encapsulation in C++. Each object of a class contains its own set of values of the underlying data and can manipulate this data by receiving a specified set of messages. The message set is defined by the methods given in the interface to the class. The usefulness of such data encapsulation can be enhanced considerably if another user (programmer) can customize the class for another application by adding to, modifying, or subtracting methods from the given class. This is particularly true if the given class is generic, such as the list or tree classes of Chapter 4. For such generic classes, the base type of data for the given set of operations is not defined. Only by creating a class derived from the generic parent class can an instance of the generic class be obtained. The feature of an object-oriented language that makes this possible is called *inheritance*. Inheritance allows programmers to reuse all or parts of an existing class in constructing a hierarchy of reusable software components.

The *derived class* construct in C++ is the basis for inheritance and provides the vehicle for customizing a parent class. Each object-oriented language handles the details of inheritance differently. C++ allows a derived class to inherit or modify all the methods of its parent or some of the methods of its parent and in addition to provide new methods not contained in the parent class that are suitable for the particular application for which the derived class will be used.

In Smalltalk, the property of inheritance forms the basis for an entire programming environment in which a hierarchy of baseline classes is available to the user. Several thousand methods have been defined and implemented from several hundred classes and subclasses. Most Smalltalk programs are constructed by sending messages to objects from existing classes or creating subclasses derived from existing classes and sending messages to these objects. Because of the enormous effort that has been invested in creating the baseline classes, many large Smalltalk systems can be constructed without having to write much new code. In order to use the language effectively, a programmer must learn and master the use of a huge base of classes and subclasses. It is no simple matter to manage such complexity, and some programmers would prefer to work in a smaller environment and have more control over building the baseline classes.

The newer C++ language offers the capability and promise of a hierarchy of classes and derived classes, but no standard set of classes and derived classes or C++ programming environment has yet been produced. Many C++ programmers are using the powerful software tools and development environment available under UNIX. It is expected that as C++ matures, C++ tool vendors will create and market libraries of classes and subclasses that will provide the basis for a generalized C++ software development environment. For now, each individual programmer and software development organization must develop and customize its own set of reusable classes and derived classes.

In C++, a class can have only one parent. In some other object-oriented languages such as Smalltalk, a class can have several parents. This is called multiple inheritance.

An important and basic issue relating to inheritance concerns the visibility of the private data of a parent class with respect to its derived classes. If a derived class were allowed to automatically access the private data of its parent (or of any ancestor class), this would severely compromise the value of data hiding. Under such conditions, the opaque shield of data-hiding could be smashed at will by creating a dummy derived class and using it to access the private data of the parent.

In C++, a derived class cannot access the private data of its parent unless specifically authorized to do so. This authorization comes in two forms. The first, discussed in Chapter 4, involves the friend construct. An entire derived class or specific methods in a derived class can be declared as friends of the parent class, thus allowing access to the private section of the parent class.

The second more applicable technique for allowing a derived class to access the private section of its parent involves the use of the *protected* mode option. All class members declared as protected are hidden in the same way as private members except with respect to derived classes.

Figure 5.1 illustrates a parent class with a protected section that can be accessed only within the scope of the parent class and all its derived classes.

5.1 The Derived Class Construct

In general, a class can be derived from a parent class as follows:

```
class derived_class_name : parent_class_name
{
    . . .
};
```

The colon separating the parent class name from the derived class name is used to establish the hierarchy between the subclass and its parent.

Figure 5.1
Derived classes.

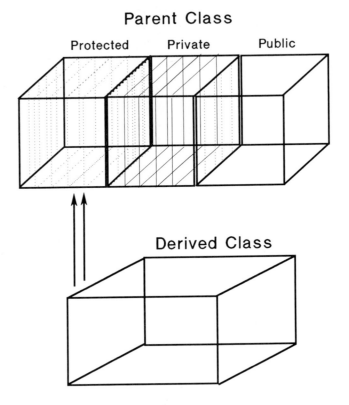

Every object of a derived class contains its own copy of the private data of its parent class as well as its own private data.

For the above derived class definition, none of the methods of the parent class can be used by objects of the derived class unless the derived class includes these methods in its public section. But it is important to note that the implementation section of the derived class can access the methods (though not the private data) of the parent class, which is desirable in many applications. This can be achieved using the following derived class definition:

```
class derived_class_name : public parent_class_name
{
    . . .
};
```

The public qualifier in the derived class definition indicates that objects of the derived class can use all the methods of the parent class, unless these methods have been redefined in the derived class. An example in Listing 5.1 illustrates these points.

Class parent_class is defined with two private data, private1 and private2. In this example, there is no constructor defined for this parent class. (Parent class constructors and their relation to derived classes are discussed in the next section.) The parent class defines and implements in-line the methods assign, inc1, inc2, and display.

A derived class named derived_class1 is defined with a single private datum, private3. Because the specifier public is not included in the derived class definition, none of the methods of the parent class are automatically available to objects of the derived class. But the methods assign and inc1, given in derived_class1, reestablish these two methods from the parent class and allow objects of this derived class to manipulate data from the parent class. The reader should note the use of the parent_class name qualifier in implementing methods assign, inc1, and display. A constructor is defined for this derived class.

It is important to note again that the implementation section of the derived class (e.g., method assign in derived_class1) can use the methods but not the private data of the parent class. Notably absent from derived_class1 is method inc2. Thus objects of derived_class1 cannot receive this message.

A derived class named derived_class2 is defined with the single private datum private4. A constructor is provided to initialize the value of this datum.

Derived_class2 is defined with the public specifier so its objects can access the methods of the parent class. We note, however, that method inc1 is redefined in this derived class. A message parent_class::inc1() can be sent to an object of derived_class2 if the programmer wishes to use the parent_class inc1 rather than the derived class inc1.

The main function declares an object p. It assigns the private data private1 and private2 the values −2 and −4. The data private1 and private2 are displayed.

An object d1 is created with private member private3 assigned the initial value −4. The data private1 and private2, also contained in object d1, are assigned the initial values 17 and 18. The message inc1() is sent to object d1, changing the value of private1 from 17 to 18. If an attempt were made to send the message inc2() to object d1, an error message such as the following would be emitted from the C++ translator:

```
''test.cpp'', line 87: error: inc2 is from private base class
```

The message display() is sent to object d1, producing the output of private1, private2, and private3.

An object d2 is created with private datum private4 assigned an initial value 5. The private data private1 and private2 are next assigned initial values −6 and −8. The message display() is sent to this object, producing the output of private1, private2, and private4. The messages inc1() and inc2() (from class derived_class2) are sent to object d2, the value of private4 is incremented by 4. and the data are displayed. The message, parent_class::inc1(), is sent to object d2, incrementing the value of private1 by one. The data are displayed.

The output of the program in Listing 5.1 is

```
private1 = -2 private2 = -4
private1 = 18 private2 = 18
private3 = -4

private1 = -6 private2 = -8
private4 = 5
private1 = -2 private2 = -7
private4 = 5
private1 = -1 private2 = -7
private4 = 5
```

Listing 5.1
First Example
Using Derived
Classes

```c
#include <stdio.h>
class parent_class
{
   private:
     int private1, private2;

   public:
     void assign( int p1, int p2 )
     {
        private1 = p1;
        private2 = p2;
     }

     int inc1() { return ++private1; }

     int inc2() { return ++private2; }

     void display()
     {
        printf( "\nprivate1 = %d private2 = %d", private1,
              private2 );
     }
};
class derived_class1 : parent_class
{
   private:
     int private3;

   public:
     derived_class1( int p3 )
     {
        private3 = p3;
     }

     void assign( int p1, int p2 )
     {
        parent_class::assign( p1, p2 );
     }

     int inc1() { return parent_class::inc1(); }

     int inc3() { return ++private3; }

     void display()
     {
```

```
            parent_class::display();
            printf( "\nprivate3 = %d\n\n", private3 );
        }
};
class derived_class2 : public parent_class
{
    private:
        int private4;

    public:
        derived_class2( int p4 )
        {
            private4 = p4;
        }

        int inc1()
        {
            int temp = parent_class::inc1();
            temp = parent_class::inc1();
            temp = parent_class::inc1();
            return parent_class::inc1();
        }

        int inc4() { return ++private4; }
        void display()
        {
            parent_class::display();
            printf( "\nprivate4 = %d", private4 );
        }
};
main()
{
    parent_class p;

    p.assign( -2, -4 );
    p.display();

    derived_class1 d1( -4 );

    d1.assign( 17, 18 );
    d1.inc1();
    // d1.inc2(); This line would be an error
    d1.display();

    derived_class2 d2( 5 );

    d2.assign( -6, -8 );
    d2.display();
    d2.inc1();
    d2.inc2();
    d2.display();
    d2.parent_class::inc1();
    d2.display();
}
```

Figure 5.2 depicts a parent class and two derived classes. The data and methods shown in italics are inherited from the parent; those in normal type are peculiar to the class.

Figure 5.2
Class hierarchy.

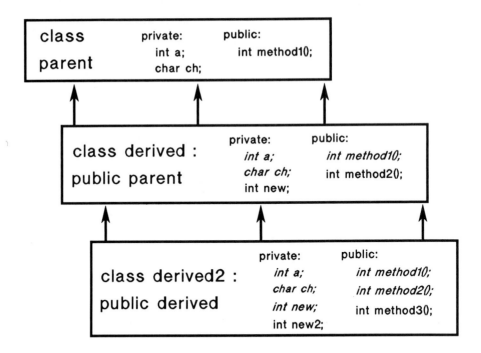

5.2   Derived Classes with Parent Class Constructors

In Listing 5.1, the parent class contains no constructor. Its private data are initialized using the method assign(int p1, int p2). This is unrealistic. Let us reconsider this example by including a constructor in the parent class. The basic issue is how we invoke this constructor in a derived class. Since objects of each derived class contain a copy of the data of the parent class, it is imperative that they have a mechanism for initializing this parent class data. This mechanism is provided through the constructor in the derived class.

A parent class acts like an unnamed member of a derived class. The private data of the parent class is initialized in the same way as that of a private class member. This problem is illustrated in Listing 5.2.

The parent class, parent_class, defines a constructor with two parameters.

The derived class contains a private member of class parent_class. This derived class defines a constructor as follows:

```
derived_class1( int p1, int p2, int p3, int p4, int p5 )
  : ( p1, p2 ), private4( p3, p4 )
{
  private3 = p5;
}
```

There are five parameters in this constructor. The first two, p1 and p2, are used to initialize the private data of the parent, private1 and private2. The activation of the parent class constructor is accomplished with the first item on the initialization list, (p1, p2). The next two parameters, p3 and p4, are used to initialize the private member private4. This is accomplished with the final element of the initialization list, private4(p3, p4). The fifth parameter of the constructor, p5, is used to initialize the private datum private3.

The constructors are activated in the order parent class first, internal class members second, and the derived class last. (C++ respects its elders and its guests.)

The main function in Listing 5.2, declares an object d with the five parameters 17, 18, 1, 2, and −5. After the message inc1( ) is sent to the object, the data are displayed. The output of the program is

```
private1 = 18 private2 = 18
private1 = 1 private2 = 2
private3 = -5
```

Listing 5.2
Constructors and
Derived Classes

```
// Constructors and derived classes
#include <stdio.h>
class parent_class
{
  private:
    int private1, private2;
  public:
    parent_class( int p1, int p2 )
    {
      private1 = p1;
      private2 = p2;
    }

    void assign( int p1, int p2 )
    {
      private1 = p1;
      private2 = p2;
    }

    int inc1(){ return ++private1; }
    int inc2(){ return ++private2; }
    void display()
    {
      printf( ''\nprivate1 = %d private2 = %d'', private1,
              private2 );
    }
};
class derived_class1 : parent_class
{
  private:
    int private3;
    parent_class private4;
```

Listing 5.2
(continued)

```
                        public:
                           derived_class1( int p1, int p2, int p3, int p4, int p5 )
                             : ( p1, p2 ), private4( p3, p4 )
                           {
                              private3 = p5;
                           }

                           void assign( int p1, int p2 )
                           {
                              parent_class::assign( p1, p2 );
                           }

                           int inc1() { return parent_class::inc1(); }

                           int inc3() { return ++private3; }
                           void display()
                           {
                              parent_class::display();
                              private4.parent_class::display();
                              printf( "\nprivate3 = %d\n\n", private3 );
                           }
                        };

                        main()
                        {
                           derived_class1 d1( 17, 18, 1, 2, -5 );

                           d1.inc1();
                           d1.display();
                        }
```

If a subclass derived_class has as a public parent parent_class, a variable declared as a pointer to class derived_class can be assigned to a variable declared
as a pointer to class parent_class without explicit type conversion. That is, an object of a derived class can be treated as if it were an object of the base class with
respect to pointers. The importance of this fact will be apparent in Chapter 6,
when virtual functions and polymorphism are introduced.

5.3   Some Examples of Derived Classes

Several examples of derived classes are presented in this section.

5.3.1   Derived counter class

As the first example in this section, a subclass is derived from the basic counter
class presented in Chapter 4. The new class, range_limited_class, allows the user
to put a fuse in a fuse box by sending in a maximum value that objects of the
derived class can attain.

Listing 5.3 presents the parent counter class. Listing 5.4 presents the interface and implementation of a derived class range_limited_counter. Listing 5.5 presents a test program that uses the derived counter class.

The derived class range_limited_counter uses the specifier public and has class counter as its parent. All the methods of the parent class counter can be sent as messages to objects of the derived class.

The constructor in the derived class assigns the private datum max_value, which sets the upper limit on the value that the private datum value can attain. The method inc( ) is redefined in the derived class to limit the private member value to max_value.

The main test program declares an object my_great_counter(10). In the for loop the message inc( ), is sent to the object my_great_counter 20 times. The message val( ), defined in the parent class, is sent to the object of the derived class in the printf statement.

The output of this program is

```
my_great_counter = 1
my_great_counter = 2
my_great_counter = 3
my_great_counter = 4
my_great_counter = 5
my_great_counter = 6
my_great_counter = 7
my_great_counter = 8
my_great_counter = 9
my_great_counter = 10
my_great_counter = 10
my_great_counter = 10
my_great_counter = 10
my_great_counter = 10
my_great_counter = 10
my_great_counter = 10
my_great_counter = 10
my_great_counter = 10
my_great_counter = 10
my_great_counter = 10
```

Clearly, the range_limited_counter object is doing its job.

Listing 5.3
Parent Counter
Class

```
// File count.h

class counter
{
    private:
       unsigned int value;
    public:
       counter(){ value = 0; }

       void inc()
       {
          if ( value < 65535 )
             value++;
       }
```

Listing 5.3
(continued)

```
                void dec()
                {
                   if ( value > 0 )
                      value--;
                }
                unsigned int val() { return value; }
          };
```

Listing 5.4
Derived Counter
Class

```
// Interface and implementation of derived class counter
#include ''count.h''
class range_limited_counter : public counter
{
  private:
     int max_value;

  public:
     range_limited_counter( int max ) : ()
     {
        max_value = max;
     }
     void inc()
     {
        if ( val() < max_value )
           counter::inc();
     }
};
```

Listing 5.5
Test Program That
Uses Derived
Counter Class

```
#include ''count1.h''
#include <stdio.h>
main()
{
  range_limited_counter my_great_counter( 10 );
  for ( int i = 0; i < 20; i++ )
  {
     my_great_counter.inc();
     printf( ''\nmy_great_counter = %d'',
             my_great_counter.val() );
  }
}
```

5.3.2 The class system at a university

Let us now consider some employee and student classes at a university. Listing 5.6 presents the interface and implementation of a parent class, data_rec, and the subclasses student, professor, and staff. The class data_rec and its derived classes are shown in Figure 5.3. The methods of subclasses are shown in italics.

class data__rec

```
private:                        public:
  char* last_name;                data_rec();
  char* first_name;               void insert_last( char* ln );
  char* street_address;           void insert_first( char* fn );
  char* city;                     void insert_street( char* st );
  char* state;                    void insert_city( char* cty );
  char* zip;                      void insert_state( char* st );
                                  void insert_zip( char* z );
                                  void print();
```

class student : public data__rec

```
private:                        public:
  char* last_name;                void insert_last( char* ln );
  char* first_name;               void insert_first( char* fn );
  char* street_address;           void insert_street( char* st );
  char* city;                     void insert_city( char* cty );
  char* state;                    void insert_state( char* st );
  char* zip;                      void insert_zip( char* z );
  char* major;                    student() : 0;
  int id_number;                  void insert_major( char* m );
  int level;                      void insert_id( int id );
                                  void insert_level( int l );
                                  void print();
```

class professor : public data__rec

```
private:                        public:
  char* last_name;                void insert_last( char* ln );
  char* first_name;               void insert_first( char* fn );
  char* street_address;           void insert_street( char* st );
  char* city;                     void insert_city( char* cty );
  char* state;                    void insert_state( char* st );
  char* zip;                      void insert_zip( char* z );
  char* dept;                     professor() : 0;
  float salary;                   void insert_dept( char* d );
                                  void insert_salary( float s );
                                  void print();
```

class staff : public professor

```
private:                        public:
  char* last_name;                void insert_last( char* ln );
  char* first_name;               void insert_first( char* fn );
  char* street_address;           void insert_street( char* st );
  char* city;                     void insert_city( char* cty );
  char* state;                    void insert_state( char* st );
  char* zip;                      void insert_zip( char* z );
  char* dept;                     void insert_dept( char* d );
  float salary;                   void insert_salary( float s );
  float hourly_wage;              staff() : 0;
                                  void insert_hrwage( float h );
                                  void print();
```

Figure 5.3
Parent class data_rec and derived classes for a university application.

The class data_rec contains fields of data that are private to all the subclasses. Each of the derived classes defines a different method, print( ), relevant to the particular subclass.

Listing 5.7 presents a test program that uses the classes of Listing 5.6. The output of this program is

```
George Smith
1234 Park Lane
Colorado Springs, CO. 80907
```

```
Major --> Computer Science
Id number --> 1234
Level --> 4
George Smith
1234 Park Lane
Colorado Springs, CO. 80907

Jones Robert
12345678 ABC Lane
Colorado Springs, CO. 80907
Department --> Computer Science
Salary --> $40000

Sears Stella
1234 Silver Lane
Manitou Springs, CO. 12345
Department --> Electrical Engineering
Salary --> $28000
Hourly wage --> $7.2
```

Listing 5.6
Classes and
Subclasses at
a University

```
// The classes and subclasses of a university
// File univ.h

#include <stream.h>
#include <string.h>

const char null = '\0';

static char *strsave( char* s )
{
  char *p;

  p = new char[ strlen( s ) + 1 ];
  strcpy( p, s );
  return ( p );
}

class data_rec
{
  private:
    char* last_name;

    char* first_name;

    char* street_address;

    char* city;

    char* state;

    char* zip;

  public:
    data_rec();
    void insert_last( char* ln )
    {
      last_name = strsave( ln );
    }
    void insert_first( char* fn )
    {
      first_name = strsave( fn );
    }
```

```
    void insert_street( char* st )
    {
       street_address = strsave( st );
    }
    void insert_city( char* cty )
    {
       city = strsave( cty );
    }
    void insert_state( char* st )
    {
       state = strsave( st );
    }
    void insert_zip( char* z ) { zip = strsave( z ); }
    void print();
};
void data_rec::print()
{
   cout << ''\n'' << last_name << '' '' << first_name << ''\n'' <<
       street_address << ''\n'' << city << '', '' << state <<
       '' '' << zip;
}
data_rec::data_rec()
{
   last_name = null;
   first_name = null;
   street_address = null;
   city = null;
   state = null;
   zip = null;
}
class student : public data_rec
// This class is derived from data_rec and inherits all the
// public members of the parent class.
{
   private:
     char* major;

     int id_number;

     int level;
   public:
     student() : () {} // Uses the same constructor as the
                       // parent class. The () is optional.

    void insert_major( char* m ) { major = strsave( m ); }

    void insert_id( int id ) { id_number = id; }

    void insert_level( int l ) { level = l; }

    void print();
};
void student::print()
{
   data_rec::print();
   cout << ''\nMajor --> '' << major;
   cout << ''\nId number --> '' << id_number << ''\nLevel --> ''
       << level;
```

Listing 5.6
(continued)

```
      data_rec::print();
  }
class professor : public data_rec
// This class is derived from data_rec and inherits all the
// public members of the parent class.
  {
    private:
      char* dept;

      float salary;

    public:
      professor() : () {}

      void insert_dept( char* d ) { dept = strsave( d ); }

      void insert_salary( float s ) { salary = s; }

      void print();
  };
void professor::print()
  {
    data_rec::print();
    cout << ''\nDepartment --> '' << dept << ''\nSalary --> $'' <<
          salary;
  }
class staff : public professor
// This class is derived from the derived class professor.
  {
    // Private data
      float hourly_wage;

    public:
      staff() : () {}

      void insert_hrwage( float h ) { hourly_wage = h; }

      void print();
  };
void staff::print()
  {
    professor::print();
    cout << ''\nHourly wage --> $'' << hourly_wage;
  }
```

Listing 5.7
Test Program That
Uses the University
Classes

```
// Test program that uses the classes and subclasses of the
// university

#include ''univ.h''

main()
{
  student my_student;
  professor my_professor;
  staff my_staff;

  my_student.insert_last( ''Smith'' );
  my_student.insert_first( ''George'' );
  my_student.insert_street( ''1234 Park Lane'' );
```

```
      my_student.insert_city( ''Colorado Springs'' );
      my_student.insert_state( ''CO.'' );
      my_student.insert_zip( ''80907'' );
      my_student.insert_major( ''Computer Science'' );
      my_student.insert_id( 1234 );
      my_student.insert_level( 4 );

      my_professor.insert_last( ''Jones'' );
      my_professor.insert_first( ''Robert'' );
      my_professor.insert_street( ''12345678 ABC Lane'' );
      my_professor.insert_city( ''Colorado Springs'' );
      my_professor.insert_state( ''CO.'' );
      my_professor.insert_zip( ''80907'' );
      my_professor.insert_dept( ''Computer Science'' );
      my_professor.insert_salary( 40000 );

      my_staff.insert_last( ''Sears'' );
      my_staff.insert_first( ''Stella'' );
      my_staff.insert_street( ''1234 Silver Lane'' );
      my_staff.insert_city( ''Manitou Springs'' );
      my_staff.insert_state( ''CO.'' );
      my_staff.insert_zip( ''12345'' );
      my_staff.insert_dept( ''Electrical Engineering'' );
      my_staff.insert_salary( 28000.0 );
      my_staff.insert_hrwage( 7.20 );

      my_student.print();
      cout << ''\n\n'';
      my_professor.print();
      cout << ''\n\n'';
      my_staff.print();
}
```

5.3.3   A stack and queue derived from a generic list

Chapter 4 presented the encapsulation of a generic list. A generic list class serves as the base for application-specific lists. In this section we show how integer stack and character queue classes can be derived from the generic list class.

Listing 5.8 presents key parts of the generic list class from Chapter 4.

Listing 5.8
Key Parts of the
Generic List Class

```
// File list.h.

#include <stdio.h>

class node
{
   friend class list;
   private:
     node* next;

     char* contents;
};

class list
{
   private:
     node* head; // Head of list
```

Listing 5.8
(continued)

```
                    int size; // Number of bytes for contents
                public:
                  void insert( char* a );
                  list( int s ) { head = 0; size = s; }
                  void append( char* a ); // Add to the tail of the list.
                  char* get(); // Remove the head of the list.
                  void clear(); // Remove all the nodes in the list.
                  ~list() { clear(); }
            };
            void list::insert( char* a )
            {
               // See Listings 4.24 and 4.25.
            }
            void list::append( char* a )
            {
               // See Listings 4.24 and 4.25
            };
            char* list::get()
            {
               // See Listings 4.24 and 4.25
            };
            void list::clear()
            {
               // See Listings 4.24 and 4.25
            };
```

Listing 5.9 presents the derived classes stack and queue and a short test program that uses these derived classes.

The derived class int_stack is given as

```
class int_stack : list
{
   public:
      void push( int a ) { list::insert( ( char * ) &a ); }
      int pop() { return *( ( int * ) list::get() ); }
      int_stack() : ( sizeof( int ) ) {}
};
```

None of the methods of the parent generic list class is available to objects of derived class int_stack.

Method push is implemented by using method insert of the parent list class and type-coercing the address of the data a to point to type char.

Method pop is implemented by using method get of the parent list class and type-coercing the return value so that it points to type int. This return value is then dereferenced to produce a type int.

The derived class char_queue is given as

```
class char_queue : list
{
  public:
    void put( char a ) { list::append( ( char * ) &a ); }
    char get() { return *( list::get() ); }
    char_queue() : ( sizeof( char ) ) {}
};
```

Methods put and get are implemented by using methods append and get from the parent generic list class.

It should be clear from Listing 5.9 that producing derived instances of a generic class is relatively easy using inheritance and derived classes.

The output of the Listing 5.9 is

```
The first item popped from the stack = 4
The second item popped from the stack = 3
The third item popped from the stack = 2
The fourth item popped from the stack = 1

The first item removed from the queue = A
The next item removed from the queue = B
The next item removed from the queue = C
```

Listing 5.9
Stack and Queue
Derived from
Generic List

```
// File listst.cpp

#include <stream.h>
#include "list.h"

class int_stack : list
{
  public:
    void push( int a ) { list::insert( ( char * ) &a ); }
    int pop() { return *( ( int * ) list::get() ); }
    int_stack() : ( sizeof( int ) ) {}
};

class char_queue : list
{
  public:
    void put( char a ) { list::append( ( char * ) &a ); }
    char get() { return *( list::get() ); }
    char_queue() : ( sizeof( char ) ) {}
};

main()
{
  int a;

  int_stack mystack;

  a = 1;
  mystack.push( a );
  a = 2;
```

Listing 5.9
(continued)

```
mystack.push( a );
a = 3;
mystack.push( a );
a = 4;
mystack.push( a );

a = mystack.pop();
cout << ''\nThe first item popped from the stack = '' << a;
a = mystack.pop();
cout << ''\nThe second item popped from the stack = '' << a;
a = mystack.pop();
cout << ''\nThe third item popped from the stack = '' << a;
a = mystack.pop();
cout << ''\nThe fourth item popped from the stack = '' << a;

char ch;

char_queue myqueue;

ch = 'A';
myqueue.put( ch );
ch = 'B';
myqueue.put( ch );
ch = 'C';
myqueue.put( ch );

ch = myqueue.get();
cout << ''\n\nThe first item removed from the queue = '' <<
    chr( ch );
ch = myqueue.get();
cout << ''\nThe next item removed from the queue = '' <<
    chr( ch );
ch = myqueue.get();
cout << ''\nThe next item removed from the queue = '' <<
    chr( ch );
}
```

Exercises

5.1 Perform a top-down decomposition of a class automobile. (See the discussion of inheritance in Chapter 1.) Specify in some detail each of the derived classes of the parent class automobile.

5.2 Explain the following program and show its output.

```
#include <stdio.h>

class parent_class
{
  private:
    int private1, private2;
  public:
    parent_class( int p1, int p2 )
    {
      private1 = p1;
      private2 = p2;
    }
```

```
      void assign( int p1, int p2 )
      {
        private1 = p1;
        private2 = p2;
      }

      int inc1() { return ++private1; }

      int inc2() { return ++private2; }

      void display()
      {
        printf( "\nprivate1 = %d private2 = %d", private1,
                private2 );
      }
};
class derived_class1 : parent_class
{
  private:
    int private3;
    parent_class private4;

  public:
    derived_class1( int p1, int p2, int p3, int p4, int p5 )
      : ( p1, p2 ), private4( p3, p4 )
    {
      private3 = p5;
    }

    void assign( int p1, int p2 )
    {
      parent_class::assign( p1, p2 );
    }

    int inc1() { return parent_class::inc1(); }

    int inc3() { return ++private3; }

    void display()
    {
      parent_class::display();
      private4.parent_class::display();
      printf( "\nprivate3 = %d\n\n", private3 );
    }
};
main()
{
  derived_class1 d1( 11, 12, 0, 1, 2 );
  d1.inc1();
  d1.display();
}
```

5.3 Show the employee classes and derived classes for a fast-food restaurant. Specify each of the derived classes in detail.

5.4 Construct derived classes for a stack and queue using the generic list that you developed in Exercise 4.10.

CHAPTER

6

Polymorphism and Virtual Functions

One of the pillars of object-oriented programming is polymorphism. In an object-oriented language, polymorphism allows a programmer to pursue a course of action by sending a message to an object without concern about how the software system is to implement the action. This capability becomes significant when the same general type of action can be accomplished in different ways by different types of objects.

Let us examine a nonsoftware analogy to polymorphism and problem solving. When an automobile driver decides to hit the brakes in order to avoid hitting a pedestrian crossing an intersection, the driver is concerned about the concept of quickly slowing down or braking. The brakes will be either drum brakes or disk brakes, which although constructed quite differently, both achieve the same effect of slowing a vehicle down while converting the vehicle's kinetic energy to heat. The driver who is about to depress the brake pedal to avoid the pedestrian is not (and should not be) thinking about the drum-versus-disk implementation of the brake but only of the desired action, slowing down quickly. The system (the car) determines how the braking action is to be implemented. Our example is illustrated in Figure 6.1.

At the design level, when a software engineer is deciding what type of action is appropriate for a given object, he or she should not be concerned about how the object interprets the action (message) and implements the method but only what the effect of the action is on the object. Object-oriented languages like C++ and Smalltalk allow a programmer to send identical messages to dissimilar but related objects and achieve identical actions while letting the software system decide how to achieve the required action for the given object.

A key issue associated with polymorphism is the timing of the software system's implementation decision. If the system decides how to implement an action at compile time, this is called *early binding*. If the decision is made dynamically at run-time, it is called late binding. Generally, early binding offers the advantage of execution speed (the compiler can optimize code before executing it), while *late binding* offers the advantages of flexibility and a high level of problem abstraction.

Both early and late binding support the general concept of polymorphism. When method names or operators are overloaded in two or more classes in C++,

Figure 6.1
Implementation
versus action
paradigm.

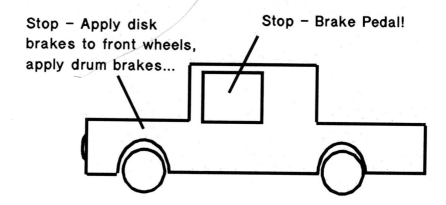

Stop – Apply disk
brakes to front wheels,
apply drum brakes...

Stop – Brake Pedal!

the compiler is able to bind a message sent to an object to the particular body of code that implements the message because it knows the type of object that the message is sent to. This early binding leads to run-time efficiency. Thus function and operator overloading is the simplest type of polymorphism.

This chapter focuses on late binding polymorphism in which the code for a method is chosen at run-time and offers the programmer a high degree of flexibility, problem abstraction, and easy maintenance. While a program is running, the system is able to choose the appropriate code implementation for a given message. With this approach a message is sent to a pointer to an object rather than directly to an object.

6.1   Virtual Functions

C++ handles late binding polymorphism through *virtual functions*. A virtual function must be declared in a parent class by using the keyword virtual in front of the usual function declaration or definition. The keyword virtual is used only once, in the parent class. Only the overloaded function name is used in derived classes. A virtual function is declared in a parent class when it is known that one or more derived classes will overload the virtual function by defining their own implementation of the function. An implementation of the virtual function must be supplied in the parent class. Not all derived classes must declare and implement the virtual function.

An issue that needs clarification is the difference between ordinary overloading of method names among classes versus overloading using a virtual function. In other words, what effect does the keyword virtual have on the overloading process?

As seen earlier, a message is sent to a pointer to an object using the notation object −> message. When the keyword virtual is not used, the system determines at compile time (early binding) the object associated with the message based on the pointer type of the object.

For example, assume that derived_class has been defined as a derived class of parent_class and that a function, print( ), has been defined for both classes. Recalling from Chapter 5 that pointers to derived classes are compatible with pointers to parent classes, consider the following code:

```
parent_class *parent;
derived_class *derived;

parent = derived;
```

When the message print( ) is sent to parent, thusly,

```
parent -> print( );
```

the system invokes function print( ) from the class parent_class. Even though parent was assigned to derived, parent is still technically a pointer to parent_class; thus the system calls methods from parent_class. Figure 6.2 illustrates this example.

Using the keyword virtual in front of the method print( ) in class parent_class tells the system not to invoke print( ) according to the type of pointer but rather according to what the pointer references (late binding). So, in the previous example, if function print( ) were to be declared as virtual, the following statement would invoke print( ) from class derived_class:

```
parent -> print( );
```

The pointer to object parent references a derived class although it is declared as a pointer to a parent class.

Listing 6.1 demonstrates the use of virtual functions. This program defines virtual function print in the class parent. This class has a protected datum, version, of type char. Because of its protected status, this datum is visible to all derived classes but hidden from all other classes.

The constructor for the parent class sets the protected datum version to 'A.' The virtual function print in the parent class prints the string "The parent. Version A."

There are three subclasses defined: class derived1, derived from parent; class derived2, derived from parent; and class derived3, derived from class derived1.

The constructor for derived class derived1 sets info to the input parameter number and sets the protected datum to the value '1.' The print method for class derived1 outputs the value of its private info and the protected version character.

Figure 6.2
Pointers to derived
class objects.

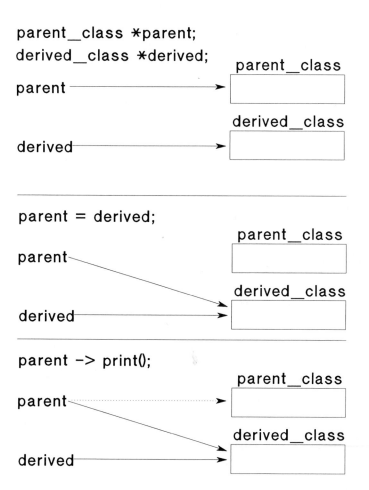

```
parent_class *parent;
derived_class *derived;
```

```
parent = derived;
```

```
parent -> print();
```

The constructor for derived class derived2 sets info to the input parameter number. The value of the protected datum version is equal to that of its parent class since its constructor does not set its own value. The print method for class derived2 outputs the value of its private info and the protected version character.

The constructor for derived class derived3 works the same as does the constructor for class derived2 except that it is required to send a value to the constructor for its parent. The print method for class derived3 outputs the value of its private info and the protected version character.

Four objects are declared in the main function: b of class parent, d1 of class derived1, d2 of class derived2, and d3 of class derived3. The main function invokes function print_info four times, sending in the addresses of b, d1, d2, and d3. Because overloaded member function print is a virtual function, the function print_info can determine the appropriate method print to use based on what is referenced by the pointer it receives.

The output of the program is

```
The parent. Version A
3. Version 1
15. Version A
-565. Version 3
```

If the keyword virtual were removed from the member function print in class parent, the output of the program would be

```
The parent. Version A
The parent. Version 1
The parent. Version A
The parent. Version 3
```

Without the keyword virtual, every address sent into function print_info would be interpreted literally as a pointer to an object of class parent, and thus the method print from the parent class would be invoked.

Listing 6.1
The Meaning of
Virtual Functions

```
// Program to illustrate the use of the virtual function
#include <stdio.h>
class parent
{
  protected:
    char version;

  public:
    parent(){ version = 'A'; }
    virtual void print()
    {
       printf( "\nThe parent. Version %c", version );
    }
};
class derived1 : public parent
{
  private:
    int info;

  public:
    derived1( int number )
    {
       info = number;
       version = '1';
    }
    void print()
    {
       printf( "\nDerived 1 info: %d. Version %c", info,
               version );
    }
};
```

```
class derived2 : public parent
{
   private:
      int info;

   public:
      derived2( int number )
      {
         info = number;
      }

      void print()
      {
         printf( "\nDerived 2 info: %d. Version %c", info,
                 version );
      }
};

class derived3 : public derived1
{
   private:
      int info;

   public:
      derived3( int number ) : ( number )
      {
         info = number;
         version = '3';
      }

      void print()
      {
         printf( "\nDerived 3 info: %d. Version %c", info,
                 version );
      }
};

void print_info( parent* info_holder )
// The virtual function print() is able to determine the
// appropriate action from the type of object referenced
// by the info_holder pointer and not from the type of pointer.
// If print() were not a virtual function, the action would
// always be determined by the type of pointer, namely
// parent pointer. Thus "The parent" would be printed out.
{
   info_holder -> print();
}

main()
{
   parent b;

   derived1 d1( 3 );
   derived2 d2( 15 );
   derived3 d3( -565 );
   print_info( &b );  // Output "The parent. Version A"
   print_info( &d1 ); // Output "3. Version 1"
   print_info( &d2 ); // Output "15. Version A"
   print_info( &d3 ); // Output "-565. Version 3"
}
```

6.2   An Object-Oriented Solution to Generating a Linked List

Virtual functions are most useful in a context in which dynamic structures are created, as in this example. Suppose we wish to build a heterogeneous linked list of nodes, each node containing one of several possible data structures. To help build our appreciation for object-oriented problem solving, the problem is first solved using a traditional nonpolymorphic approach. It is then resolved using virtual functions and polymorphism. The two approaches to this example are contrasted, with emphasis on the ease of maintenance made possible by virtual functions and polymorphism.

For our linked list example, let us again use a university environment. Included in this population are students, staff members, and professors. If records of all these classes of people are maintained, there are some common information requirements. For example it may be desirable to keep a record of a person's last name, first name, age, and social security number (the number of data fields is kept small to keep the system manageable) regardless of the subclass they are associated with. In addition, for the subclass of students, records of the grade point average and level must be kept. For the subclass professor, a record of the annual salary is maintained. Finally, for the subclass staff, a record of the hourly salary is required.

The three basic operations that are implemented in the heterogeneous linked list are insert, remove, and print. The insert operation adds either a student, professor, or staff member to the list. The remove operation deletes either a student, professor, or staff member from the list. The print operation displays all the records in the list.

6.2.1   Nonpolymorphic solution to heterogeneous linked list

Our first approach to our university lists is a nonpolymorphic solution. In the traditional, C-like construction of a heterogeneous linked list, a single node type that accommodates all the subclasses in the system is defined using an anonymous union. Each node in the linked list has the same structure. A discriminant field (private datum in the class node) allows the system to choose the appropriate code for inserting and printing.

The code that shows the class definition of a node and list is given in Listing 6.2.

The private section of a node contains

```
char last_name[ 15 ];
char first_name[ 15 ];
int age;
long social_security_number;
node_type discriminant;
union
{
```

```
      student_type s;
      float annual_salary;
      float hourly_salary;
    };
    node* next;
```

This data structure suggests that all nodes in the list have a last_name field, a first_name field, an age field, a social_security_number field, a discriminant field (either student, staff, or professor) and one of the three fields s (of type student_type) annual_salary, or hourly_salary. The memory storage required of the union is equal to the largest component in the union, clearly in this case the field s of type student_type. The field next is a pointer to the next node in the list.

The public methods in class node allow a programmer to set the values of the private data.

The interface to the list class contains only one private datum, root, a pointer to the first node in the linked list. The public methods insert, remove, and print_list provide the basic operations required of the linked list.

Listing 6.2
Class Definition of
a Node and List—
Nonpolymorphic
Solution

```
// Linked list of university employees using
// nonpolymorphic representation.
// File list1.h

enum node_type{ student, staff, professor };

struct student_type
{
   float grade_point_average;
   int level;
};

class node
{
   friend class list;

   private:
     char last_name[ 15 ];
     char first_name[ 15 ];
     int age;
     long social_security_number;
     node_type discriminant;

     union
     {
        student_type s;
        float annual_salary;
        float hourly_salary;
     };

     node* next;

   public:
     node( char* ln, char* fn, int a, long ss, node_type nt )
     {
        strcpy( last_name, ln );
        strcpy( first_name, fn );
        age = a;
```

Listing 6.2
(continued)

```
        social_security_number = ss;
        discriminant = nt;
        next = 0;
    }
    node()
    {
        last_name[ 0 ] = '\0';
        first_name[ 0 ] = '\0';
        age = 0;
        social_security_number = 0;
        next = 0;
    }
    void set_node_type( node_type nt )
    {
        discriminant = nt;
    }
    void set_last_name( char* last_n )
    {
        strcpy( last_name, last_n );
    }
    void set_first_name( char* first_n )
    {
        strcpy( first_name, first_n );
    }
    void set_age( int a ) { age = a; }
    void set_social_security_number( long soc_sec )
    {
        social_security_number = soc_sec;
    }
    void set_average( float av )
    {
        s.grade_point_average = av;
    }
    void set_level( int l )
    {
        s.level = l;
    }
    void set_annual_salary( float as )
    {
        annual_salary = as;
    }
     void set_hourly_salary( float hs )
     {
        hourly_salary = hs;
     }
};
class list
{
  private:
    node* root;

  public:
    list() { root = 0; }
```

```
        void insert( node* n );
        void remove( char* last_name );
        void print_list( );
};
```

The implementation of the methods of class list are given in Listing 6.3.
It is assumed that the list is ordered on the last name field of each node.

Let us examine the implementation of method insert. The key feature of this
implementation is the switch statement,

```
switch ( n -> discriminant )
{
   case student:
     new_node -> s.level = n -> s.level;
     new_node -> s.grade_point_average =
       n -> s.grade_point_average;
     break;
   case professor:
     new_node -> annual_salary = n -> annual_salary;
     break;
   case staff:
     new_node -> hourly_salary = n -> hourly_salary;
}
```

This statement occurs after a new_node is dynamically constructed while data
for last_name, first_name, age, social_security_number, and discriminant are
embedded in the new_node. The switch statement adds additional data to the
newly constructed node. In the case in which the new_node is a student node, the
additional data, level, and grade_point_average are added. If the new_node is a
professor, annual_salary is added. Finally, in the case in which the new_node is
staff, hourly_salary is added.

The rest of the code for insert closely follows the usual insertion algorithm
for a linked list. The last name of the person being inserted is compared with the
last name of the nodes already in the list until this last name is no longer alpha-
betically less than a last name of a linked list node, at which time the new node
containing the appropriate information is created. This new node is connected
to the previous node and following node appropriately.

The method remove follows the usual algorithm for linked list deletion. The
list is searched until the last name being deleted matches the same last name in
the linked list. The list is relinked using the previous and following nodes appropriately, and finally the storage associated with the node to be deleted is
deallocated.

The method print_list uses a switch statement as its key feature. This switch
statement, given below, occurs just after method print_list displays the data
fields common to all the specialized classes.

```
switch ( cur -> discriminant )
{
```

```
        case student:
          printf( ''\ngrade point average: %.2f level: %d'',
                  cur -> s.grade_point_average,
                  cur -> s.level );
          break;
        case professor:
          printf( ''\nAnnual salary: $%.2f'',
                  cur -> annual_salary );
          break;
        case staff:
          printf( ''\nHourly wage: $%.2f'',
                  cur -> hourly_salary );
      }
```

The discriminant field of the node being printed is used to determine which block of code is to be executed.

The reader with experience in C programming should feel very much at home with this solution.

Listing 6.3
Implementation of Linked List Methods—Nonpolymorphic Solution

```
// Implementation of list operations
// Nonpolymorphic solution
// File list1.cpp
void list::insert( node* n )
{
  // The last_name is the key for maintaining an ordered
  // list
  char key[ 15 ];
  strcpy( key, n -> last_name );

  node* current_node = root;
  node* previous = 0;

  while ( current_node != 0 &&
          strcmp( current_node -> last_name, key ) < 0 )
  {
    previous = current_node;
    current_node = current_node -> next;
  }

  node* new_node = new node( n -> last_name,
                             n -> first_name,
                             n -> age,
                             n -> social_security_number,
                             n -> discriminant
                           );
  switch ( n -> discriminant )
  {
    case student:
      new_node -> s.level = n -> s.level;
      new_node -> s.grade_point_average =
        n -> s.grade_point_average;
      break;
    case professor:
      new_node -> annual_salary = n -> annual_salary;
      break;
```

```
      case staff:
        new_node -> hourly_salary = n -> hourly_salary;
    }
    new_node -> next = current_node;
    if ( previous == 0 )
      root = new_node;
    else
      previous -> next = new_node;
}
void list::remove( char* last_name )
{
node* current_node = root;
node* previous = 0;

while ( current_node != 0 &&
        strcmp( current_node -> last_name,
                last_name ) != 0 )
{
    previous = current_node;
    current_node = current_node -> next;
}
  if ( current_node != 0 && previous == 0 )
  {
    root = current_node -> next;
    delete current_node;
  }
  else if ( current_node != 0 && previous != 0 )
  {
    previous -> next = current_node -> next;
    delete current_node;
  }
}
void list::print_list()
{
  node* cur = root;

  while ( cur != 0 )
  {
    printf( ''\n\n%s %s\nAge %d\nSocial Security # %ld'',
            cur -> last_name, cur -> first_name,
            cur -> age, cur -> social_security_number );
    switch ( cur -> discriminant )
    {
      case student:
        printf( ''\ngrade point average: %.2f level: %d'',
                cur -> s.grade_point_average,
                cur -> s.level );
        break;
      case professor:
        printf( ''\nAnnual salary: $%.2f'',
                cur -> annual_salary );
        break;
      case staff:
        printf( ''\nHourly wage: $%.2f'',
                cur -> hourly_salary );
    }
    cur = cur -> next;
  }
}
```

A main driver program that tests this implementation of the node and linked list classes is given in Listing 6.4.

The output of this program is

```
Marshall Law
Age 27
Social Security # 123456789
grade point average: 1.36 level: 4

Steele Hard
Age 66
Social Security # 987654321
Annual salary: $56789.13

Work Do
Age 26
Social Security # 123454321
Hourly wage: $8.24

Steele Hard
Age 66
Social Security # 987654321
Annual salary: $56789.13
```

Listing 6.4
Main Driver
Program—
Nonpolymorphic
Solution

```
// Main test program for nonpolymorphic solution
// File main1.cpp

#include "list1.h"

main()
{
   list people;
   node temp;

   temp.set_last_name( "Steele" );
   temp.set_first_name( "Hard" );
   temp.set_age( 66 );
   temp.set_social_security_number( 987654321 );
   temp.set_node_type( professor );
   temp.set_annual_salary( 56789.13 );
   people.insert( &temp );

   temp.set_last_name( "Marshall" );
   temp.set_first_name( "Law" );
   temp.set_age( 27 );
   temp.set_social_security_number( 123456789 );
   temp.set_node_type( student );
   temp.set_level( 4 );
   temp.set_average( 1.36 );
   people.insert( &temp );

   temp.set_last_name( "Work" );
   temp.set_first_name( "Do" );
   temp.set_age( 26 );
   temp.set_social_security_number( 123454321 );
   temp.set_node_type( staff );
   temp.set_hourly_salary( 8.24 );
   people.insert( &temp );

   people.print_list();
```

```
        people.remove( ''Garbage'' );
        people.remove( ''Marshall'' );
        people.remove ( ''Work'' );

        people.print_list();
}
```

6.2.2   Object-oriented solution to heterogeneous linked list

The linked list construction employed in this section starts by defining a parent class univ_community that contains the data fields common to all the subclasses. Then the subclasses student, professor, and staff are defined as derived classes, each containing a private section with appropriate data that distinguishes the subclass from the other subclasses.

The definitions of the parent class, its derived classes, and the list class are presented in Listing 6.5.

Let us examine the parent class, univ_community. It contains a protected section, which includes:

```
        char last_name[ 15 ];
        char first_name[ 15 ];
        int age;
        long social_security_number;
        static univ_community* ptr;

        univ_community* next;
```

The fields last_name, first_name, age, and social_security_number are data fields required of all the derived classes. The pointer next is declared as a pointer to the parent class.

Figure 6.3 illustrates the heterogeneous list of members of the university community, containing nodes of different derived classes.

We recall from Chapter 5 that a pointer to a derived class can be assigned to a variable declared as a pointer to the parent class without explicit type conversion. That is, objects of derived classes can be used as if they were objects of the parent class when assignments are made through pointers. This is a key fact in the object-oriented implementation.

Figure 6.3
Example of heterogeneous linked list in university system.

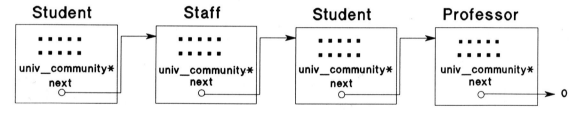

The static field univ_community* ptr will be explained later. For now it is noted that because this data member is declared as static, only one copy is made. All objects of the parent class and derived class share the same pointer value.

Two virtual functions are declared in the public section of class univ_community;

```
virtual void print()
{
  printf( ''\n\n%s %s\nAge %d\nSocial Security # %ld'',
          last_name, first_name, age,
          social_security_number );
}
virtual void insert() {};
```

The first virtual function, print, displays the data in the fields common to all the derived classes. Each derived class object has its own method print that outputs the unique data appropriate to its class.

The second virtual function establishes that each derived class will have its own method insert. The body of code for the parent method is empty.

The current solution differs dramatically from the previous solution. In the current solution, the methods insert and print are associated with an object of each subclass. In Section 6.2.1, all objects of class node have exactly the same methods insert and print. The older approach has one big "computing engine" for insert and another for print, which work for all classes of records. The newer approach distributes smaller computing engines into each derived class. The system determines the appropriate method at run-time based on the nature of the pointer to the object sending the message.

Let us examine the derived class student in detail. The other derived classes, professor and student, are similar.

Because of the designator public, all the public methods of the parent class univ_community are available to objects of class student.

The private section of class student contains the data grade_point_average and level, unique to this class.

The methods insert and print are given as:

```
void print()
{
  univ_community::print();
  printf( ''\ngrade point average: %.2f level: %d'',
          grade_point_average, level );
}
void insert()
{
  ptr = new student( last_name,
                     first_name,
                     age,
                     social_security_number,
                     grade_point_average,
                     level );
}
```

Method print first displays the common data fields last_name, first_name, age, and social_security_number by calling method print from the parent class, using

```
univ_community::print();
```

Then the unique fields of data (grade_point_average and level) are output.

Method insert allocates space for a new student node while filling this node with the following data: last_name, first_name, age, social_security_number, grade_point_average, and level. We note that we are assigning to a student node a pointer to a variable that expects a pointer to a univ_community node. The pointer ptr returned by the memory allocation function new is stored in the static (common) location declared in the protected section of the parent class. This datum is accessed by function insert_person of class list.

Listing 6.5
Definition of Parent
Class, Subclasses,
and List

```
// University community class and derived classes
// File list2.h

#include <stdio.h>
#include <string.h>

class univ_community
{
   friend class list;

   protected:
      char last_name[ 15 ];
      char first_name[ 15 ];
      int age;
      long social_security_number;
      static univ_community* ptr;

      univ_community* next;

   public:
      univ_community( char* ln, char* fn, int a, long ss )
      {
         strcpy( last_name, ln );
         strcpy( first_name, fn );
         age = a;
         social_security_number = ss;
         next = 0;
      }

      univ_community()
      {
         last_name[ 0 ] = '\0';
         first_name[ 0 ] = '\0';
         age = 0;
         social_security_number = 0;
         next = 0;
      }

      void set_last_name( char* last_n )
      {
         strcpy( last_name, last_n );
      }
```

Listing 6.5
(continued)

```
                  void set_first_name( char* first_n )
                  {
                     strcpy( first_name, first_n );
                  }

                  void set_age( int a ) { age = a; }

                  void set_social_security_number( long soc_sec )
                  {
                     social_security_number = soc_sec;
                  }

                  virtual void print()
                  {
                     printf( ''\n\n%s %s\nAge %d\nSocial Security # %ld'',
                             last_name, first_name, age,
                             social_security_number );
                  }

                  virtual void insert() {}
            };

            class student : public univ_community
            {
               friend class list;

               private:
                  float grade_point_average;
                  int level;

               public:
                  student( char* ln, char* fn, int a, long ss, float av,
                           int l ) : ( ln, fn, a, ss )
                  {
                     grade_point_average = av;
                     level = l;
                  }

                  student() : ()
                  {
                     grade_point_average = 0.0;
                     level = 0;
                  }

                  void set_average( float av )
                  {
                     grade_point_average = av;
                  }

                  void set_level( int l )
                  {
                     level = l;
                  }
                  void print()
                  {
                     univ_community::print();
                     printf( ''\ngrade point average: %.2f level: %d'',
                             grade_point_average, level );
                  }

                  void insert()
                  {
```

```
            ptr = new student( last_name,
                               first_name,
                               age,
                               social_security_number,
                               grade_point_average,
                               level );
      }
};
class professor : public univ_community
{
   friend class list;

   private:
     float annual_salary;

   public:
     professor( char* ln, char* fn, int a, long ss, float s
                ) : ( ln, fn, a, ss )
     {
        annual_salary = s;
     }

     professor() : ()
     {
        annual_salary = 0.0;
     }

     void set_annual_salary( float as ) { annual_salary = as; }

     void print()
     {
        univ_community::print();
        printf( ''\nAnnual salary: $%.2f'', annual_salary );
     }

     void insert()
     {
        ptr = new professor( last_name,
                             first_name,
                             age,
                             social_security_number,
                             annual_salary );
     }
};
class staff : public univ_community
{
   friend class list;

   private:
     float hourly_salary;

   public:
     staff( char* ln, char* fn, int a, long ss, float s ) :
           ( ln, fn, a, ss )
     {
        hourly_salary = s;
     }

     staff() : ()
     {
```

Listing 6.5
(continued)

```
      hourly_salary = 0.0;
    }
    void set_hourly_salary( float hs ) { hourly_salary = hs; }
    void print()
    {
      univ_community::print();
      printf( ''\nHourly salary: $%.2f'', hourly_salary );
    }
    void insert()
    {
      ptr = new staff( last_name,
                       first_name,
                       age,
                       social_security_number,
                       hourly_salary );
    }
};
class list
{
  private:
    univ_community* root;
  public:
    list() { root = 0; }
    void insert_person( univ_community* n );
    void remove( char* last_name );
    void print_list();
};
```

The implementation of methods insert_person, remove, and print_list from class list are given in Listing 6.6.

Method print_list sends the message

```
cur -> print()
```

to all the node pointers in the list. The polymorphic behavior is achieved when the system determines at run-time the correct method print to use from the type of object the pointer cur references.

The method remove is the same as the one in Section 6.2.1.

The method insert_person sends the message

```
n -> insert()
```

to the object pointed to by n. The polymorphic behavior is achieved when the system determines at run-time the correct method insert to use from the type of object pointer referenced by n.

The common datum ptr, whose value is set by the insert method of each derived class, is the memory address of the new node being inserted. This memory address is used in method insert_person to forge the links of the new node into the linked list, as follows:

```
n -> insert();
n -> ptr -> next = current_node;
if ( previous == 0 )
  root = n -> ptr;
  else
    previous -> next = n -> ptr;
```

The reader is urged to review the traditional implementation given in Section 6.2.1 and compare it carefully to the implementation given in this section.

Listing 6.6
Implementation
of Linked List
Methods—
Object-Oriented
Solution

```
// Implementation of linked list methods
// Object-oriented solution
// File list2.cpp
void list::print_list()
{
    univ_community* cur = root;

    while ( cur != 0 )
    {
        cur -> print();
        cur = cur -> next;
    }
}

void list::remove( char* last_name )
{
    univ_community* current_node = root;
    univ_community* previous = 0;

    while ( current_node != 0 &&
            strcmp( current_node -> last_name,
                    last_name ) != 0 )
    {
        previous = current_node;
        current_node = current_node -> next;
    }
    if ( current_node != 0 && previous == 0 )
    {
        root = current_node -> next;
        delete current_node;
    }
    else if ( current_node != 0 && previous != 0 )
    {
        previous -> next = current_node -> next;
        delete current_node;
    }
}

void list::insert_person( univ_community* n )
{
    // The last_name is the key for maintaining an ordered
    // list
    char key[ 15 ];
    strcpy( key, n -> last_name );
```

Listing 6.6
(continued)

```
univ_community* current_node = root;
univ_community* previous = 0;

while ( current_node != 0 &&
        strcmp( current_node -> last_name, key ) < 0 )
{
   previous = current_node;
   current_node = current_node -> next;
}
n -> insert();
n -> ptr -> next = current_node;
if ( previous == 0 )
   root = n -> ptr;
else
   previous -> next = n -> ptr;
}
```

A main driver program that tests the implementation of the node and linked list classes is given in Listing 6.7. The output of this program is the same as the program in Listing 6.4, namely:

```
Marshall Law
Age 27
Social Security # 123456789
grade point average: 1.36 level: 4

Steele Hard
Age 66
Social Security # 987654321
Annual salary: $56789.13

Work Do
Age 26
Social Security # 123454321
Hourly wage: $8.24

Steele Hard
Age 66
Social Security # 987654321
Annual salary: $56789.13
```

Listing 6.7
Main Driver
Program—
Object-Oriented
Solution

```
// Test program for object-oriented solution to list
// File main2.cpp

#include "list2.h"

main()
{
   // Object declarations
   list people;

   student stu( "Marshall", "Law", 27, 123456789, 1.36, 4 );
   staff stf( "Work", "Do", 26, 123454321, 8.24 );
   professor prof( "Steele", "Hard", 66, 987654321, 56789.13 );

   people.insert_person( &stf );
   people.insert_person( &prof );
   people.insert_person( &stu );
```

```
        people.print_list();

        people.remove( ''Garbage'' );
        people.remove( ''Marshall'' );
        people.remove ( ''Work'' );

        people.print_list();
}
```

6.2.3   Maintenance on the non—object-oriented and object-oriented systems

The main benefit of the object-oriented solution is demonstrated by doing some maintenance on it and on the non–object-oriented system, for comparison.

The university community has thus far been defined to include students, professors, and staff. Although some people (particularly professors) would argue that these groups are sufficient, most universities have another group called administrators, which is supposed to serve the previous groups.

To illustrate software maintenance, suppose we wish to add the subclass called dean to each system. This subclass is defined in Listing 6.8 using the object-oriented approach.

Like the other subclasses presented in Section 6.2.2, the derived class dean has its own method print and its own method insert.

After we add the code in Listing 6.8 to the file list2.h, our maintenance is finished, and a new main driver program can insert objects of class dean into object(s) of class list.

If we wish to add additional subclasses of people to the university community (e.g., provosts, chancellors, registrars, etc.) we only have to define the new derived classes and specify their appropriate methods print and insert. The remaining code in the software system stays intact. Polymorphism has enabled us to perform reliable and highly localized maintenance.

Listing 6.8
Definition of the
Derived Class
Dean

```
class dean : public univ_community
{
    friend class list;
    private:
      int years_in_service;
      int college; // 1 Engineering, 2 Business, 3 Education
                   // 4 Letters, arts, and sciences, etc.
    public:
      dean( char* ln, char* fn, int a, long ss, int yr,
            int c ) : ( ln, fn, a, ss )
      {
        years_in_service = yr;
        college = c;
      }
```

Listing 6.8
(continued)

```
dean() : ()
{
    years_in_service = 0;
    college = 0;
}
void set_years( int yr ) { years_in_service = yr; }

void set_college( int c ) { college = c; }

void print()
{
    univ_community::print();
    printf( "\nCollege: %d\nYears in service %d",
            college, years_in_service );
}

void insert()
{
    ptr = new dean( last_name,
                    first_name,
                    age,
                    social_security_number,
                    years_in_service,
                    college );
}
};
```

In contrast, let us examine this maintenance task on the system presented in Section 6.2.1. In Listing 6.9, the modified system that does not use an object-oriented approach is presented. The definition and implementation of class list are combined in Listing 6.9. Can you spot the half-dozen or so changes that are scattered throughout the code?

Another enumeration type, dean, is added to node_type. The struct dean_type is added as a global type definition, and the field dean_type d is added to the union in the private section of class node. The methods set_years and set_college are added to the public section of class node. An additional block of code, given below, is appended to the switch statement in function insert of class list.

```
case dean:
new_node -> d.years_of_service = n ->
            d.years_of_service;
new_node -> d.college = n -> d.college;
```

The block of code given below is added to the switch statement in function print_list of class list.

```
case dean:
    printf( "\nCollege: %d\nYears in service %d",
            cur -> d.college, cur -> d.years_of_service
            );
```

In our view, the contrast is clear. Maintenance on the object-oriented system is much easier than maintenance on the non–object-oriented system. This is because the methods insert and print are attached to each subclass.

Listing 6.9
Modified Code
for System of
Section 6.2.1

```cpp
// Linked list of university employees using
// non-object-oriented representation
// File list1.h
enum node_type{ student, staff, professor, dean };
struct student_type
{
   float grade_point_average;
   int level;
};
struct dean_type
{
   int years_of_service;
   int college;
};
class node
{
   friend class list;

   private:
      char last_name[ 15 ];
      char first_name[ 15 ];
      int age;
      long social_security_number;
      node_type discriminant;

      union
      {
         student_type s;
         float annual_salary;
         float hourly_salary;
         dean_type d;
      };

      node* next;
   public:
      node( char* ln, char* fn, int a, long ss, node_type nt )
      {
         strcpy( last_name, ln );
         strcpy( first_name, fn );
         age = a;
         social_security_number = ss;
         discriminant = nt;
         next = 0;
      }

      node()
      {
         last_name[ 0 ] = '\0';
         first_name[ 0 ] = '\0';
         age = 0;
```

Listing 6.9
(continued)

```cpp
            social_security_number = 0;
            next = 0;
        }
    void set_node_type( node_type nt )
    {
        discriminant = nt;
    }
    void set_last_name( char* last_n )
    {
        strcpy( last_name, last_n );
    }
    void set_first_name( char* first_n )
    {
        strcpy( first_name, first_n );
    }
    void set_age( int a ) { age = a; }
    void set_social_security_number( long soc_sec )
    {
        social_security_number = soc_sec;
    }
    void set_average( float av )
    {
        s.grade_point_average = av;
    }
    void set_level( int l )
    {
        s.level = l;
    }
    void set_annual_salary( float as )
    {
        annual_salary = as;
    }
    void set_hourly_salary( float hs )
    {
        hourly_salary = hs;
    }
    void set_years( int yr ) { d.years_of_service = yr; }
    void set_college( int c ) { d.college = c; }
};
class list
{
  private:
    node* root;

  public:
    list() { root = 0; }

    void insert( node* n );

    void remove( char* last_name );

    void print_list();
};
```

```
void list::insert( node* n )
{
  // The last_name is the key for maintaining an ordered
  // list
  char key[ 15 ];
  strcpy( key, n -> last_name );

  node* current_node = root;
  node* previous = 0;

  while ( current_node != 0 &&
          strcmp( current_node -> last_name, key ) < 0 )
  {
    previous = current_node;
    current_node = current_node -> next;
  }

  node* new_node = new node( n -> last_name,
                             n -> first_name,
                             n -> age,
                             n -> social_security_number,
                             n -> discriminant
                           );
  switch ( n -> discriminant )
  {
    case student:
      new_node -> s.level = n -> s.level;
      new_node -> s.grade_point_average =
        n -> s.grade_point_average;
      break;
    case professor:
      new_node -> annual_salary = n -> annual_salary;
    case staff:
      new_node -> hourly_salary = n -> hourly_salary;
    case dean:
      new_node -> d.years_of_service = n ->
                  d.years_of_service;
      new_node -> d.college = n -> d.college;
  }
  new_node -> next = current_node;
  if ( previous == 0 )
    root = new_node;
  else
    previous -> next = new_node;
}
void list::remove( char* last_name )
{
  node* current_node = root;
  node* previous = 0;
  while ( current_node != 0 &&
          strcmp( current_node -> last_name,
                  last_name ) != 0 )
  {
    previous = current_node;
    current_node = current_node -> next;
  }
  if ( current_node != 0 && previous == 0 )
  {
```

Listing 6.9
(continued)

```
                               root = current_node -> next;
                               delete current_node;
                           }
                           else if ( current_node != 0 && previous != 0 )
                           {
                               previous -> next = current_node -> next;
                               delete current_node;
                           }
                       }
                       void list::print_list( )
                       {
                           node* cur = root;

                           while ( cur != 0 )
                           {
                               printf( "\n\n%s %s\nAge %d\nSocial Security # %ld",
                                       cur -> last_name, cur -> first_name,
                                       cur -> age, cur -> social_security_number );
                               switch ( cur -> discriminant )
                               {
                                 case student:
                                   printf( "\ngrade point average: %.2f level: %d",
                                           cur -> s.grade_point_average,
                                           cur -> s.level );
                                   break;
                                 case professor:
                                   printf( "\nAnnual salary: $%.2f",
                                           cur -> annual_salary );
                                   break;
                                 case staff:
                                   printf( "\nHourly wage: $%.2f",
                                           cur -> hourly_salary );
                                   break;
                                 case dean:
                                   printf( "\nCollege: %d\nYears in service %d",
                                            cur -> d.college, cur -> d.years_of_service
                                           );
                               }
                               cur = cur -> next;
                           }
                       }
```

6.3   A Heterogeneous Search Tree Using Polymorphism

Having seen the benefits of polymorphism in Section 6.2, we examine here another example, the construction of a search tree using polymorphism. The subclasses from Section 6.2, will be used in building the search tree. Each node of the search tree is either of class student, professor, staff, or dean.

In Listing 6.10, the interface and implementation of classes univ_community, student, professor, staff, dean, node, and tree are given.

There are slight modifications to the previously introduced parent and derived classes. The method insert is no longer a virtual function. The method insert_person, from class tree, does not need to send a message insert to objects from each of the subclasses. The static (common) protected datum ptr is no longer required, nor is the protected datum next.

The algorithm for search tree insertion is the same as introduced earlier in Chapter 4.

In Listing 6.11, the code for a main driver program is shown. The output is the same as given in Section 6.2.

Listing 6.10
Interface and
Implementation of
Polymorphic
Search Tree

```cpp
// University community class and derived classes
// File univ.h

#include <stdio.h>
#include <string.h>

class univ_community
{
  friend class tree;

  protected:
    char last_name[ 15 ];
    char first_name[ 15 ];
    int age;
    long social_security_number;

  public:
    univ_community( char* ln, char* fn, int a, long ss )
    {
      strcpy( last_name, ln );
      strcpy( first_name, fn );
      age = a;
      social_security_number = ss;
    }

    univ_community()
    {
      last_name[ 0 ] = '\0';
      first_name[ 0 ] = '\0';
      age = 0;
      social_security_number = 0;
    }

    void set_last_name( char* last_n )
    {
      strcpy( last_name, last_n );
    }

    void set_first_name( char* first_n )
    {
      strcpy( first_name, first_n );
    }
    void set_age( int a ) { age = a; }

    void set_social_security_number( long soc_sec )
    {
      social_security_number = soc_sec;
    }
```

Listing 6.10
(continued)

```
        virtual void print()
        {
          printf( ''\n\n%s %s\nAge %d\nSocial Security # %ld'',
                  last_name, first_name, age,
                  social_security_number );
        }
};
class student : public univ_community
{
   friend class tree;

   private:
     float grade_point_average;
     int level;

   public:
     student( char* ln, char* fn, int a, long ss, float av,
              int l ) : ( ln, fn, a, ss )
     {
       grade_point_average = av;
       level = l;
     }

     student() : ()
     {
       grade_point_average = 0.0;
       level = 0;
     }

     void set_average( float av )
     {
       grade_point_average = av;
     }

     void set_level( int l )
     {
       level = l;
     }

     void print()
     {
       univ_community::print();
       printf( ''\ngrade point average: %.2f level: %d'',
               grade_point_average, level );
     }
};
class professor : public univ_community
{
   friend class tree;

   private:
     float annual_salary;

   public:
     professor( char* ln, char* fn, int a, long ss, float s
                ) : ( ln, fn, a, ss )
     {
       annual_salary = s;
     }
```

```cpp
      professor() : ()
      {
         annual_salary = 0.0;
      }
      void set_annual_salary( float as ) { annual_salary = as; }
      void print()
      {
         univ_community::print();
         printf( "\nAnnual salary: $%.2f", annual_salary );
      }
};
class staff : public univ_community
{
   friend class tree;

   private:
      float hourly_salary;

   public:
      staff( char* ln, char* fn, int a, long ss, float s ) :
            ( ln, fn, a, ss )
      {
         hourly_salary = s;
      }
      staff() : ()
      {
         hourly_salary = 0.0;
      }
      void set_hourly_salary( float hs ) { hourly_salary = hs; }
      void print()
      {
         univ_community::print();
         printf( "\nHourly salary: $%.2f", hourly_salary );
      }
};
class dean : public univ_community
{
   friend class tree;

   private:
      int years_in_service;
      int college; // 1 Engineering, 2 Business, 3 Education
                   // 4 Letters, arts, and sciences, etc.

   public:
      dean( char* ln, char* fn, int a, long ss, int yr,
            int c ) : ( ln, fn, a, ss )
      {
         years_in_service = yr;
         college = c;
      }
      dean() : ()
      {
         years_in_service = 0;
         college = 0;
      }
```

Listing 6.10
(continued)

```
void set_years( int yr ) { years_in_service = yr; }
void set_college( int c ) { college = c; }
void print()
{
  univ_community::print();
  printf( "\nCollege: %d\nYears in service %d",
          college, years_in_service );
}
};
// Search tree construction
class node
{
  friend class tree;
  private:
    node *left, *right;
    univ_community* data;
};
class tree
{
  private:
    node* root;
    node* left;
    node* right;

  public:
    tree() { root = left = right = 0; }

    void insert_person( univ_community* a );

    void display( node* n = 0, int first = 1 );
};

void tree::display( node* n, int first )
{
  node* current;

  if ( first )
  {
    current = root;
    first = 0;
  }
  else
    current = n;
  if ( current != 0 )
  {
    display( current -> left, first );
    current -> data -> print();
    display( current -> right, first );
  }
}

void tree::insert_person( univ_community* a )
{
  node *parent,
       *current;
  int found = 0;
```

```
      parent = 0;
      current = root;
      while ( current && !found )
      {
         if ( strcmp( current -> data -> last_name,
              a -> last_name ) == 0 )
            found = 1;
         else
         {
            parent = current;
            if ( strcmp( a -> last_name,
                 current -> data -> last_name ) < 0 )
            current = current -> left;
         else
            current = current -> right;
         }
      }
      if ( !found )
      {
         if ( !parent )
         {
            // First node in tree
            root = new node;
            root -> left = root -> right = 0;
            root -> data = new univ_community;
            root -> data = a;
         }
         else
         {
            if ( strcmp( a -> last_name,
                      parent -> data -> last_name ) < 0 )
            {
               // Add new node to the left of parent
               node* new_node = new node;
               new_node -> data = a;
               new_node -> left = new_node -> right = 0;
               parent -> left = new_node;
            }
            else
            {
               // Add new node to the right of parent
               node* new_node = new node;
               new_node -> data = a;
               new_node -> left = new_node -> right = 0;
               parent -> right = new_node;
            }
         }
      }
}
```

Listing 6.11
Main Driver
Program for
Search Tree

```
// Test program for object-oriented solution to list
#include ''univ.h''

main()
{
```

Listing 6.11
(continued)

```
// Object declarations
tree people;

student stu( "Marshall", "Law", 27, 123456789, 1.36, 4 );

staff stf( "Work", "Do", 26, 123454321, 8.24 );

professor prof( "Steele", "Hard", 66, 987654321, 56789.13 );

dean d( "Nose", "Hard", 78, 11111, 1, 2 );

people.insert_person( &stf );
people.insert_person( &prof );
people.insert_person( &stu );
people.insert_person( &d );

people.display();
}
```

6.4   Finite-State Machine Using Polymorphism

Finite-state machines are an important design tool in software engineering.

As the final example in this chapter, a finite-state machine that can be used to verify that an input string matches a specified pattern is constructed.

Suppose that we wish to test a string for the pattern

$$A\,E^n\,I \parallel B\,F^n\,J \parallel B\,F^n\,M\,G^n\,K \parallel C\,G^n\,K \parallel D\,H^n\,L \parallel D\,H^n\,O\,E^n\,I \parallel$$
$$D\,H^n\,N\,G^n\,K.$$

The symbol $\parallel$ means *or*. The superscript n, as in E^n, means E occurring zero or more times.

Given a string, we wish to determine whether the string is valid or invalid according to the rules specified above.

The above specification can be modeled using the finite-state machine shown in Figure 6.4. From state 1, the character 'A' takes the system to state 2; the character 'B' takes the system to state 3, and so forth.

A structure, parent, is defined as that which contains data common to all subclasses in the system—namely, a string expression, an index into the string, and two boolean values end_state and doom_state that are set to the value 1 when the system enters state 6 or fails. If the input expression takes the system to state 6, the expression is valid. If the input expression takes the system into the doom state, the expression is invalid.

The parent class defines a virtual function, transition, that returns a pointer to a parent state.

Derived classes state1, state2, state3, state4, and state5 are defined.

The interface and implementation of the parent class and the derived classes are given in Listing 6.12.

Figure 6.4
Finite-state
machine for
verifying an
input string.

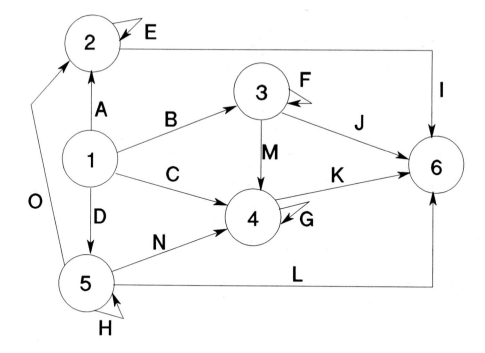

Examining the code for method transition in class 3 as a typical case, we see that the switch statement, given below, determines the return value of function transition. If starting in state 3 the character 'F' is input, the function returns a pointer to state 3 (itself). If character 'M' is input, the function returns a pointer to state 4. If character 'J' is input, the function sets the value of end_state to 1. If the null terminating character is input, the function sets the value of doom_state to 1—the expression has ended without getting the system into state 6, the end state. If any other character is input, the function sets the value of doom_state to 1.

```
switch ( expression[ index++ ] )
{
  case 'F' :
    return ptr3;
  case 'M' :
    return ptr4;
  case 'J' :
    end_state = 1;
    break;
  case '\0' :
    doom_state = 1;
  default:
    doom_state = 1;
}
```

Listing 6.12

Interface and
Implementation of
Parent Class and
Derived Classes
for a Finite-State
Machine

```
// Interface and implementation of state machine classes
// File finite.h
#include <string.h>
struct parent
{
    static char *expression;
    static index;
    static end_state;   // 1 when last state is reached, 0
                        // otherwise
    static doom_state; // 1 when illegal input occurs, 0
                        // otherwise

    parent( char* expr )
    {
      expression = new char[ strlen( expr ) ];
      strcpy( expression, expr );
      end_state = 0;
      doom_state = 0;
      index = 0;
    }
    virtual parent* transition() {};
};
struct state1 : public parent
{
    parent *ptr2, *ptr3, *ptr4, *ptr5;
    state1() : ( expression ) {}

    parent* transition();
};
struct state2 : public parent
{
    parent *ptr2;

    state2() : ( expression ) {}

    parent* transition();
};
struct state3 : public parent
{
    parent *ptr3, *ptr4;

    state3() : ( expression ) {}

    parent* transition();
};
struct state4 : public parent
{
    parent *ptr4;

    state4() : ( expression ) {}

    parent* transition();
};
struct state5 : public parent
{
    parent *ptr2, *ptr4, *ptr5;

    state5() : ( expression ) {}
```

```
      parent* transition();
};
parent* state1::transition()
{
   switch ( expression[ index++ ] )
   {
     case 'A' :
       return ptr2;
     case 'B' :
       return ptr3;
     case 'C' :
       return ptr4;
     case 'D' :
       return ptr5;
     case '\0' :
       doom_state = 1;
     default:
       doom_state = 1;
   }
}
parent* state2::transition()
{
   switch ( expression[ index++ ] )
   {
     case 'E' :
       return ptr2;
     case 'I' :
       end_state = 1;
       break;
     case '\0' :
       doom_state = 1;
     default:
       doom_state = 1;
   }
}
parent* state3::transition()
{
   switch ( expression[ index++ ] )
   {
     case 'F' :
       return ptr3;
     case 'M' :
       return ptr4;
     case 'J' :
       end_state = 1;
       break;
     case '\0' :
       doom_state = 1;
     default:
       doom_state = 1;
   }
}
     parent* state4::transition()
     {
       switch ( expression[ index++ ] )
       {
```

Listing 6.12
(continued)

```
                    case 'G' :
                       return ptr4;
                    case 'K' :
                      end_state = 1;
                      break;
                    case '\0' :
                      doom_state = 1;
                    default:
                      doom_state = 1;
                }
            }
            parent* state5::transition()
            {
              switch ( expression[ index++ ] )
              {
                case 'O' :
                  return ptr2;
                case 'H' :
                  return ptr5;
                case 'L' :
                  end_state = 1;
                  break;
                case 'N' :
                  return ptr4;
                case '\0' :
                  doom_state = 1;
                default:
                  doom_state = 1;
              }
            }
```

In Listing 6.13 the code that builds the finite-state machine and tests an input expression is shown.

Because of virtual function transition and polymorphism, the following statements are used to determine the validity of the input expression:

```
ptr = s1.transition();
while ( ptr -> end_state != 1 && ptr -> doom_state != 1 )
{
   ptr = ptr -> transition();
}
if ( ptr -> end_state == 1 )
   printf( ''\nValid input expression'' );
else
   printf( ''\nInvalid input expression'' );
```

The message transition is sent to ptr, a pointer to the parent class. The system determines the appropriate method transition, at run-time, based on the type of object referenced by pointer ptr.

Listing 6.13
Code for Building
Finite-State
Machine and
Testing Input
Expressions

```
// Main program for finite-state machine

#include <stdio.h>
#include "finite.h"

state1 s1;
state2 s2;
state3 s3;
state4 s4;
state5 s5;

void build_state_machine()
{
   s1.ptr2 = &s2;
   s1.ptr3 = &s3;
   s1.ptr4 = &s4;
   s1.ptr5 = &s5;
   s2.ptr2 = &s2;
   s3.ptr3 = &s3;
   s3.ptr4 = &s4;
   s4.ptr4 = &s4;
   s5.ptr2 = &s2;
   s5.ptr4 = &s4;
   s5.ptr5 = &s5;
}

main()
{
   build_state_machine();
   char input_string[ 80 ];

   printf( "Enter input expression: " );
   scanf( "%s", input_string );

   parent state_machine( input_string );

   parent* ptr;
   ptr = s1.transition();
   while ( ptr -> end_state != 1 && ptr -> doom_state != 1 )
   {
      ptr = ptr -> transition();
   }
   if ( ptr -> end_state == 1 )
      printf( "\nValid input expression" );
   else
      printf( "\nInvalid input expression" );
}
```

Exercises

6.1 Explain what a virtual function is in C++.

6.2 Explain Listing 6.10 in detail.

6.3 Describe three applications in which virtual functions may be useful. For each of these applications, specify the parent classes and derived classes.

7

Case Studies in Object-Oriented Programming

We present three case studies in this chapter that illustrate the object-oriented features of C++ and problem decomposition using data encapsulation, inheritance, and polymorphism.

7.1 A "Super Fast" Spelling Checker

In our first case study, we wish to construct a "super fast" spelling checker. This application highlights the use in C++ of data abstraction and data encapsulation, which contribute significantly to ease of use and maintenance.

7.1.1 Specifications for spelling checker

Our spelling checker system is to be designed to maximize throughput, the number of words that can be checked per second. Specifications in addition to speed, such as requirements for text files and user input, must also be considered.

A separate program for building a dictionary file must be designed. The dictionary file is to be built from the ASCII text files A.TEX, B.TEX, C.TEX, . . . , Z.TEX. Each of these text files contains words beginning with the given letter of the alphabet. These text files contain a total of approximately 20,000 root words.

For the purpose of this application, words are defined as strings of alphabetic characters (a . . . z or A . . . Z). Any nonalphabetic character serves as a word delimiter. As a consequence of this simple definition, a word such as *can't* will be parsed into two words: *can* and *t,* which is an occasional problem we will live with in exchange for the simplicity of our definition. Later maintenance on this program might substitute a more complex definition for a word.

The user inputs the name of the input text file to be spell-checked on the program command line. As the input text file is processed, words not found in the dictionary file are stored in a search table, which maintains an ordered collection of words. After the input file has been processed, all potentially misspelled words deposited in the search table are printed out in alphabetical order. The user can then use a text editor to correct the truly misspelled words.

7.1.2   High-level design of spelling checker

The basic entities that define the spelling checker problem space are a dictionary, words associated with a particular input text file, and a search table. At the high level of design, we define a class abstraction for each entity in the problem space.

The dictionary class must include the following methods (with parameters shown):

1. `void load_dictionary()`—Used by spelling checker. This method loads the dictionary files from disk to RAM.

2. `void save_dictionary()`—Used by dictionary builder. This method transfers the dictionary files from RAM to disk.

3. `int check( char* wd )`—Used by spelling checker. This method returns 1 if the character string *wd* is found in the RAM dictionary; otherwise it returns 0.

4. `void insert( char* wd )`—Used by dictionary builder. This method adds the character string *wd* to the existing dictionary in RAM.

The word class must include the following methods (with parameters shown):

1. A constructor that allocates memory for a buffer. This buffer is used to store all or parts of the input text file.

2. `int open_file( char* filename )`—Used by spelling checker and dictionary builder. This method returns 1 if the filename exists and is successfully opened; otherwise it returns 0.

3. `int get_next_word( char* wd )`—Used by spelling checker and dictionary builder. This method returns 1 if a next word, delimited by non-alphabetic characters, is found in the filename associated with the class; otherwise it returns 0. If a next word is found, it is returned in the character string *wd*.

The search_table class must include the following methods (with parameters shown):

1. A constructor that initializes the search table to empty.

2. `void insert( char* wd )`—Used by spelling checker. This method adds a character string *wd* to the search table.

3. `void display( )`—Used by spelling checker. This method prints an alphabetized list of character strings contained in the search table.

We translate the informal descriptions of each class to formal class definitions. These definitions are given in files dict.h, word.h, and table.h and are presented in Listings 7.1, 7.2, and 7.3.

Listing 7.1
Class Dictionary
Interface

```
// Interface to class dictionary
// File dict.h
class dictionary
{
    private:
        void compute( char* wd,
                      unsigned &majorkey,
                      unsigned &minorkey );
        /* The virtual hash function compute is used by the
           methods insert and check. This method returns two
           hash values, majorkey and minorkey, for a given
           character string wd. */

    public:
        void load_dictionary();
        // Loads the dictionary files from disk into RAM.

        void save_dictionary();
        // Saves the dictionary files stored in RAM.

        void insert( char* wd );
        // Inserts the character string wd into the
        // dictionary.

        int check( char* wd );
        // Checks the character string wd. Returns 1 if the
        // string is present; otherwise, returns 0.
};
```

Listing 7.2
Class Word
Interface

```
// Interface to class word
// File word.h
#include <stdio.h>
class word
{
    private:
        char* buffer;      // Buffer for holding parts of text
                           // file.
        int pos;           // Current location in the buffer.
        int size;          // Number of bytes in buffer.
        int file_open;     // 1 if file is open, 0 if closed.
        FILE* fp;          // File pointer for filename.

        int allowable( char ch );
        // Returns 1 if ch is a letter, otherwise returns 0.
```

```
      void load_buffer();
      // Sequentially loads buffer from file fp, sets size to
      // the number of bytes actually read, and sets pos to 0.
      // Sets file_open to 0 when the input file is fully
      // loaded into the buffer.
    public:
      word( char* filename ); // Constructor

      word();                    // Constructor

      ~word();

      int open_file( char* filename );
      // Returns 1 if filename exists and is opened; otherwise
      // 0.

      int get_next_word( char* wd );
      // Returns 1 if a next word exists. This word is
      // returned in the character string wd. Otherwise,
      // returns 0.
};
```

The class search_table required for this application is a subclass derived from the generic tree class. We repeat the interface to this generic tree in Listing 7.3 and show the derived class search_table.

Listing 7.3
Class Search_Table
Interface Derived
from the Generic
Tree

```
// Interface to generic search tree and derived search_table
// File table.h

// Function type definitions for the user-defined lessthan,
// equal and visit functions.
typedef int ( *lessthantype )( char*, char* );
typedef int ( *equaltype )( char*, char* );
typedef void ( *visittype )( char* );

class node
{
  friend class tree;

  //Private data
    node *left, *right;
    char* contents; // Space for contents is dynamically allocated.
};
class tree
{
  private:
    node* root;             // Root node of tree
    int size;               // Number of bytes for contents
    lessthantype lessthan;  // Pointer to a function
    equaltype equal;        // Pointer to a function
    visittype visit;        // Pointer to a function
  public:
    tree( int s, lessthantype l, equaltype e, visittype v )
    {
```

Listing 7.3
(continued)

```
        root = 0;
        size = s;
        lessthan = l;
        equal = e;
        visit = v;
    }
    void insert( char* a ); // Add a node to the tree.

    void remove( char* a ); // Remove a node from the tree.

    int is_present( char* a );
    // Returns 1, if a is present; otherwise 0.

    void process_nodes( node* n = 0, int first = 1 );
    // Call process_nodes without any parameters

    void clear( node* n = 0, int first = 1 );
    // Call clear without any parameters

    ~tree(){clear();}
};
class search_table : tree
// The only methods that can be invoked by objects of class
// search_table are insert and display.
{
  public:
    search_table( int s, lessthantype l, equaltype e, visittype v
    ( s, l, e, v ){}// Invokes the constructor of the
                     // parent class

    void insert( char* wd ){tree::insert( wd );}

    void display(){tree::process_nodes();}
};
```

7.1.3 Low-level design of spelling checker

We turn now to low-level design considerations.

There are two dictionary files stored on disk, "HASH.DTA" and "SMALL.DTA." Both files are arrays of unsigned integers. The first file, of size 32767 (the largest integer in the 16-bit implementation being used), represents a hash table. The second file is a minimal hash table for words of length 3 or less.

The run-time efficiency of the spelling checker is dependent on the implementation of the method check, in class dictionary. This method uses the private member function compute. An array of unsigned integers stored in a dictionary file is used as a hash table. Each English word to be spell-checked is hashed into a major key and a minor key. The major key represents the index in the hash array; the minor key represents the value stored in the major key index location. The same hash function, compute, is used in building the hash array. Since character strings map to unsigned integers in the hash array, the possibility of an English word that is not in the hash table producing the same major and minor key as an English word that is in the hash array exists. Such a potentially misspelled English word would be identified as correctly spelled. It can be shown that the probability of such an error is very small.

The theory of virtual hashing and the algorithm developed by Richard Wiener are described in detail in Chapter 10 of *Data Structures Using Modula-2* by Sincovec and Wiener (Wiley, 1986). The implementation details of the private function compute follow the discussion and algorithm given in that book.

As a brief overview of *virtual hashing,* the algorithm mimics many random number generators in order to distribute both major and minor keys uniformly across their allowable range of values. Pairs of characters are formed into long integers. Products of long integers are taken until all characters are accounted for. The middle bits of the long integer products are used to continue the chain of products. This effectively scrambles the information in the major and minor keys to produce the uniform distribution of values.

The class word contains a pointer to a buffer whose memory is allocated in the heap in the constructor for word. When the message open_file is sent by an object of class word or from a word constructor, the buffer is filled with characters from the input text file. If the buffer is larger than the input text file, the input file is closed and the private datum file_open is set to 0. If the buffer is smaller than the input text file, the input file is left open and the datum file_open is set to 1. The private datum pos is initialized to 0, and the private datum size is set equal to the number of bytes from the input file that are read into the buffer. The pointer to the file that is opened is stored as part of the private data of an object of class word.

The design of class word allows words from many different files to coexist. Although not required in this application, such a reusable class might be useful in building a text editor with windows in which several files are displayed at the same time.

The method get_next_word, in class word, scans the buffer of characters, reloads it when necessary using the private member function load_buffer (using nonalphabetic characters as delimiters), and loads the next word, if any, into the character string *wd.*

7.1.4   Implementation of spelling checker

After design comes implementation. The program for building a dictionary is given in Listing 7.4. This program uses an object d of class dictionary and an object w of class word. Files "A.TEX," "B.TEX," . . . , "Z.TEX" are loaded in sequence. For each of these files the message open_file(filename) is sent to the object w. After opening a file, the message get_next_word(wd) is sent to object w. If the value returned is 1 (true), the counter is incremented and the message insert(wd) is sent to the object d. This process is continued until the current file contains no more words. Then the next file in the sequence is loaded and its words are inserted into the dictionary.

The program build is easy to read and understand because of the extensive use of data abstraction and encapsulation. Indeed, a nonspecialist could write this program using the reusable class components dictionary and word. A common characteristic in a properly organized object-oriented software system is a main driver program that is easy to read and easy to maintain.

Listing 7.4
Program for
Building a
Dictionary

```cpp
// Build dictionary
// File build.cpp

#include ''word.h''
#include ''dict.h''
#include <string.h>

// Objects required in this application
dictionary d;
word w;

main()
{
  char wd[ 25 ];
  char filename[ 6 ];
  long count = 0;
  for ( int i = 'A'; i <= 'Z'; i++ )
  {
    printf( ''\nBuilding dictionary for letter %c'', i );
    filename[ 0 ] = ( char ) i;
    filename[ 1 ] = '\0';
    strcat( filename, ''.tex'' );
    printf( ''\nLoading %s'', filename );
    if ( w.open_file( filename ) )
    {
      int result = w.get_next_word( wd );
      while( result )
      {
        count++;
        d.insert( wd );
        result = w.get_next_word( wd );
      }
    }
  }
  d.save_dictionary();
}
```

In Listing 7.5, the main spelling checker program is given. This program, like the build dictionary program, is easy to read and maintain due to data abstraction and encapsulation. The three objects used in this program are d of class dictionary, w of class word, and table of subclass search_table.

The filename of the file to spell-check is obtained from the command line using argv[1]. The message open_file is sent to object w. The message get_next_word(wd) is sent to object w. As long as there is another word in the input file, the message check(wd) is sent to object d, the dictionary. If the value 1 is returned (true), the word is in the dictionary and another word, wd, is obtained. If the word wd is not in the dictionary, the message insert(wd) is sent to the object table.

After all the words in the file have been checked, the number of misspelled words is output and the message display( ) is sent to the object table. As indicated previously, a properly constructed object-oriented program is very easy to read. The complexity is hidden in the implementation of the various classes.

Listing 7.5
Main Spelling
Checker Program

```cpp
// Spelling checker implementation.
// File spell.cpp
#include ''word.h''
#include ''dict.h''
#include ''table.h''

extern lessthan( char* str1, char* str2 );
extern equal( char* str1, char* str2 );
extern void visit( char* str );

char wd[ 25 ];

// Objects required in this application
dictionary d;
word w;
search_table table( 25, lessthan, equal, visit );

main( int argc, char* argv[] )
{
    long count = 0;
    int misspelled = 0;

    if ( argc != 2 )
      printf( ''\nUsage: spell filename'' );
    else
    {
      d.load_dictionary();
      if ( w.open_file( argv[ 1 ] ) )
      {
        int result = w.get_next_word( wd );
        while( result )
        {
          count++;
          if ( !d.check( wd ) )
          {
            table.insert( wd );
              printf( ''\nInserting %s in table'', wd );
            misspelled++;
          }
          result = w.get_next_word( wd );
        }
      }
      printf( ''\n\n%d words not found in dictionary\n\n'', misspelled );
      printf( ''The words not found in the dictionary\n'' );
      table.display();
    }
}

int lessthan( char* str1, char* str2 )
{
```

Listing 7.5
(continued)

```
    if ( strcmp( str1, str2 ) < 1 )
       return 1;
    else
       return 0;
}

int equal( char* str1, char* str2 )
{
    if ( strcmp( str1, str2 ) == 0 )
       return 1;
    else
       return 0;
}

void visit( char* str )
{
    printf( "\n%s", str );
}
```

The implementation of class word is given in Listing 7.6. Although two constructors are implemented, only the constructor without parameters is used in this application.

Listing 7.6
Implementation of
Class Word

```
// Implementation of class word.
// File word.cpp
#include "word.h"
const int buffer_size = 10000;
word::word()
{
    buffer = new char[ buffer_size ];
}
word::word( char* filename )
{
    int result = open_file( filename );
    if ( result )
       buffer = new char[ buffer_size ];
}
word::~word()
{
    delete buffer;
}
int word::allowable( char ch )
{
    // Returns 1 if ch is an alphabet character, otherwise 0
    return ( ( ch >= 'A' && ch <= 'Z' ) ||
             ( ch >= 'a' && ch <= 'z' ) );
}
int word::open_file( char* filename )
{
    if ( ( fp = fopen( filename, "rt" ) ) == 0 )
    {
```

```
        filename[ 0 ] = '\0';
        file_open =0;
        printf( "\n%c%s does not exist", '\07', filename );
        return 0;
    }
    else
    {
        file_open = 1;
        load_buffer();
        return 1;
    }
}

void word::load_buffer()
{
    if ( file_open == 1 )
    {
        size = fread( buffer, 1, buffer_size, fp );
        if ( size < buffer_size )
        {
            file_open = 0;
            fclose( fp );
        }
        pos = 0;
    }
}

int word::get_next_word( char* w )
{
    int index = 0;
    // Move to the beginning of a word
    while ( ( pos < size ) &&
            ( !allowable( buffer[ pos ] ) ) )
        pos++;
    if ( pos >= size && file_open == 0 )
        return 0;
    else if ( pos >= size && file_open == 1 )
    {
        load_buffer();
        while ( ( pos < size ) &&
                ( !allowable( buffer[ pos ] ) ) )
            pos++;
    }
    // Move to the end of a word
    while ( ( pos < size ) &&
            ( allowable( buffer[ pos ] ) ) )
        w[ index++ ] = buffer[ pos++ ];
    if ( pos >= size && file_open == 1 )
    {
        load_buffer();
        while ( ( pos < size ) &&
                ( allowable( buffer[ pos ] ) ) )
            w[ index++ ] = buffer[ pos++ ];
    }
    w[ index ] = '\0';
    for ( int i = 0; i < strlen( w ); i++ )
        w[ i ] = tolower( w[ i ] );
    return 1;
}
```

The implementation of class dictionary is given in Listing 7.7.

Listing 7.7
Implementation of
Class Dictionary

```cpp
// Implementation of class dictionary.
// File dict.cpp
#include "dict.h"
#include <stdio.h>

const int hashsize = 32767;
const int smallsize = 18280;
const int c2 = 26;
const int c3 = 26 * 26;
const int c4 = 96;

unsigned hash[ hashsize ];
unsigned small[ smallsize ];

#define getbits(x,pos,nbits) (x>>pos+1-nbits) & ~( ~0 <<nbits)

unsigned int makeword( unsigned card1, unsigned card2 )
// Combines the upper 8 bits of card1 with the lower 8 bits
// of card2.
{
    return ( ( card1 << 8 ) | ( card2 & 0x00FF ) );
}

unsigned int hilong( long l )
// Extracts the upper 16 bits of the long integer l
{
    return ( ( l >> 16 ) & ( 0xFFFF ) );
}
long makelong( unsigned card1, unsigned card2 )
{ // Combines two cardinals into a long
    long temp1, temp2;

    temp1 = ( long ) card1;
    temp2 = ( long ) card2;
    return ( ( temp1 << 16 ) | temp2 );
}

unsigned int lolong ( long l )
// Extracts the lower 16 bits of the long integer l
{
    return ( ( l ) & ( 0xFFFF ) );
}

void dictionary::compute( char* w, unsigned &majorkey,
                          unsigned &minorkey )
{

    /* Returns the minorkey and majorkey of a word using the
       virtual hash algorithm developed by Richard Wiener.*/

    int even;
    int temp;
    int iteration;
    int numberit;
    long w1, w2, w3;
    unsigned hiwd, lowd, hibyte, lobyte;

    int len = strlen( w );
    if ( len % 2 == 1 )
    {
```

```
         temp = len - 1;
         even = 0;
      }
      else
      {
         temp = len;
         even = 1;
      }
      numberit = temp / 2 - 2;
      w1 = makelong( w[ 0 ], w[ 1 ] );
      w2 = makelong( w[ 2 ], w[ 3 ] );
      w3 = w1 * w2;
      hiwd = hilong( w3 );
      lowd = lolong( w3 );
      lobyte = getbits( hiwd, 15, 8 );
      hibyte = getbits( lowd, 7, 8 );
      for ( iteration = 1; iteration <= numberit; iteration++ )
      {
         w1 = makelong( 0, makeword( hibyte, lobyte ) );
         w2 = makelong( w[ 2 * iteration + 2 ],
                    w[ 2 * iteration + 3 ] );
         w3 = w1 * w2;
         hiwd = hilong( w3 );
         lowd = lolong( w3 );
         lobyte = getbits( hiwd, 15, 8 );
         hibyte = getbits( lowd, 7, 8 );
      }
      if ( ! even )
      {
         w1 = makelong( w[ 1 ], makeword( hibyte, lobyte ) );
         w2 = makelong( w[ 0 ], w[ len - 1 ] );
         w3 = w1 * w2;
      }
      hiwd = hilong( w3 );
      lowd = lolong( w3 );
      lobyte = getbits( hiwd, 15, 8 );
      hibyte = getbits( lowd, 7, 7 );
      majorkey = makeword( hibyte, lobyte );
      lobyte = getbits( hiwd, 7, 8 );
      hibyte = getbits( lowd, 15, 8 );
      minorkey = makeword( hibyte, lobyte );
}
void dictionary::load_dictionary()
{
   FILE *h, *s;

   h = fopen( ''HASH.DTA'', ''rb'' );
   int size = fread( ( char * ) hash, sizeof( int ),
                 hashsize, h );
   fclose( h );
   s = fopen( ''SMALL.DTA'', ''rb'' );
   size = fread( ( char * ) small, sizeof( int ), smallsize,
              s );
   fclose( s );
}
```

Listing 7.7
(continued)

```
                          h = fopen( ''HASH.DTA'', ''wb'' );
                          fwrite( ( char * ) hash, sizeof( int ), hashsize, h );
                          fclose( h );
                          s = fopen( ''SMALL.DTA'', ''wb'' );
                          fwrite( ( char * ) small, sizeof( int ), smallsize, s );
                          fclose( s );
                      }
                      void dictionary::insert( char* w )
                      // Returns 1 if w in dictionary otherwise returns 0
                      {
                          unsigned int majorkey, minorkey, tablevalue, len;

                          if ( strlen( w ) != 0 )
                          {
                            len = strlen( w );
                            if ( len <= 3 )
                            {
                              /* Table lookup */
                              if ( len == 1 ) small[ w[ 0 ] - c4 ] = 1;
                              else
                                if ( len == 2 )
                                  small[ w[ 0 ] - c4 + c2 * ( w[ 1 ] - c4 ) ] = 1;
                                else
                                  small[ w[ 0 ] - c4 + c2 * ( w[ 1 ] - c4 ) +
                                              c3 * ( w[ 2 ] - c4 ) ] = 1;
                            }
                            else
                            {
                              /* Virtual hashing */
                              compute( w, majorkey, minorkey );
                              tablevalue = hash[ majorkey ];
                              while ( ( tablevalue != 0 ) &&
                                      ( tablevalue != minorkey ) )
                              {
                                majorkey = ( majorkey + 1 ) % hashsize;
                                tablevalue = hash[ majorkey ];
                              }
                              if ( tablevalue == minorkey ) return;
                              else
                              {
                                hash[ majorkey ] = minorkey;
                              }
                            }
                          }
                      }

                      int dictionary::check( char *w )
                      // Returns 1 if w in dictionary otherwise returns 0
                      {
                          unsigned majorkey, minorkey, tablevalue, len;

                          if ( strlen( w ) != 0 )
                          {
                            len = strlen( w );
                            if ( len <= 3 )
                            {
                              /* Direct table lookup for small words */
                              if ( len == 1 ) return ( small[ w[ 0 ] - c4 ] );
                              else
```

```
            if ( len == 2 )
               return ( small[ w[ 0 ] - c4 +
                        c2 * ( w[ 1 ] - c4 ) ] );
            else
               return ( small[ w[ 0 ] - c4 +
                        c2 * ( w[ 1 ] - c4 ) +
                        c3 * ( w[ 2 ] - c4 ) ] );
        }
        else
        {
           /* Virtual hashing */
           compute( w, majorkey, minorkey );
           majorkey = majorkey % hashsize;
           tablevalue = hash[ majorkey ];
           while ( ( tablevalue != 0 ) &&
                   ( tablevalue != minorkey ) )
           {
              majorkey = ( majorkey + 1 ) % hashsize;
              tablevalue = hash[ majorkey ];
           }
           return ( tablevalue == minorkey );
        }
    }
}
```

The implementation of class search_table is given in Listing 7.8. This is actually the implementation of the generic search tree class. The derived class definition, given in Listing 7.3, implements all its methods in terms of the parent class methods of the generic search tree.

Listing 7.8
Implementation
of Class
Search_Table

```
// Implementation of generic tree class
// File table.cpp

#include ''table.h''

void tree::process_nodes( node* n, int first )
{
   node* current;

   if ( first )
   {
      current = root;
      first = 0;
   }
   else
      current = n;
   if ( current != 0 )
   {
      process_nodes( current -> left, first );
      ( *visit )( current -> contents );
      process_nodes( current -> right, first );
   }
}
```

Listing 7.8
(continued)

```
void tree::insert( char* a )
{
    node *parent,
         *current;
    int found = 0;

    parent = 0;
    current = root;
    while ( current && !found )
    {
        if ( ( *equal )( current -> contents, a ) )
            found = 1;
        else
        {
            parent = current;
            if ( ( *lessthan )( a, current -> contents ) )
                current = current -> left;
            else
                current = current -> right;
        }
    }
    if ( !found )
    {
        if ( !parent )
        {
            // First node in tree
            root = new node;
            root -> left = root -> right = 0;
            // Allocate space for the contents
            root -> contents = new char[ size ];
            // Do a byte-by-byte transfer of data from a to
            // contents.
            for ( int i = 0; i < size; i++ )
                root -> contents[ i ] = a[ i ];
        }
        else
        {
            if ( ( *lessthan )( a, parent -> contents ) )
            {
                // Add new node to the left of parent
                node* new_node = new node;
                // Allocate space for the contents
                new_node -> contents = new char[ size ];
                // Do a byte-by-byte transfer of data from a to
                // contents.
                for ( int i = 0; i < size; i++ )
                    new_node -> contents[ i ] = a[ i ];
                new_node -> left = new_node -> right = 0;
                parent -> left = new_node;
            }
            else
            {
                // Add new node to the right of parent
                node* new_node = new node;
                // Allocate space for the contents
                new_node -> contents = new char[ size ];
                // Do a byte-by-byte transfer of data from a to
                // contents.
```

```
                 for ( int i = 0; i < size; i++ )
                     new_node -> contents[ i ] = a[ i ];
                 new_node -> left = new_node -> right = 0;
                 parent -> right = new_node;
             }
         }
     }
}
int tree::is_present( char* a )
{
    node *parent,
         *current;
    int found = 0;

    parent = 0;
    current = root;
    while ( current && !found )
    {
        if ( ( *equal )( current -> contents, a ) )
            found = 1;
        else
        {
            parent = current;
            if ( ( *lessthan )( a, current -> contents ) )
                current = current -> left;
            else
                current = current -> right;
        }
    }
    return found;
}
void tree::clear( node* n, int first )
{
    node* current;
    if ( first )
    {
        current = root;
        first = 0;
    }
    else
        current = n;
    if ( current != 0 )
    {
        clear( current -> left, first );
        clear( current -> right, first );
        delete current -> contents;
        delete current;
    }
}
void tree::remove( char* a )
{
    node *previous,
         *present,
         *replace,
         *s,
         *parent;
    int found = 0;
```

Listing 7.8
(continued)

```
previous = 0;
present = root;
while ( present && !found )
{
  if ( ( *equal )( a, present -> contents ) )
    found = 1;
  else
  {
    previous = present;
    if ( ( *lessthan )( a, present -> contents ) )
      present = present -> left;
    else
      present = present -> right;
  }
}
if ( found )
{
  if ( present -> left == 0 )
    replace = present -> right;
  else
    if ( present -> right == 0 )
      replace = present -> left;
    else
    {
      parent = present;
      replace = present -> right;
      s = replace -> left;
      while ( s != 0 )
      {
        parent = replace;
        replace = s;
        s = replace -> left;
      }
      if ( parent != present )
      {
        parent -> left = replace -> right;
        replace -> right = present -> right;
      }
      replace -> left = present -> left;
    }
  if ( previous == 0 )
    root = replace;
  else
    if ( present == previous -> left )
      previous -> left = replace;
    else
      previous -> right = replace;
  delete present -> contents;
  delete present;
}
}
```

7.2 Bank Teller Discrete Event Simulation

In our second case study, we simulate the waiting lines that form in front of bank tellers in a typical bank. The discrete event simulation will provide information helpful to time efficiency for both the bank teller and the bank customer and as an example for the reader will demonstrate the use of inheritance in object-oriented programming as a means of achieving easy, localized maintenance.

7.2.1 Specifications for queue simulation

The number of working hours that are simulated is a user input parameter. The basic unit of time in the simulation is the minute.

We assume that customers arrive at the bank according to a Poisson arrival process with a user-specified average interarrival time. The Poisson arrival process yields an exponential interarrival probability density function.

We also assume that each teller serves his or her customers with an exponential service time probability density function. The user must specify the average service time for each server, as part of the input data.

We wish to model and compare two distinct types of queuing systems, which we will call Bank Simulation 1 and Bank Simulation 2. In the first system, a single queue is formed that serves n servers. The number of servers is a user input parameter. If one or more servers is unoccupied, the first customer in the queue enters service. The choice of server when more than one server is free is determined randomly, with each server having an equal likelihood of being chosen.

The second queuing model assumes that each of the n servers has a separate waiting line. If one or more servers is free and their respective line is empty when a customer enters the bank, the choice of server is determined randomly, as before, with each server having an equal likelihood of being chosen. If all the servers are occupied, the customer joins the shortest line. In the event that two or more lines have the same number of customers, the customer joins the lowest-numbered line.

From the bank's point of view, the efficiency of each system can be estimated by examining the time-average size of the single queue or the separate queues. The bank is also interested in estimating the fraction of time that each server is occupied over a given working day for each of the queuing models. The simulation is required to maintain statistics that allow such estimates to be made.

From the customer's point of view, the efficiency of each system can be estimated by examining the average time waiting in line for each of the two queuing models.

We assume that when the simulated clock time is equal to or greater than the user-specified number of minutes that the bank is to be open, each customer currently in line is allowed to complete his or her transaction. Thus the bank is assumed to begin its working day with each server unoccupied and is assumed to end its working day with each server unoccupied. The simulation is required to send its output report to the screen upon the completion of the simulation (just after the last customer leaves the bank).

The user must specify the following parameters as input for each of the queuing models:

1. The average interarrival time of customers

2. The number of servers

3. The average service time for each of the servers.

4. The number of minutes of working time that the system is to be simulated

The output required of the simulation is the following:

1. The percentage of time that each server is busy

2. The total number of customers served by each server

3. The time-average size of each queue

4. The maximum size of each queue over the period of the simulation

5. The average waiting time in the queue for each queue

6. The average waiting time in the queue over all customers

7.2.2 High-level design of queue simulation

An object-oriented solution to a problem requires that we map the problem space into a set of objects and operations in the solution space. We must first identify the major components of the problem space before we can attempt this high-level mapping.

The problem space for the bank simulation includes the following entities:

1. Customers

2. One or more customer queues

3. Clock time, which advances from one event to another

4. One or more servers

5. The bank that contains either one big line or several smaller lines

Each entity will be mapped to a class of abstract objects in the solution space. As we have seen before, the class construct in C++ supports the encapsulation of data and the decomposition of a problem into objects and operations. We discuss each of the classes that make up the object-oriented solution space for this bank simulation.

The customer class contains the only important feature associated with each customer, his or her arrival time in the system. This arrival_time datum is part of the private section of the class. Since we plan to have one or more queues of customers, we must designate the class customer_queue to be a friend of class customer so that objects of class customer_queue can access the private data (arrival_time) of class customer. The class customer has no methods.

The class customer_queue contains the following private data:

1. A static array of customers.

2. Integer index values first and last that control insertion and deletion in the queue.

3. The real value last_event_time, representing the time of the last customer arrival or departure from the queue.

4. The integer value cum_customers, representing the current total number of customers arriving in the queue.

5. The integer value current_queue_size, representing the current size of the queue.

6. The integer value peak_queue, representing the largest size, to date, of the queue.

7. The real value cum_queue_size_time, representing the current sum of products of queue size multiplied by the time that the queue is the given size. This value must be updated every time a customer joins the queue or departs from the queue. The sum of products of queue size and time the queue is the given size divided by the total run-time of the simulation provides an estimate of the average queue size.

8. The real value cum_wait_time, representing the current sum of all customer waiting times for the queue. At the end of the simulation, this value divided by the total run-time provides an estimate of the average queue wait time per customer.

The public methods (and their parameters) that are defined for class customer_queue are the following:

1. A constructor that initializes much of the private data associated with the queue.

2. `void insert( time t )`—This method inserts a customer into the queue at time t and updates appropriate queue statistics.

3. `void remove( time t )`—This method removes a customer from the queue at time t and updates appropriate queue statistics.

4. `int total_customers()`—This method returns the private datum cum_customers.

5. `float average_queue_size( time t )`—This method returns the ratio of the private data cum_queue_size_time and the current clock time.

6. `int size()`—This method returns the private datum current_queue_size.

7. `int maximum_queue_size()`—This method returns the value of the private datum peak_queue.

8. `float average_queue_wait_time()`—This method returns the ratio of the private data cum_wait_time and cum_customers.

9. `float total_wait_time()`—This method returns the private datum cum_wait_time.

The class time contains the private datum current_time and the following methods (with their parameters):

1. `float get_time()`—This method returns the private datum current_time.

2. `void set_time( float t )`—This method assigns the private datum current_time to the value t.

The class server contains the following private data:

1. An integer, available, that has the value 1 if the server is free, otherwise the value 0.

2. The real value cum_service_time that represents the current cumulative time that the server is busy.

3. The real value next_available that represents the time at which the server will be done serving and will be free.

4. The integer value total_customers_served that represents the total number of customers served by the server to date.

5. The real value av_service_time, the key parameter that determines the shape of the exponential service probability density function.

The public methods (and their parameters) that are defined for class server are the following:

1. A constructor that initializes some of the private data.

2. `void set_av_service_time( float average_service_time )`—This method assigns the private datum av_service_time, to the value of the parameter sent in.

3. `void add_to_total_served()`—This method increments the private datum total_customers_served by 1.

4. `void set_server_free()`—This method sets the private datum available to 1 and sets the private datum next_available to the constant large, a number chosen to be larger than the clock time to be encountered in any reasonable simulation experiment.

5. `void set_server_busy()`—This method sets the private datum available to 0.

6. `int busy()`—This method returns 1 (true) if the private datum available is 0; otherwise, it returns 1.

7. `int get_total_served()`—This method returns the private datum total_customers_served.

8. `void add_to_service_time( float t )`—This method increments the private datum cum_service_time by t.

9. `float fraction_of_time_service( time t )`—This method returns the ratio of the private datum cum_service_time and the time t.

10. `void set_next_available( float t )`—This method assigns the value t to the private datum next_available.

11. `float get_next_available()`—This method returns the current value of the private datum next_available.

12. `void serve_cust( time t )`—This method computes the service time for the current customer, updates the value of next_available using the current clock time t and the exponential service time, sets the server to busy, and updates the appropriate server statistics.

We translate the informal descriptions of each class given above to formal class definitions. These definitions are given in files cust.h, time.h, queue.h, and server.h and are presented, along with their implementations, in Listings 7.9, 7.10, 7.11, and 7.12. As noted, a drawback of the customer_queue implementation is that the maximum size must be specified in advance.

Listing 7.9
Definition and
Implementation of
Class Customer

```
// Interface to class customer
// File cust.h
class customer
{
    friend class customer_queue;
    private:
        float arrival_time;   // Time when customer joins line
};
```

Listing 7.10
Definition and
Implementation of
Class Time

```
// Interface to class time
// File time.h
class time
{
    private:
        float current_time;
    public:
```

Listing 7.10
(continued)

```
time()
{
   current_time = 0.0;
}
float get_time() { return current_time; }
void set_time( float t ) { current_time = t; }
};
```

Listing 7.11
Interface to Class
Customer_Queue

```
// Interface to customer_queue - static version
// This implementation suffers from the fact that
// the maximum size must be specified in advance.
// File queue.h

#include ''time.h''
#include ''cust.h''

const max_queue = 200; // Capacity of waiting line

class customer_queue
{
   private:
      customer line[ max_queue ];
      int first, last;
      float last_event_time;       // Time of last customer
                                   // arrival or departure
      int cum_customers;           // Cumulative number of customers
      int current_queue_size;
      int peak_queue;
      float cum_queue_size_time;   // Cumulative sum of products of
                                   // size of queue × time
      float cum_wait_time;         // Cumulative wait time for all
                                   // patrons

   public:
      customer_queue()
      {
         first = 0;
         last = max_queue - 1;
         last_event_time = 0.0;
         cum_customers = 0;
         current_queue_size = 0;
         peak_queue = 0;
         cum_queue_size_time = 0.0;
         cum_wait_time = 0.0;
      }
      void insert( time t );

      void remove( time t );

      int total_customers() { return cum_customers; }

      float average_queue_size( time t )
      {
         return ( cum_queue_size_time / t.get_time() );
      }
      int size() { return current_queue_size; }

      int maximum_queue_size() { return peak_queue; }
```

```
    float average_queue_wait_time()
    {
      return ( cum_wait_time / cum_customers );
    }
    float total_wait_time() { return cum_wait_time; }
};
```

Listing 7.12
Definition and
Implementation
of Class Server

```
// Interface to class server
// File server.h
#include <math.h>
const float large = 999999.9;
extern float rand_real();
class server
{
  private:
    int available;            // 1 if server if free, otherwise 0
    float cum_service_time;   // Cumulative service time
    float next_available;     // Time when server is free
    int total_customers_served;
    float av_service_time;
  public:
    server()
    {
      cum_service_time = 0.0;
      total_customers_served = 0;
      next_available = large;
      available = 1;
    }

    void add_to_total_served() { total_customers_served++; }

    void set_server_free()
    {
      available = 1;
      next_available = large;
    }

    void set_server_busy() { available = 0; }

    int busy()
    {
      if ( available )
        return 0;
      else
        return 1;
    }

    int get_total_served() { return total_customers_served; }

    void add_to_service_time( float t )
    {
      cum_service_time += t;
    }

    float fraction_of_time_service( time t )
    {
      return ( cum_service_time / ( t.get_time() ) );
    }
```

Listing 7.12
(continued)

```
void set_next_available( float t ) { next_available = t; }
float get_next_available() { return next_available; }
void serve_cust( time t )
{
    float r = -av_service_time * log( rand_real() );
    set_next_available( t.get_time() + r );
    add_to_service_time( r );
    add_to_total_served();
    set_server_busy();
}
void set_av_service_time( float average_service_time )
{
    av_service_time = average_service_time;
}
};
```

7.2.3 Low-level design of queue simulation

The low-level design details of the bank case study are not complicated. None of the classes defined in the previous section requires complex algorithms for its implementation. The queue is defined as a static array of customers. The index parameters first and last are used to control insertion and deletion from the queue thusly: initial values of first and last, first = 0, last = max_queue − 1; for insertion, last = ++last % max_queue; and for deletion, first = ++first % max_queue.

7.2.4 Implementation of queue simulation

The implementation of class customer_queue is given in Listing 7.13.

Listing 7.13
Implementation
of Class
Customer_Queue

```
// Implementation of class customer_queue
// File queue.cpp
#include ''queue.h''
void customer_queue::insert( time t )
{
    float current_time = t.get_time();
    last = ++last % max_queue;
    line[ last ].arrival_time = current_time;
    cum_customers++;
    cum_queue_size_time += current_queue_size *
        ( current_time - last_event_time );
    current_queue_size++;
```

```
   if ( current_queue_size > peak_queue )
     peak_queue = current_queue_size;
   last_event_time = current_time;
}
void customer_queue::remove( time t )
{
   float current_time = t.get_time();
   float wait = current_time - line[ first ].arrival_time;

   cum_wait_time += wait;
   cum_queue_size_time += current_queue_size *
     ( current_time - last_event_time );
   current_queue_size --;
   last_event_time = current_time;
   first = ++first % max_queue;
}
```

Figure 7.1(a) shows the physical configuration for the first of the two simulation models, a single queue feeding n servers. Figure 7.1(b) shows the physical configuration for the second simulation model, n queues with n servers.

Figure 7.1
Physical configuration for (a) single-queue and (b) multiline simulation models.

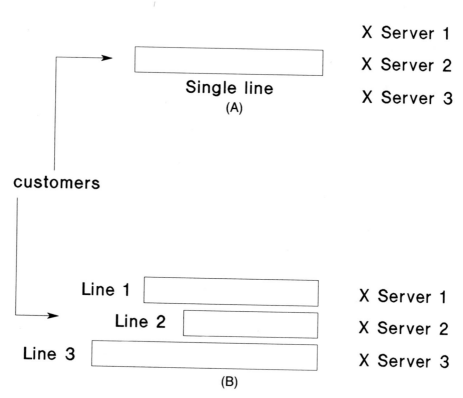

In the first simulation model, the following objects are declared:

```
customer_queue q;
time t;
server *s;
```

The last declaration represents an array of servers. Memory for this array of objects is allocated at run-time in the heap, after the user has specified the number of servers. The memory allocation is performed using

```
s = new server[ number_servers ];
```

As emphasized before, a properly constructed object-oriented solution should be easy to read and to maintain. In this spirit, let us examine an important loop in the main driver program of the first bank simulation that controls the objects of the problem during business hours. This loop, reproduced in Listing 7.14, is paraphrased in the following paragraphs.

The first arrival time is generated. The next event is computed using the function get_next_event. This function returns the value 0 if the next event is a customer arrival, returns the value 1 if the next event is server 1 completing service, returns the value 2 if the next event is server 2 completing service, and returns the value n if the next event is server n completing service. The function get_next_event is discussed later in this section.

If the next_event_time, also returned from function get_next_event, is less than the user input simulation_time, we set the clock to the next event time.

If the next event is the completion of service and the size of the queue is greater than one (at least one customer is waiting in line for service), the message remove is sent to the object q, and then the message serve_cust(t) is sent to the object s[next_event − 1].

If the next event is the completion of service and the size of the queue is zero (no customers are in line waiting for service), the message set_server_free( ) is sent to the object s[next_event − 1].

If the next event is a customer arrival, we determine whether one or more servers is free. The function server_avail(server_no) is used for this purpose. If this function returns the value 1, then the available server is returned in the reference parameter server_no. If this function returns 0, this implies that all the servers are busy.

If one or more servers is free and the server number is given by server_no, the message insert(t) is sent to the object q. Immediately following this, the message remove(t) is sent to the object q. This is done to update the statistics for the queue. Then the message serve_cust(t) is sent to the object s[server_no].

If none of the servers is free, the message insert(t) is sent to the object q.

A new value for the important variable arrival_time is set if the next event is the arrival of a customer.

Listing 7.14
The Loop That
Controls the
Objects During
Business Hours for
Bank Simulation 1

```
centermessage( ''Simulating . . . '' );
arrival_time = generate_iat( t );
do
{  // During business hours . . .
   // Determine the next event
   next_event = get_next_event( next_event_time );
   #ifdef debug
      printf( ''\n\nThe next_event = %d'', next_event );
      printf( '' next_event_time = %f'', next_event_time );
   #endif
   if ( next_event_time <= simulation_time )
   {
      t.set_time( next_event_time );
      if ( next_event > 0 && q.size() > 0 )
      {  // Take a customer from the queue
         q.remove( t );
         s[ next_event - 1 ].serve_cust( t );
         #ifdef debug
            printf( ''\nThe queue size = %d\n\n'', q.size() );
            spacebar();
            clrscreen();
         #endif
      }
      else if ( next_event > 0 && q.size() == 0 )
      {
         s[ next_event - 1 ].set_server_free();
         #ifdef debug
            printf( ''\nThe queue size = %d\n\n'', q.size() );
            spacebar();
            clrscreen();
         #endif
      }
   else // Next event is a customer arrival
   {
      if ( q.size() == 0 && server_avail( server_no ) )
      {  // Customer goes directly to server server_no
         q.insert( t );
         q.remove( t ); // Insert and remove to update stats
         s[ server_no ].serve_cust( t );
         #ifdef debug
            printf( ''\nThe queue size = %d\n\n'', q.size() );
            spacebar();
            clrscreen();
         #endif
      }
      else // Customer joins queue
      {
         q.insert( t );
         #ifdef debug
            printf( ''\nThe queue size = %d\n\n'', q.size() );
            spacebar();
            clrscreen();
         #endif
      }
      arrival_time = generate_iat( t );
   }
}
} while ( next_event_time <= simulation_time );
```

The function get_next_event is given in Listing 7.15. This function returns the value 0 if the next event is a new customer arrival or n = 1, 2, . . . , n if the next event is the completion of service for server n.

The value min is initialized to arrival_time. The value of choice is initialized to 0. In a for loop, the message get_next_available( ) is sequentially sent to the objects s[i − 1], and the returned value temp is compared to min. If temp is less than min, new values for choice and min are assigned. After the loop, the value of choice is returned and the value min returned as a reference parameter.

Listing 7.15
The Function
Get_Next_Event

```
int get_next_event( float &n_event_time )
{
    float min = arrival_time;
    int choice = 0;
    float temp;
    for ( int i = 1; i <= number_servers; i++ )
    {
        if ( ( temp = s[ i - 1 ].get_next_available() ) < min )
        {
            choice = i;
            min = temp;
        }
    }
    n_event_time = min;
    return choice;
}
```

In Listing 7.16, the important function server_avail is given. In a for loop, the message busy( ) is sent to the objects s[i]. If a free server is found, the number of the server is placed into the local array choice and the value of the local integer variable number_free is incremented. If at the end of the loop the value of number_free is 0, the function server_avail returns 0. If the value of number_free is greater than 0, the function server_avail returns 1 and the reference parameter n is computed using the code

```
n = choice[ random( 0, number_free - 1 ) ];
```

The function random(0, number_free − 1), taken from file util.h, returns a uniformly distributed integer from 0 to number_free − 1.

Listing 7.16
Function
Server_Avail

```
int server_avail( int &n )
{   // Returns 0 if no server is available
    // Otherwise returns 1 and number of available server
    int choice[ 30 ];
    int number_free = 0;

    for ( int i = 0; i < number_servers; i++ )
    {
```

```
      if ( !s[ i ].busy() )
      {
         choice[ number_free ] = i;
         number_free++;
      }
   }
   if ( number_free == 0 )
      return 0;
   else
   {
      // Choose a random server among available servers
      n = choice[ random( 0, number_free - 1 ) ];
      return 1;
   }
}
```

The loop that controls the objects of the problem after the doors of the bank have closed but customers may still be waiting for service is given in Listing 7.17.

In this loop, the arrival_time is set to the constant large, which ensures that the function get_next_event will return the value 0 only if all the servers are free. The function get_next_event is invoked. While the next event is not 0, the message set_time(next_event_time) is sent to object t. The message size( ) is sent to the object q. If the return value is greater than 0, the message remove(t) is sent to the object q. Then the message serve_cust(t) is sent to the object s[next_event − 1]. If the return value is 0, the message set_server_free( ) is sent to the object s[next_event − b1]. Finally a new next_event number is computed.

Upon the termination of this final loop, the function report_stats is called, and the object q is sent as a parameter.

Listing 7.17
The Loop That Controls the Objects in Bank 1 after It Has Closed Its Doors

```
arrival_time = large; // Bank is now closed
next_event = get_next_event( next_event_time );
#ifdef debug
   printf( ''\nBank closed\n'' );
   printf( ''\nThe next_event = %d'', next_event );
   printf( '' next_event_time = %f'', next_event_time );
   printf( ''\nCurrent queue size = %d'', q.size() );
   spacebar();
   clrscreen();
#endif
// Determine whether all servers are free
while ( next_event != 0 )
{
   t.set_time( next_event_time );
   if ( q.size() > 0 )
   {
      q.remove( t );
      s[ next_event - 1 ].serve_cust( t );
   }
   else
      s[ next_event - 1 ].set_server_free();
   next_event = get_next_event( next_event_time );
}
report_stats( q );
```

The reader is urged to study Listing 7.18, which includes all the code for Bank Simulation 1. The code segments that are delimited by #ifdef debug and #endif are present for debugging purposes. If the user includes the statement

```
#define debug
```

before any of the debug segments, they will be compiled with the rest of the program. If the #define debug statement is not present, the debug statements will not be compiled with the program.

Listing 7.18
Bank Simulation 1
Driver Program

```
// Main bank simulation program
// This program simulates a bank with one waiting line
// and n servers. When one or more servers is free,
// the server is chosen randomly.
// File bank1.cpp
#include "queue.h"
#include "server.h"
#include <util.h>

float average_iat;              // Average interarrival time
float simulation_time;          // Time, in minutes, bank is open
int number_servers;             // Number of servers in system
float *average_service_time;    // Array of av_serv_times
float arrival_time;

// Object declarations
customer_queue q;
time t;
server *s; // Array of servers

void get_input()
{
   gotoxy( 0, 10 );
   printf( "\nEnter the number of servers: " );
   scanf( "%d", &number_servers );

   average_service_time = new float[ number_servers ];
   s = new server[ number_servers ];

   for ( int z = 0; z < number_servers; z++ )
   {
      printf( "\nEnter average service time for server %d: ",
            z + 1 );
      scanf( "%f", &average_service_time[ z ] );
      s[ z ].set_av_service_time( average_service_time[ z ] );
   }
   printf( "\nEnter the average interarrival time: " );
   scanf( "%f", &average_iat );
   printf( "\nNumber of minutes for the simulation: " );
   scanf( "%f", &simulation_time );
}

main()
{
   extern int get_next_event( float &n_event_time );
   extern int server_avail( int &n );
   extern void report_stats( customer_queue q );
```

```
extern void title();
extern float generate_iat( time t );

float next_event_time;
int next_event;
int server_no;

clrscreen();
title();
get_input();
clrscreen();
title();
gotoxy( 0, 10 );
centermessage( ''Simulating . . . '' );
arrival_time = generate_iat( t );
do
{ // During business hours . . .
  // Determine the next event
  next_event = get_next_event( next_event_time );
  #ifdef debug
    printf( ''\n\nThe next_event = %d'', next_event );
    printf( '' next_event_time = %f'', next_event_time );
  #endif
  if ( next_event_time <= simulation_time )
  {
    t.set_time( next_event_time );
    if ( next_event > 0 && q.size() > 0 )
    { // Take a customer from the queue
      q.remove( t );
      s[ next_event - 1 ].serve_cust( t );
      #ifdef debug
        printf( ''\nThe queue size = %d\n\n'', q.size() );
        spacebar();
        clrscreen();
      #endif
    }
    else if ( next_event > 0 && q.size() == 0 )
    {
      s[ next_event - 1 ].set_server_free();
      #ifdef debug
        printf( ''\nThe queue size = %d\n\n'', q.size() );
        spacebar();
        clrscreen();
      #endif
    }
    else // Next event is a customer arrival
    {
      if ( q.size() == 0 && server_avail( server_no ) )
      { // Customer goes directly to server server_no
        q.insert( t );
        q.remove( t ); // Insert and remove to update stats
        s[ server_no ].serve_cust( t );
        #ifdef debug
          printf( ''\nThe queue size = %d\n\n'', q.size() );
          spacebar();
          clrscreen();
        #endif
      }
      else // Customer joins queue
      {
```

Listing 7.18
(continued)

```
                              q.insert( t );
                              #ifdef debug
                                 printf( ''\nThe queue size = %d\n\n'', q.size() );
                                 spacebar();
                                 clrscreen();
                              #endif
                           }
                           arrival_time = generate_iat( t );
                       }
                   }
               } while ( next_event_time <= simulation_time );
               arrival_time = large; // Bank is now closed
               next_event = get_next_event( next_event_time );
               #ifdef debug
                  printf( ''\nBank closed\n'' );
                  printf( ''\nThe next_event = %d'', next_event );
                  printf( '' next_event_time = %f'', next_event_time );
                  printf( ''\nCurrent queue size = %d'', q.size() );
                  spacebar();
                  clrscreen();
               #endif
               // Determine whether all servers are free
               while ( next_event != 0 )
               {
                  t.set_time( next_event_time );
                  if ( q.size() > 0 )
                  {
                     q.remove( t );
                     s[ next_event - 1 ].serve_cust( t );
                  }
                  else
                     s[ next_event - 1 ].set_server_free();
                  next_event = get_next_event( next_event_time );
               }
               report_stats( q );
           }

           float generate_iat( time t )
           {  // Exponential distribution with mean given by av_
              // interarrival_time
              return ( -average_iat * log( rand_real() ) +
                       t.get_time() );
           }

           int get_next_event( float &n_event_time )
           {
              float min = arrival_time;
              int choice = 0;
              float temp;

              for ( int i = 1; i <= number_servers; i++ )
              {
                 if ( ( temp = s[ i - 1 ].get_next_available() ) < min )
                 {
                    choice = i;
                    min = temp;
                 }
              }
              n_event_time = min;
              return choice;
           }
```

```
int server_avail( int &n )
{  // Returns 0 if no server is available
   // otherwise returns 1 and number of available server
   int choice[ 30 ];
   int number_free = 0;

   for ( int i = 0; i < number_servers; i++ )
   {
      if ( !s[ i ].busy( ) )
      {
         choice[ number_free ] = i;
         number_free++;
      }
   }
   if ( number_free == 0 )
      return 0;
   else
   {
      // Choose a random server among available servers
      n = choice[ random( 0, number_free - 1 ) ];
      return 1;
   }
}

void report_stats( customer_queue q )
{
   clrscreen( );
   centermessage( ''Output Statistics'' );
   printf( ''\n'' );
   centermessage( ''------------------'' );
   printf( ''\n\nAverage queue size      : %-8.3f'',
           q.average_queue_size( t ) );
   printf( ''\n\nAverage queue wait time : %-8.3f'',
           q.average_queue_wait_time( ) );
   printf(
   ''\n\nMaximum queue size      : %-d'', q.maximum_queue_size( ) );
   printf(
   ''\n\nTotal customers         : %-d'', q.total_customers( ) );
   for ( int i = 0; i < number_servers; i++ )
   {
      printf(
      ''\n\nServer %d service time : %-8.3f%c'',
        i + 1, s[ i ].fraction_of_time_service( t ) * 100, 37 );
      printf(
         ''\n\nServer %d total served : %-d'', i + 1,
         s[ i ].get_total_served( ) );
   }
}

void title( )
{
   gotoxy( 0, 4 );
   centermessage( ''Discrete Event Simulation Of Bank Queue'' );
   printf( ''\n'' );
   centermessage( ''-------------------------------------'' );
}
```

In the second simulation model, the following objects are declared:

```
customer_queue *q; // Array of queues
time t;
server *s;          // Array of servers
```

Memory for the arrays of objects *q and *s are allocated at run-time in the heap, after the user has specified the number of servers. The memory allocation is performed using

```
s = new server[ number_servers ];
```

and

```
q = new customer_queue[ number_servers ];
```

Bank Simulation 2 also contains two important loops that control the objects of the simulation during business hours and after the doors of the bank are closed. These two loops are given in Listings 7.19 and 7.20. Because of the extensive level of abstraction employed in both simulation models and the sharing of class abstractions between the two models, these two loops are very similar to the loops given earlier for the first simulation model.

The major difference from the earlier implementation is that every time a message is sent to a queue object, the object q[next_event −1] or q[server_no] is used instead of the object q.

The else statement in Listing 7.19 that refers to the customer joining the shortest queue requires that the smallest queue size be computed. The local variable choice is introduced for this purpose. The message insert(t) is sent to the object q[choice] after the correct value of choice is found.

In Listing 7.20, the same change from object q to object q[next_event − 1] or q to q[server_no] is evident.

Listing 7.19
The Loop That Controls the Objects During Business Hours for Bank Simulation 2

```
centermessage( ''Simulating . . . '' );
arrival_time = generate_iat( t );
do
{ // During business hours . . .
    // Determine the next event
    next_event = get_next_event( next_event_time );
    #ifdef debug
        printf( ''\n\nThe next_event = %d'', next_event );
        printf( '' next_event_time = %f'', next_event_time );
    #endif
    if ( next_event_time <= simulation_time )
    {
        t.set_time( next_event_time );
        if ( next_event > 0 && q[ next_event − 1 ].size() > 0 )
        { // Take a customer from the queue
            q[ next_event − 1 ].remove( t );
            s[ next_event − 1 ].serve_cust( t );
            #ifdef debug
```

```
            printf( ''\nThe queue size = %d\n\n'',
                      q[ next_event - 1 ].size() );
            spacebar();
            clrscreen();
          #endif
        }
        else if ( next_event > 0 && q[ next_event - 1 ].size() == 0 )
        {
          s[ next_event - 1 ].set_server_free();
          #ifdef debug
            printf( ''\nThe queue size = %d\n\n'',
                      q[ next_event - 1 ].size() );
            spacebar();
            clrscreen();
          #endif
        }
        else // Next event is a customer arrival
        {
          if ( server_avail( server_no ) )
          { // Customer goes directly to server server_no
            q[ server_no ].insert( t );
            q[ server_no ].remove( t ); // Insert and remove to
                                        //    update stats
            s[ server_no ].serve_cust( t );
            #ifdef debug
              printf( ''\nThe queue size = %d\n\n'',
                        q[ server_no ].size() );
              spacebar();
              clrscreen();
            #endif
          }
          else // Customer joins shortest queue. In case two or
               //   more queues are the same, the customer joins
               //   the lowest-number queue.
          {
            int min_size = q[ 0 ].size();
            int choice = 0;
            if ( number_servers > 1 )
              for ( int i = 1; i < number_servers; i++ )
                if ( q[ i ].size() < min_size )
                {
                  choice = i;
                  min_size = q[ i ].size();
                }
            q[ choice ].insert( t );
            #ifdef debug
              printf( ''\nThe queue size = %d\n\n'',
                        q[ choice ].size() );
              spacebar();
              clrscreen();
            #endif
          }
          arrival_time = generate_iat( t );
        }
      }
    } while ( next_event_time <= simulation_time );
```

Listing 7.20
The Loop That
Controls the
Objects in Bank 2
after It Has Closed
Its Doors

```
arrival_time = large; // Bank is now closed
next_event = get_next_event( next_event_time );
#ifdef debug
    printf( ''\nBank closed\n'' );
    printf( ''\nThe next_event = %d'', next_event );
    printf( '' next_event_time = %f'', next_event_time );
    spacebar();
    clrscreen();
#endif
// Determine whether all servers are free
while ( next_event != 0 )
{
    t.set_time( next_event_time );
    if ( q[ next_event - 1 ].size() > 0 )
    {
        q[ next_event - 1 ].remove( t );
        s[ next_event - 1 ].serve_cust( t );
    }
    else
        s[ next_event - 1 ].set_server_free();
    next_event = get_next_event( next_event_time );
}
report_stats( q );
```

The reader is urged to carefully examine Listing 7.21 that contains the code for the complete Bank Simulation 2.

Listing 7.21
Bank Simulation 2
Driver Program

```
// Main bank simulation program
// This program simulates a bank with n waiting lines
// and n servers. When one or more servers is free,
// the server is chosen randomly.
// File bank1.cpp

#include ''queue.h''
#include ''server.h''
#include <util.h>
float average_iat;       // Average interarrival time
float simulation_time;   // Time, in minutes, bank is open
int number_servers;      // Number of servers in system
float *average_service_time; // Array of av_serv_times
float arrival_time;

// Object declarations
customer_queue *q; // Array of queues
time t;
server *s;               // Array of servers

void get_input()
{
    gotoxy( 0, 10 );
    printf( ''\nEnter the number of servers: '' );
    scanf( ''%d'', &number_servers );

    average_service_time = new float[ number_servers ];
    s = new server[ number_servers ];
    q = new customer_queue[ number_servers ];
```

```
        for ( int z = 0; z < number_servers; z++ )
        {
            printf( ''\nEnter average service time for server %d: '',
                z + 1 );
            scanf( ''%f'', &average_service_time[ z ] );
            s[ z ].set_av_service_time( average_service_time[ z ] );
        }
        printf( ''\nEnter the average interarrival time: '' );
        scanf( ''%f'', &average_iat );
        printf( ''\nNumber of minutes for the simulation: '' );
        scanf( ''%f'', &simulation_time );
}

main()
{
    extern int get_next_event( float &n_event_time );
    extern int server_avail( int &n );
    extern void report_stats( customer_queue* q );
    extern void title();
    extern float generate_iat( time t );

    float next_event_time;
    int next_event;
    int server_no;

    clrscreen();
    title();
    get_input();
    clrscreen();
    title();
    gotoxy( 0, 10 );
    centermessage( ''Simulating . . . '' );
    arrival_time = generate_iat( t );
    do
    {   // During business hours . . .
        // Determine the next event
        next_event = get_next_event( next_event_time );
        #ifdef debug
            printf( ''\n\nThe next_event = %d'', next_event );
            printf( '' next_event_time = %f'', next_event_time );
        #endif
        if ( next_event_time <= simulation_time )
        {
            t.set_time( next_event_time );
            if ( next_event > 0 && q[ next_event - 1 ].size() > 0 )
            {   // Take a customer from the queue
                q[ next_event - 1 ].remove( t );
                s[ next_event - 1 ].serve_cust( t );
                #ifdef debug
                    printf( ''\nThe queue size = %d\n\n'',
                        q[ next_event - 1 ].size() );
                    spacebar();
                    clrscreen();
                #endif
            }
            else if ( next_event > 0 &&
                    q[ next_event - 1 ].size() == 0 )
                {
```

Listing 7.21
(continued)

```
                            s[ next_event - 1 ].set_server_free();
                        #ifdef debug
                            printf( ''\nThe queue size = %d\n\n'',
                                    q[ next_event - 1 ].size() );
                            spacebar();
                            clrscreen();
                        #endif
                    }
                    else  // Next event is a customer arrival
                    {
                        if ( server_avail( server_no ) )
                        { // Customer goes directly to server server_no
                            q[ server_no ].insert( t );
                            q[ server_no ].remove( t );  // Insert and remove to
                                                         // update stats
                            s[ server_no ].serve_cust( t );
                        #ifdef debug
                            printf( ''\nThe queue size = %d\n\n'',
                                    q[ server_no ].size() );
                            spacebar();
                            clrscreen();
                        #endif
                        }
                        else // Customer joins shortest queue. In case two or
                             // more queues are the same, the customer joins
                             // the lowest-number queue.
                        {
                            int min_size = q[ 0 ].size();
                            int choice = 0;
                            if ( number_servers > 1 )
                                for ( int i = 1; i < number_servers; i++ )
                                    if ( q[ i ].size() < min_size )
                                    {
                                        choice = i;
                                        min_size = q[ i ].size();
                                    }
                            q[ choice ].insert( t );
                        #ifdef debug
                            printf( ''\nThe queue size = %d\n\n'',
                                    q[ choice ].size() );
                            spacebar();
                            clrscreen();
                        #endif
                        }
                        arrival_time = generate_iat( t );
                    }
                }
            } while ( next_event_time <= simulation_time );
            arrival_time = large; // Bank is now closed
            next_event = get_next_event( next_event_time );
            #ifdef debug
                printf( ''\nBank closed\n'' );
                printf( ''\nThe next_event = %d'', next_event );
                printf( '' next_event_time = %f'', next_event_time );
                spacebar();
                clrscreen();
            #endif
            // Determine whether all servers are free
```

```
   while ( next_event != 0 )
   {
     t.set_time( next_event_time );
     if ( q[ next_event - 1 ].size() > 0 )
     {
       q[ next_event - 1 ].remove( t );
       s[ next_event - 1 ].serve_cust( t );
     }
     else
       s[ next_event - 1 ].set_server_free();
     next_event = get_next_event( next_event_time );
   }
   report_stats( q );
}

float generate_iat( time t )
{  // Exponential distribution with mean given by av_
   // interarrival_time
   return ( -average_iat * log( rand_real() ) +
            t.get_time() );
}

int get_next_event( float &n_event_time )
{
   float min = arrival_time;
   int choice = 0;
   float temp;

   for ( int i = 1; i <= number_servers; i++ )
   {
     if ( ( temp = s[ i - 1 ].get_next_available() ) < min )
     {
       choice = i;
       min = temp;
     }
   }
   n_event_time = min;
   return choice;
}

int server_avail( int &n )
{  // Returns 0 if no server is available
   // otherwise returns 1 and number of available server
   int choice[ 30 ];
   int number_free = 0;

   for ( int i = 0; i < number_servers; i++ )
   {
     if ( !s[ i ].busy() )
     {
       choice[ number_free ] = i;
       number_free++;
     }
   }
   if ( number_free == 0 )
     return 0;
   else
   {
```

Listing 7.21
(continued)

```
                    // Choose a random server among available servers
                    n = choice[ random( 0, number_free - 1 ) ];
                    return 1;
                }
            }
        void report_stats( customer_queue* q )
        {
          clrscreen();
          centermessage( ''Output Statistics'' );
          printf( ''\n'' );
          centermessage( ''-----------------'' );
          for ( int i = 0; i < number_servers; i++ )
          {
            printf(
            ''\n\nServer %d service time : %-8.3f%c'',
              i + 1, s[ i ].fraction_of_time_service( t ) * 100, 37 );
            printf(
              ''\n\nServer %d total served : %-d'', i + 1,
              s[ i ].get_total_served() );
          }
          for ( i = 0; i < number_servers; i++ )
          {
            printf( ''\n\nAverage queue size %d : %-8.3f'', i + 1,
                  q[ i ].average_queue_size( t ) );
            printf( ''\n\nAverage queue wait time %d : %-8.3f'', i + 1,
                  q[ i ].average_queue_wait_time() );
            printf( ''\n\nMaximum queue size %d : %-d'', i + 1,
                  q[ i ].maximum_queue_size()
            );
            printf( ''\n\nTotal customers %d       : %-d'', i + 1,
                  q[ i ].total_customers() );
            // Compute average wait time
            float total_wait_time = 0.0;
            float total_customers = 0.0;
            for ( int j = 0; j < number_servers; j++ )
            {
              total_wait_time += q[ j ].total_wait_time();
              total_customers += q[ j ].total_customers();
            }
            printf(
            ''\n\nThe average wait time : %-8.3f'',
              total_wait_time / total_customers );
          }
        }
        void title()
        {
          gotoxy( 0, 4 );
          centermessage( ''Discrete Event Simulation Of Bank Queue'' );
          printf( ''\n'' );
          centermessage( ''--------------------------------------'' )
        }
```

7.2.5 Simulation output

It is interesting to compare the performance of the single-line multiserver system with the multiline multiserver system. By running each system repeatedly with comparable values for average customer service times and average inter-arrival times, we can draw statistical inferences. The single-line multiserver system consistently performs better than the multiline multiserver system.

We present two sets of output statistics that are typical. The first is for a three-server system in which the first server has an average service time of 1 minute, the second server has an average service time of 2 minutes, and the third server has an average service time of 3 minutes. For this system, we assume that the average interarrival time is 0.8 minutes.

In the second system, we have five servers, each with an average service time of 5 minutes. We assume that the average interarrival time is 1 minute. Typical simulation results are given in Tables 7.1 and 7.2.

TABLE 7.1 Output Results for Single-Line versus Multiline Queuing Systems

Statistics for Single-Line System		Statistics for Multiline System	
2000 minutes of simulated time. 3 servers.		2000 minutes of simulated time. 3 servers.	
Average service times	1 −> 1 minute	Average service times	1 −> 1 minute
	2 −> 2 minutes		2 −> 2 minutes
	3 −> 3 minutes		3 −> 3 minutes
Average interarrival time	0.8 minutes	Average interarrival time	0.8 minute
Average queue size	1.715	Server 1 service time	62.337%
Average queue wait time	1.325	Server 1 total served	1258
Maximum queue size	19	Server 2 service time	71.126%
Total customers	2598	Server 2 total served	696
Server 1 service time	66.726%	Server 3 service time	77.000%
Server 1 total served	1346	Server 3 total served	497
Server 2 service time	76.774%	Average size queue 1	0.575
Server 2 total served	728	Average wait time	
Server 3 service time	80.390%	queue 1	0.916
Server 3 total served	524	Maximum size queue 1	8
		Total customers 1	1258
		The average wait time	1.422
		Average size queue 2	0.564
		Average wait time	
		queue 2	1.624
		Maximum size queue 2	7
		Total customers 2	696
		The average wait time	1.422
		Average size queue 3	0.600
		Average wait time	
		queue 3	2.421
		Maximum size queue 3	7
		Total customers 3	497
		The average wait time	1.422

TABLE 7.2   Output Results for Single-Line versus Multiline Queuing Systems

Statistics for Single-Line System		Statistics for Multiline System	
2000 minutes of simulated time. 5 servers.		Server 1 service time	53.061%
Average service times	1 —> 5 minutes	Server 1 total served	223
	2 —> 5 minutes	Server 2 service time	51.851%
	3 —> 5 minutes	Server 2 total served	187
	4 —> 5 minutes	Server 3 service time	50.400%
	5 —> 5 minutes	Server 3 total served	207
Average interarrival time	2 minutes	Server 4 service time	51.569%
Average queue size	0.224	Server 4 total served	189
Average queue wait time	0.439	Server 5 service time	49.334%
Maximum queue size	9	Server 5 total served	198
Total customers	1026	Average size queue 1	0.142
Server 1 service time	50.376%	Average wait time queue 1	1.279
Server 1 total served	208	Maximum size queue 1	2
Server 2 service time	50.174%	Total customers 1	223
Server 2 total served	214	The average wait time	0.618
Server 3 service time	51.020%	Average size queue 2	0.079
Server 3 total served	189	Average wait time queue 2	0.845
Server 4 service time	53.367%	Maximum size queue 2	2
Server 4 total served	206	Total customers 2	187
Server 5 service time	49.936%	The average wait time	0.618
Server 5 total served	209	Average size queue 3	0.059
		Average wait time queue 3	0.569
		Maximum size queue 3	2
		Total customers 3	207
		The average wait time	0.618
		Average size queue 4	0.017
		Average wait time queue 4	0.183
		Maximum size queue 4	1
		Total customers 4	189
		The average wait time	0.618
		Average size queue 5	0.012
		Average wait time queue 5	0.125
		Maximum size queue 5	1
		Total customers 5	198
		The average wait time	0.618

7.2.6   Maintenance of queue simulation

The implementations presented for the two simulation models in Section 7.2.4 use a static representation for the important abstraction customer_queue. The software imposes a limit of 200 customers for each customer_queue. Although for most practical simulation experiments this upper limit is more than sufficient, it may not always suffice. If the traffic intensity, the ratio of mean server time over all the servers divided by the average customer interarrival time, is greater than 1, the queuing system is said to be unstable. Under such conditions it is possible in a long simulation experiment for one or more queues to exceed the value 200.

The concept of a queue involves no upper bound on the number of objects that can be stored in the queue. It is therefore philosophically undesirable for the software implementation to impose an arbitrary limit if this can be avoided, although computer hardware often unavoidably imposes size limitations on the data structures used to implement abstract concepts.

In this section, we illustrate the simplicity of software maintenance on a properly constructed object-oriented program and tout the benefits of inheritance as we perform maintenance on the implementation of the customer_queue class. We focus on files queue.h and queue.cpp. The reader is urged to review Listings 7.11 and 7.13.

Before discussing the changes to this customer_queue implementation that removes the arbitrary upper limit, we observe that as long as we do not change the interface to the methods (function prototypes) in the class customer_queue, there will be no fall-out effects resulting from our changes. Indeed, no changes to code and no recompilation will be required outside of the single file queue.cpp. The linker will have to be invoked to couple the new object code of the revised queue.cpp to the rest of the system.

This kind of localized maintenance, which limits changes to a single software module and protects the remainder of the software system from fall-out effects, has long been a major goal in software design. The proper use of the object-oriented paradigm guarantees localized maintenance. In C++, the sharp separation that can be created between the interface to the public members of a class (the class methods) and the implementation of these methods is responsible for ensuring localized maintenance. This aspect of the object-oriented paradigm represents a most significant contribution to modern software technology.

For our revised customer_queue, we derive a class queue from the generic class slist. We reproduce the interface and implementation of this class in Listing 7.22.

Listing 7.22
Generic Class Slist

```
// This code defines a generic class for a singly linked list.
// Both the interface and implementation are contained
// in this file.
// File list.h.

#include <stdio.h>

class node
{
  friend class slist;

  private:
    node* next;
    char* contents; // Space dynamically allocated.
};
```

Listing 7.22
(continued)

```cpp
class slist
{
  private:
    node* head;  // Head of list
    int size;    // Number of bytes for contents

  // Public data
  public:
    void insert( char* a );  // Add to the head of the list.
    slist( int s ) { head = 0; size = s; }
    void append( char* a );  // Add to the tail of the list.
    char* get();             // Remove the head of the list.
    void clear();            // Remove all the nodes in the list.
    ~slist() { clear(); }
};

void slist::insert( char* a )
{
  node* temp;
  temp = new node;
  temp -> contents = new char[ size ];
  for ( int i = 0; i < size; i++ )
    temp -> contents[ i ] = a[ i ];
  if ( head )
  {
    temp -> next = head;
    head = temp;
  }
  else
  {
    temp -> next = 0;
    head = temp;
  }
}

void slist::append( char* a )
{
node *previous, *current, *newnode;

if ( head )
{
  previous = head;
  current = head -> next;
  while ( current != 0 )
  {
    previous = current;
    current = current -> next;
  }
  newnode = new node;
  newnode -> contents = new char[ size ];
  newnode -> next = 0;
  for ( int i = 0; i < size; i++ )
    newnode -> contents[ i ] = a[ i ];
  previous -> next = newnode;
}
else
{
  head = new node;
  head -> contents = new char[ size ];
  head -> next = 0;
```

```
        for ( int i = 0; i < size; i++ )
            head -> contents[ i ] = a[ i ];
    }
};
char* slist::get()
{
    if ( head == 0 )
        printf( "Error --> get() from empty slist" );
    else
    {
        char* r;
        r = new char[ size ];
        node* f = head;
        for ( int i = 0; i < size; i++ )
            r[ i ] = f -> contents[ i ];
        head = head -> next;
        delete f;
        return r;
    }
};
void slist::clear()
{
    node* l = head;
    if ( l == 0 ) return;
    do {
        node* ll = l;
        l = l -> next;
        delete ll;
    } while ( l != 0 );
};
```

The file containing the new customer queue interface is given in Listing 7.23.

The derived class queue does not use the designator public in its declaration and therefore passes only the methods redefined in its own public section to objects declared to be of class queue. This is reasonable because a queue is a specialization, not generalization, of a generic linked list.

The public section of the revised customer_queue class is unchanged. This is essential in order to localize changes to just the file queue.cpp. The private section of the revised file queue.h contains an object of derived class queue. The remaining private members are the same as before. The only significant change is the conversion from a static implementation of a queue of customers to a dynamic implementation.

Listing 7.23
Class
Customer_Queue
Derived from a
Generic List

```
// Interface to dynamic queue class
// This queue is derived from a generic list class
// There is no limitation on the queue size except the size
// of the heap.
// File queue.h

#include "list.h"
#include "time.h"
#include "cust.h"
```

Listing 7.23
(continued)

```
class queue : slist
// A private derived class to serve only class customer_queue
{
    friend class customer_queue;
    // The operations of put and get are accessible only
    // by the friend class customer_queue.

    private:
        void put( customer *c ) { slist::append( ( char * ) c ); }

        customer* get() { return ( customer* ) slist::get(); }

    public:
        queue() : ( sizeof( customer ) ) {}
};
class customer_queue
{
    private:
        queue q; // A private queue derived from a generic list
        float last_event_time; // Time of last customer
                                //   arrival or departure
        int cum_customers;         // Cumulative number of customers
        int current_queue_size;
        int peak_queue;
        float cum_queue_size_time; // Cumulative sum of products
                                   //   of size of queue x time
        float cum_wait_time;       // Cumulative wait time for
                                   //   all patrons

    public:
        void insert( time t );

        void remove( time t );

        customer_queue();

        int total_customers() { return cum_customers; }

        float average_queue_size( time t )
        {
            return ( cum_queue_size_time / t.get_time() );
        }

        int size() { return current_queue_size; }

        int maximum_queue_size() { return peak_queue; }

        float average_queue_wait_time()
        {
            return ( cum_wait_time / cum_customers );
        }

        float total_wait_time() { return cum_wait_time; }
};
```

The implementation of the revised queue is given in Listing 7.24.

The reader should note the invocation of the constructor q() in the constructor for the customer_queue. By specifying : q() after the usual constructor interface, the constructor for the private member class queue is invoked. The code contained between the braces represents the main body of initialization code for the customer_queue class.

The method put, from the derived class queue, is used in implementing method insert. The method get, from the derived class queue, is used in implementing method remove. Most of the implementation of methods insert and remove is as before. (See Listing 7.13.)

Listing 7.24
Revised
Implementation
of Class
Customer_Queue

```
// Implementation of class customer_queue
#include "queue.h"
customer_queue::customer_queue( ) : q()
{
    last_event_time = 0.0;
    cum_customers = 0;
    current_queue_size = 0;
    peak_queue = 0;
    cum_queue_size_time = 0.0;
    cum_wait_time = 0.0;
}

void customer_queue::insert( time t )
{
    float current_time = t.get_time();
    customer temp;

    temp.arrival_time = current_time;
    q.put( &temp );
    cum_customers++;
    cum_queue_size_time += current_queue_size *
        ( current_time - last_event_time );
    current_queue_size++;
    if ( current_queue_size > peak_queue )
        peak_queue = current_queue_size;
    last_event_time = current_time;
}

void customer_queue::remove( time t )
{
    float current_time = t.get_time();
    customer* temp;
    temp = q.get();
    float wait = current_time - temp -> arrival_time;

    cum_wait_time += wait;
    cum_queue_size_time += current_queue_size *
        ( current_time - last_event_time );
    current_queue_size--;
    last_event_time = current_time;
}
```

7.3 Interactive Function Evaluator

If the cliche "saving the best for last" is applicable to this book, our last case study, creating an interactive function evaluator, is best because it shows all the pillars of object-oriented programming and the advanced features of C++ in action. Data hiding, encapsulation, inheritance, and polymorphism are central to the design of the system we are to describe.

The problem we confront here is a little more technical than the previous case studies and requires that we take a brief excursion into the world of data structures and algorithms related to expression trees. As with the first two case studies, the means are as important as the end. That is, the object-oriented methodology used in the design and implementation of the end product is as important as the end product. For this last case study, the end product is quite useful in its own right.

Few programming languages allow a user to input a mathematical expression "on the fly" (while a program is running). Normally a programmer must "hard wire" or embed a function definition into the body of the program. This is most inconvenient when, for example, the program is to perform numerical integration or plot a graph of the user's function. For such applications it would be much more useful if the user could enter his or her mathematical function as a character string while the program is running or have the program read the character string from a file, and interpret it as a function, and perform function evaluation on the fly. We call such a system an interactive function evaluator.

7.3.1 Specifications for function evaluator

We wish to design and implement a multivariable interactive algebraic expression evaluator as a class called function. The constructor for this class must allow an algebraic function of up to six independent variables to be specified as a character string using a prescribed syntax. A destructor for this class must also be provided. This ensures that when the block in which a function object is declared is exited, the memory associated with the object is automatically deallocated.

The algebraic expressions can include the binary operators $+$, $-$, $*$, and $/$. No unary operators are allowed. Thus the unary negation operator would be disallowed in this implementation. We restrict variable names to single lowercase letters from a to z.

The syntax of the character string that describes an algebraic expression of up to six variables is illustrated by the following examples:

```
function f1( ''x : 2 * x - 7'' );
function f2( ''x : 2.4 * x * x / ( 2 + 4.6 * x )'' );
function f3( ''a, b : 2 * a / ( 3 * a * b ) * 1.6'' );
function f4( ''x, y, z : 2 * x + 4 * z - 7.1 * y'' );
function f5( ''u,v,w,x,y,z:100*u/(v+w)-x*y*x'' );
function f6( ''x : 17'' );
```

Each algebraic expression string begins with a list of independent variables given in the order in which the parameters are to be specified when the function is invoked. Each string must include at least one independent variable, and each independent variable is separated by a comma from the next variable on the list. White space is ignored. A colon is used as a delimiter for the list. Following the colon, the algebraic expression is written exactly as it would be if it were embedded in the program as a function definition. In the case where the function contains only constants (function f6 above), one variable must be indicated as an independent variable.

The class function is to overload the operator ( ) so that the user can invoke functions—send the message ( ) to objects of class function—in a natural way. We illustrate this with the following function calls using the six function definitions given previously.

```
float r = f1( 29.8 );
r = f1( 32 * y * z );    // y and z have been assigned values
r = f3( u, v );          // u and v have been assigned values
r = f3( 2.1 * x, y );    // x and y have been assigned values
r = f4( a, 2 * b, c );   // a, b, c have been assigned values
r = f4( 4, 3, 2.7 );
r = f5( 1.6, 2.7, 7.1, 2.4, 6.8, 7.9 );
r = f5( a, b, c, d, e, f ); // a..f have meaningful values
```

In the case of r = f3(2.1 * x, y), the first value 2.1 * x goes to the variable a and the value y goes to the variable b in the expression

```
2 * a / ( 3 * a * b ) * 1.6
```

In the case of r = f5(1.6, 2.7, 7.1, 2.4, 6.8, 7.9), the value 1.6 goes to variable u, the value 2.7 goes to the variable v, the value 7.1 goes to the variable w, the value 2.4 goes to the variable x, the value 6.8 goes to the variable y, and the value 7.9 goes to the variable z, in the expression

```
100 * u / ( v + w ) - x * y * x
```

In a typical application that requires class function, the user inputs one or more algebraic expressions while the program is running. This is illustrated with the following code segment:

```
char expression[ 200 ];
printf( ''\nEnter the first algebraic expression: '' );
scanf( ''%s'', expression );
function f1( expression );

printf( ''\nEnter the second algebraic expression: '' );
scanf( ''%s'', expression );
```

```
function f2( expression );
. . .
```

The class function must be able to test the portion of the string representing the algebraic expression for syntactic validity. Thus it must include a method,

```
int valid( char *expr )
```

that returns a 1 if the string expr represents a bonafide algebraic expression, and 0 otherwise.

The class function must, in fact, include the following public methods:

```
function( char* s );
-function();
int valid( char *expr );
void delete_function();
float operator ()( float u = 0, float v = 0,
                   float w = 0, float x = 0,
                   float y = 0, float z = 0 );
```

The first method, the constructor, allows the user to specify the names and order of the independent variables and the algebraic expression to be evaluated. The second method, the destructor, automatically deallocates storage for a function object when the block containing the function object is exited. The third method, valid, as described earlier, allows the user to determine whether the expression defined in the constructor is properly constructed. The fourth method, operator ( ), allows up to six arguments, depending on the number of independent variables defined in the constructor. The use of default values allows the user the option of sending in only the required number of parameters when the method ( ) is sent to a function object.

Class function presents a simple interface to the programmer, which is as it should be. The complexity of class function is in the implementation, happily hidden from the programmer. A software engineer who is not an expression tree or data structures specialist and who does not wish to divert his or her attention from the problem being solved is delighted to use the extension to the C++ language that class function provides. Once the relatively simple syntax of algebraic expression strings is learned, such a software engineer can go about his or her business in a normal way. Objects of class function, such as f1 through f6 above, can be manipulated in a totally natural way. Such a programmer might quickly forget that class function and algebraic expression strings are not part of the C++ language.

Before we plunge into the theory, design, and implementation of class function, let us consider the overhead associated with interactive function evaluation. How much longer does it take to perform function evaluation on objects of class function than on "hard-wired" functions embedded in our program?

The following test program, Listing 7.25, provides us with such an estimate. It also further demonstrates the simplicity of using class function.

Listing 7.25
Comparison of
Hard-Wired and
Interactive
Function
Evaluation

```
#include ''function.h''
#include <util.h>

main()
{
   extern float f2( float x, float y, float z );

   function f1( ''x, y, z : 2 / ( 2.6 - x - y - z )'' );
   float r;

   rpttiming( begin );
   for ( int i = 0; i < 10000; i++ )
     r = f1( 3.7, 2.8, 9.123 );
   rpttiming( end );
   rpttiming( begin ); // From util
   for ( i = 0; i < 10000; i++ )
     r = f2( 3.7, 2.8, 9.123);
   rpttiming( end ); // From util
   printf( ''\n\nThe value of f1 = %f'', r );
   printf( ''\n\nThe value of f2 = %f'', r );
}
float f2( float x, float y, float z )
{
   return 2 / ( 2.6 - x - y - z );
}
```

The program in Listing 7.25, run on a COMPAQ 386 computer using the Guidelines C++ system, shows approximately a 4-to-1 run-time penalty for using class function. This penalty will vary with the specific function that is defined. Since a penalty of over 10-to-1 had been expected based on previous implementations in other languages, the authors were pleasantly surprised and encouraged by the results. In some applications, a run-time penalty of 4-to-1 would be intolerable, while in other applications it would be more than compensated for by the advantage of interactive function evaluation.

7.3.2   Review of expression trees

We digress, briefly, from the object-oriented development of class function in order to review the data structure and algorithms associated with expression trees. The reader already familiar with this subject may wish to skim this section quickly. The reader desiring additional background may wish to consult *Data Structures Using Modula-2,* by Sincovec and Wiener (Wiley, 1986) or any other data structures book that discusses algebraic expression trees.

An *expression tree* is a complete binary (in which each nonleaf node has two children) tree consisting of nodes that represent operands (numeric constants or variables) or operators ($+$, $-$, $*$, or $/$). Parentheses are notably absent from an expression tree.

Figure 7.2
Tree representing
an algebraic
expression.

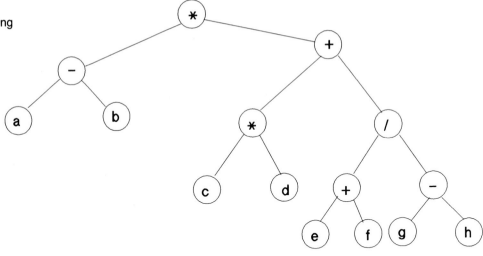

Consider the expression tree shown in Figure 7.2. From this expression tree we can immediately write down the algebraic expression that the tree represents, namely,

$$(a - b) * ((c * d) + ((e + f) / (g - h)))$$

The reader should note that the leaf nodes of the expression tree are operand nodes, whereas the interior nodes are operator nodes. The challenging question is, how can we obtain the expression tree shown in Figure 7.2 if we are given the expression shown above? In particular, how can we produce a tree that contains no parentheses when the expression contains parentheses? We present an algorithm in pseudocode in Listing 7.26.

Listing 7.26
Pseudocode
Algorithm for
Building an
Algebraic
Expression
Tree

```
We assume that each node of our expression tree
contains the fields:

info -> character // The type of operator if the
                  // node is an operator node.
paren -> integer  // Value of totalparen when node is formed
value -> real     // The value of the operand if the node
                  // is an operand node.
left -> pointer to another tree node
right -> pointer to another tree node

Algorithm parenthesis( ch : char ) returns an integer
// This algorithm modifies the global variable total_paren,
// which represents the current value of the total number of
// left parentheses minus the total number of right
// parentheses. The function returns the value 1 if ch is
// either a left or right parenthesis.
```

```
    if ( ch = '(' )
    then
      increment total_paren;
      return 1;
    else if ( ch = ')'
    then
      decrement total_paren;
      return 1;
    else
      return 0;
end algorithm.
```

Algorithm precedence(op1 : pointer to tree node,
                      op2 : character) returns an integer
// Computes the algebraic precedence of the operators
// op1 -> info and op2. The function returns the value 1 if
// op1 -> info has a higher precedence than ch.

```
    if ( op1 -> paren < totalparen )
    then
      return 1;
    else if ( op1 -> paren > totalparen )
    then
      decrement op1 -> paren;
      return 1;
    else
      flag := 1;
      if ( ( op1 -> info = '+' ) or ( op1 -> info = '-' ) )
          and ( ( op2 = '*' ) or ( op2 = '/' ) )
      then
        flag := 0;
    return flag;
end algorithm.
```

Algorithm addoperator(p, n : pointer to tree nodes,
                       ch : character) returns void
// This algorithm adds the operator node ch to the
// expression tree.

```
    if ( n = 0 )
    then
      root := makenode( ch ); // Make a root node
    else
      if ( precedence( n, ch ) = 0 )
      then
      if ( n -> right = 0 )
      then
        setright( n, ch ); // Make a node as the right child
                           // of node n with operator ch.
      else
        p := n;
        addoperator( p, n -> right, ch );
      end(* if then *);
    else
      if ( p = 0 )
      then
        dynamically allocate space for node r
        r -> info := ch;
        r -> left := n;
        r -> right := 0;
        r -> paren := totalparen;
        root := r;
```

Listing 7.26
(continued)

```
        else
          dynamically allocate space for node r
          r -> info := ch;
          r -> left := n;
          r -> right := 0;
          r -> paren := totalparen;
          p -> right := r;
        end(* if then *);
      end(* if then *);
    end(* if then *);
  end algorithm.

Algorithm build_tree( expr : a string ) returns void
// This algorithm constructs an expression tree from the
// string expr.

    root := 0;
    totalparen := 0;
    index := 0;
    ch := expr[ index ];
    while ( ch # terminating character of expr )
      if ( ch = ' ' )
      then
        increment index;
        ch := expr[ index ];
      else if ( ch is a numeric literal or variable )
      // ch is an operand
      then
        insert the value of the operand into operand queue.
        // If the operand is a variable, insert either 100000,
        // 100001, 100002, 100003, 100004, or 100005 based on
        // whether the variable is the first, second, third,
        // fourth, fifth, or sixth variable.
        increment index;
        ch := expr[ index ];
      else if ( parenthesis( ch ) = 1 )
      then
        increment index;
        ch := expr[ index ];
      else if ( ch is an operator )
      then
        addoperator( 0, root, ch );
        increment index;
        ch := expr[ index ];
      end(* if then *);
    end(* while loop *);
    addoperands( root ); // Removes the operand values
    // from the queue and forms leaf nodes from left to right
    // in the expression tree.
  end algorithm.

Algorithm eval( tree : pointer to node ) returns real
// Returns the value of an expression tree. Before
// evaluating the expression tree, the values of any operand
// nodes that represent variables are computed from the
// values of the parameters that are sent in.
```

```
     if ( tree -> info is an operator )
     then
       case tree -> info
         '+' : return eval( tree -> left ) +
                     eval( tree -> right );
         '-' : return eval( tree -> left ) -
                     eval( tree -> right );
         '*' : return eval( tree -> left ) *
                     eval( tree -> right );
         '/' : return eval( tree -> .left ) /
                     eval( tree -> right );
       end(* case *);
     else
       return value( tree -> info );
     end(* if then *);
end algorithm.
```

To understand better the algorithm in Listing 7.26, let us walk through the construction of an expression tree.

Suppose we are given the expression string

```
''x, y : ( x + 12.6 ) * y''
```

The portion of the string that is used in algorithm build_tree is "(x + 12.6) * y".

The first character, ch, is a left parenthesis, '('. The value of totalparen is incremented from 0 to 1. Algorithm build_tree skips over white space.

The second nonblank character is x. Because x is the first variable, the value 100000 is inserted into the operand queue.

The next nonblank value of ch is '+'. The algorithm addoperator is called. Because the parameter n is 0, the root node of the expression tree is formed as an operator node containing the '+' operator, as shown in Figure 7.3(a). The value 1 is assigned to the paren field of the '+' node since the current value of totalparen is 1.

The next nonblank value of ch is 1. This represents the beginning of a numeric literal. After scanning forward until the first nonnumeric character is encountered, the value of the numeric literal, 12.6, is obtained. This value is inserted in the operand queue.

The next nonblank value of ch is ')'. This causes the value of totalparen to be decremented from 1 back to 0.

The next nonblank value of ch is '*'. The algorithm addoperator is called. The parameter n is a pointer to the root node of the tree. The algorithm for precedence compares the precedence of the operator in the root node, '+', with the operator '*'. Normally, the '+' operator has a lower precedence than the '*' operator. But because of the parentheses around the '+' operator, the precedence function returns the value 1, indicating that the addition operation is to take precedence over the multiplication operation.

Control, in algorithm addoperator, shifts to the else clause directly above the line if (p = 0). A new node is allocated. Its info field is set to ch. Its left child

Figure 7.3
Expression tree
analysis 1.

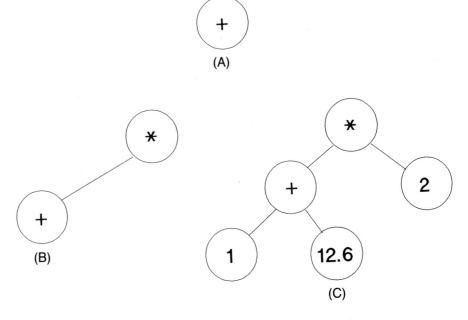

(A)

(B)

(C)

pointer is set to the old root node, and its right child is set to 0. The value of the root pointer is set to this new node containing the '*'operator. This leads to the expression tree shown in Figure 7.3(b).

Finally, the last nonblank value of ch is y, a variable. Because y is the second variable, the value 100001 is inserted into the operand queue.

The function addoperands is called. The three values stored in the operand queue, 100000, 12.6, and 100001, are removed in order from the operand queue and put into leaf nodes from left to right in the expression tree. Upon encountering the preset values 100000 and 100001, the actual values of the variables x and y, say 1 and 2, are substituted. This results in the completed expression tree shown in Figure 7.3(c).

We leave it to the reader to verify that the short recursive algorithm eval, given in Listing 7.26, computes the value 27.2 for the expression tree.

Let us make one final walk through of the algorithms of Listing 7.26. Suppose that we are given the expression string

```
''x, y : x + 12.6 * y''
```

This expression string is almost the same as the previous one except for the omission of the parentheses. Let us see what change occurs in the resulting expression tree because of the absence of these parentheses.

The first nonblank character, ch, is x in the portion of the expression string of relevance to algorithm build_tree, "x + 12.6 * y". Because the variable x is the first variable, the value 100000 is inserted into the operand queue.

Figure 7.4
Expression tree
analysis 2.

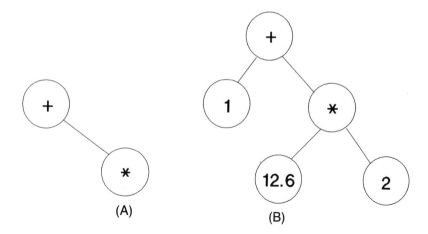

(A)

(B)

The next nonblank character is '+'. The algorithm addoperator creates a root node with the '+' operator. The next nonblank value of ch is 1. As before, the value of the numeric literal, 12.6, is inserted into the operand queue.

The next nonblank character is '*'. The algorithm precedence determines that the root node operator '+' has lower precedence than the ch operator '*'. Thus the new operator node containing '*' is set to the right of the existing root node operator '+'. The expression tree is shown in Figure 7.4(a).

The final nonblank value of ch is y. Because the variable y is the second variable, the value 100001 is inserted into the operand queue.

Function addoperands removes the operand values, in order, from the operand queue and creates leaf nodes from left to right with these values (except for the variable nodes, which take the values of the variables that are sent in, say 1 and 2). The completed expression tree is as shown in Figure 7.4(b).

Clearly, the use of the paren field in the expression tree nodes and of the global variable totalparen, enables the addoperator algorithm to respond appropriately to parentheses in the original expression.

The reader may wish to walk through the construction of a more complex tree in order to explore the branch paths of the addoperator algorithm not yet exercised.

7.3.3 High-level design of function evaluator

We begin our high-level design of the interactive function evaluator with a main driver program that uses the class function. This program allows a user to input an expression string representing an algebraic function of up to six variables. An inner loop allows the user to evaluate the expression any number of times before possibly entering a new expression.

The main driver program sets the stage for the design of the system. It represents the tip of the iceberg that is visible to the user. This program, presented in Listing 7.27, illustrates the importance of destructors. Each time around the main while loop, memory for an object f is allocated in the last statement in the segment,

```
printf( "\n\nEnter the algebraic expression: " );
readstring( str );
function f( str ); // Allocate object of class function
```

Because this declaration is inside the block that defines the while loop, the destructor is automatically activated each time one iteration of the loop is completed. Were it not for this fact, multiple iterations of the outside while loop might cause a stack overflow error.

Notice again the simplicity of using class function and the naturalness with which the user can evaluate functions (objects of class function).

Listing 7.27
Main Driver
Program That
Uses Class
Function

```
// Algebraic function evaluation driver program
// File exprtst.cpp

#include "function.h"
#include <util.h>

main()
{
   char str[ 200 ];

   float v[ 6 ]; // Values of independent variables
   int num_var; // Number of possible independent variables

   clrscreen();
   printf( "\n\nDo you wish to enter an expression (y/n)? " );
   while ( yes() )
   {
      printf( "\n\nEnter the algebraic expression: " );
      readstring( str );
      function f( str ); // Allocate object of class function
      printf( "\nNumber of independent variables: " );
      scanf( "%d", &num_var );
      if ( f.valid( str ) )
      {
         printf( "\n\nEvaluate %s (y/n)? ", str );
         while ( yes() )
         {
            for ( int i = 0; i < num_var; i++ )
            {
               printf( "\nEnter value of independent variable %d: "
                     i + 1 );
               scanf( "%f", &v[ i ] );
            }
            switch ( num_var )
            {
               case 1:
                  printf( "\n\nThe function evaluates to %f",
                        f( v[ 0 ] ) );
                  break;
```

```
            case 2:
              printf( ''\n\nThe function evaluates to %f'',
                      f( v[ 0 ], v[ 1 ] ) );
              break;
            case 3:
              printf( ''\n\nThe function evaluates to %f'',
                      f( v[ 0 ], v[ 1 ], v[ 2 ] ) );
              break;
            case 4:
              printf( ''\n\nThe function evaluates to %f'',
                      f( v[ 0 ], v[ 1 ], v[ 2 ], v[ 3 ] ) );
              break;
            case 5:
              printf( ''\n\nThe function evaluates to %f'',
                      f( v[ 0 ], v[ 1 ], v[ 2 ], v[ 3 ],
                         v[ 4 ] ) );
              break;
            case 6:
              printf( ''\n\nThe function evaluates to %f'',
                      f( v[ 0 ], v[ 1 ], v[ 2 ], v[ 3 ],
                         v[ 4 ], v[ 5 ] ) );
              break;
          }
          printf( ''\n\nEvaluate %s again (y/n)? '', str );
        }
        printf( ''\n\n'' );
      }
      else
        printf( ''\n%c             Invalid expression'', '\07' );
        printf( ''\n\nEnter a new expression (y/n)? '' );
        // Destructor deallocates object
    }
}
```

Now we are ready to plunge into the depths of the system. We expect that in order to achieve the simplicity of the function interface that is evident in the main driver program in Listing 7.27, there will be complexity at the lower levels. Our expectation is correct!

The classes that define the problem space are function and symbol_table. The latter is used by class function to store the symbols and values associated with variables. In addition, we will need another class, to be introduced later, that is used in implementing method valid in class function.

Based on the algorithms shown earlier, we define class function as shown in Listing 7.28.

The private section of this class contains a statically implemented operand queue (an array of 100 real numbers). It contains a datum root of class node (described below) that points to the root node of an expression tree, and also a datum sym_tab of class symbol_table that contains the symbols and values for each variable in the tree. It contains integer index values first and last for controlling the operand_queue. It comprises the datum total_paren, required in the expression tree algorithms. In addition, the private section of class function includes the following member functions, some of which implement algorithms given in Listing 7.26:

1. `int parenthesis( char ch );`—This function implements algorithm parenthesis.

2. `void add_operator( node *p, node *n, char ch );`—This function implements algorithm addoperator.

3. `void checkandadd( node *n );`—This function is used by add_operands.

4. `int precedence( node *op1, char op2 );`—This function implements algorithm precedence.

5. `void add_operands( node *n );`—This function removes values, in order, from the operand_queue and creates leaf nodes from left to right in the expression tree.

6. `void build_tree( char* s );`—This function implements algorithm build_tree.

The public section of class function was described in Section 7.3.2. We comment only on the overloaded operator, ( ). This operator is declared with six parameters, u, v, w, x, y, and z, each given a default value of 0.0.

We could just as well declare this operator with an unspecified number of parameters, as follows:

```
float operator ( ) ( int n . . . );
```

This specification introduces some problems that are not present when default parameters are used. We discuss the nature of these problems in Section 7.3.4, when we consider a possible implementation of this operator with an unspecified number of parameters. We believe that functions with an unspecified number of parameters should be used only when both the number and the type of the parameters are not known in advance. Here the number of parameters is not known, but the type of each parameter (float) is known. Using default values effectively allows the user to send in any number of parameters, from 1 to 6.

Listing 7.28
Interface to Class Function

```
// Interface of class function
class function
{
  private:
    float operand_queue[ 100 ];
    // Stores operand constants. The values 100,000 . .
    // 100,005 are reserved to indicate a variable.

    node* root;

    symbol_table sym_tab;

    int first, last;
```

```
       int total_paren;

       int parenthesis( char ch );

       void add_operator( node *p, node *n, char ch );

       void checkandadd( node *n );

       int precedence( node *op1, char op2 );

       void add_operands( node *n );

       void build_tree( char* s );
       // Constructs an algebraic expression tree from a valid
       // expression. If the expression is invalid, no tree
       // is built.
   public:
       function( char* s ); // Constructor

       ~function(); // Destructor

       int valid( char *expr );
       // Returns 1 if expr is a valid algebraic expression
       // Otherwise returns 0

       void delete_function( node *n = 0, int start = 1 );
       // Call this method with no parameters
       // Deallocates an algebraic expression tree

       float operator ()( float u = 0, float v = 0,
                          float w = 0, float x = 0,
                          float y = 0, float z = 0 );
       // Used to evaluate an object of class function
};
```

The data structure for the expression tree, given in Listing 7.26, reflects a non–object-oriented design of the system. In this design, all nodes are outwardly the same with the different types of nodes perhaps being differentiated by a discriminant field (a variant record in Pascal, a union in C). Operand nodes use the value field, whereas operator nodes use an info field. The recursive algorithm eval uses a case statement to determine the particular type of node (either operator or operand). The problem with this older style of design is that as new classes of nodes are added to the tree during maintenance, the case statement(s) discriminating the type of node in question must be modified. At best, this type of maintenance is awkward, and at worst it is prone to error.

Polymorphism can be employed to great advantage here by creating a parent class node that contains the information set needed by all types of nodes. This parent class declares a virtual function eval that returns a real number. In addition to the parent class node, we define a group of derived classes of specialized nodes, each with its own method eval. Thus instead of an expression tree with homogeneous nodes, we create an expression tree with many different classes of nodes. During the recursive traversal of the heterogeneous expression tree, each node responds in a manner appropriate to the method eval sent to the object of class node. In a sense, each node has its own eval "engine" rather than the system having one large centralized eval engine.

What types of specialized nodes do we need? We must look at the problem space—algebraic expressions. Such expressions contain the following entities: constants, variables, and plus, minus, multiply, and divide operators. Therefore we need operand nodes of class constant that contain the values of the numeric literals contained in the original expression string. We also need operand nodes of class variable that contain the indices in the symbol table where their numeric values are stored. And we need operator nodes of class plus for addition, class minus for subtraction, class multiply for multiplication, and class divide for division.

In Listing 7.29, we show the code for the entire file function.h, which includes the interface to class function and the interface and implementation of class node, and the derived classes constant, variable, plus, minus, multiply, and divide.

Parent class node has a protected section that contains all the data required of each of the more specialized derived classes. This data includes info, paren, operand, and two pointers to other derived class nodes. Such data is strictly private for all outside classes except derived classes, for which the protected data is public. Some of the derived classes declare class function as a friend because the implementation of some of class function's methods require access to the private section of these derived classes.

Listing 7.29
File Function.h

```
// Interface of class function, class node, and derived
// classes constant, variable, plus, minus, multiply, and
// divide.
// File function.h

#include ''symbol.h''

class node
{
    friend class function;
    protected:
        node *right, *left;
        char info;
        int paren;
        int operand; // 1 if true, 0 if not true

    public:
        virtual float eval() { return 0.0; }
};

class function
{
    friend class variable;

    private:
        float operand_queue[ 100 ];
        // Stores operand constants. The values 100,000 . .
        // 100,005 are reserved to indicate a variable.

    node* root;

    symbol_table sym_tab;
```

```
        int first, last;

        int total_paren;

        int parenthesis( char ch );

        void add_operator( node *p, node *n, char ch );

        void checkandadd( node *n );

        int precedence( node *op1, char op2 );

        void add_operands( node *n );

        void build_tree( char* s );
        // Constructs an algebraic expression tree from a valid
        // expression. If the expression is invalid, no tree
        // is built.
    public:
        function( char* s ); // Constructor

        ~function(); // Destructor

        int valid( char *expr );
        // Returns 1 if expr is a valid algebraic expression
        // Otherwise returns 0

        void delete_function( node *n = 0, int start = 1 );
        // Call this method with no parameters
        // Deallocates an algebraic expression tree

        float operator ()( float u = 0, float v = 0,
                           float w = 0, float x = 0,
                           float y = 0, float z = 0 );
        // Used to evaluate an object of class function
};
class variable : public node
{
    friend class function;

    private:
        int index; // Index in symbol table
        function* f; //

    public:
        float eval() { return f -> sym_tab.get_value( index ); }
};
class constant : public node
{
    friend class function;

    private:
        float value;

    public:
        float eval() { return value; }
};
class plus : public node
{
    public:
        float eval() { return left -> eval() + right -> eval(); }
};
```

Listing 7.29
(continued)

```
class minus : public node
{
  public:
    float eval(){ return left -> eval() - right -> eval(); }
};

class multiply : public node
{
  public:
    float eval(){ return left -> eval() * right -> eval(); }
};

class divide : public node
{
  public:
    float eval(){ return left -> eval() / right -> eval(); }
};
```

7.3.4 Low-level design of function evaluator

In looking at the low-level design of the interactive function evaluator, we first consider the implementation of the overloaded operator method, ( ). This implementation is given in Listing 7.30. Here we can see the magic of polymorphism! After depositing the values of the parameters sent into method ( ) into the symbol table, the method eval( ) is invoked from the pointer to the root node, using root $->$ eval( ). The root node might be a constant node, it might be a variable node, or it might be one of the four types of operator nodes. The system will invoke the appropriate method eval based on the pointer that is stored in the private datum root.

Listing 7.30
Implementation of
Operator ()

```
float function::operator ()( float u = 0, float v = 0,
                             float w = 0, float x = 0,
                             float y = 0, float z = 0 )
{
  sym_tab.add_value( 0, u );
  sym_tab.add_value( 1, v );
  sym_tab.add_value( 2, w );
  sym_tab.add_value( 3, x );
  sym_tab.add_value( 4, y );
  sym_tab.add_value( 5, z );
  return root -> eval();
}
```

If we were to use an unspecified number of parameters in the operator declaration, the implementation might be as given in Listing 7.31. This implementation suffers from several serious problems. The user must send the address of a floating point parameter rather than the value of the parameter into ( ). Thus it would no longer be legal to make a call such as

```
f( 2.34, -5.67 )
```

to an object of class function defined with two independent variables. Instead, one would have to make a call such as

```
f( &x, &y )
```

if x and y were the independent variables.

Another serious problem with this implementation is that if the value of any of the parameters equals 0.0, the system assumes that there are no additional parameters to be input. This problem could be overcome by requiring the user to send in a special sentinel value to terminate the parameter list. Such a requirement is clumsy. Therefore, we prefer the implementation of operator ( ) given in Listing 7.30 that uses default values to achieve variability in the number of parameters.

Listing 7.31
Implementation of
Operator () with
an Unspecified
Number of
Parameters

```
Replace previous code with float function::operator ()( int
u . . . )
{
  va_list arg_lst;
  va_start( arg_lst, u );
  for ( int i = 0; ; i++ )
  {
    float *arg = va_arg( arg_lst, float* );
    if ( *arg == 0 ) break;
    sym_tab.add_value( i, *arg );
  }
  va_end( arg_lst );
  return root -> eval();
}
```

Listing 7.32 contains the code for implementing method add_operands, from class function. This method is invoked by method build_tree after all the interior operator nodes have been inserted into the expression tree. Method add_operands removes operand values from the operand_queue and creates leaf nodes from left to right with these values. In the case of the variable values 100000 to 100005, the index location (v − 100000) is stored in the private datum index and is the index location in the symbol table where the variable's value is stored. Only if the pointer to a node is not 0 and the node is an operator node (operand = 0) does the recursion continue.

Listing 7.32
Implementation
of Method
Add_Operands

```
void function::add_operands( node *n )
{
  if ( root == 0 )
  {
    float v = queue[ first++ ];
    if ( v < 100000 || v > 100005 )
    {
```

Listing 7.32
(continued)

```
            constant *newnode = new constant;
            newnode -> value = v;
            newnode -> left = newnode -> right = 0;
            newnode -> paren = total_paren;
            newnode -> operand = 1;
            root = newnode;
        }
        else
        {
            variable *newnode = new variable;
            newnode -> index = ( int ) ( v - 100000 );
            newnode -> f = this;
            newnode -> left = newnode -> right = 0;
            newnode -> paren = total_paren;
            newnode -> operand = 1;
            root = newnode;
        }
    }
    else
    {
        if ( n != 0 && n -> operand == 0 )
        {
            node *temp = n;

            add_operands( temp -> left );
            checkandadd( temp );
            add_operands( temp -> right );
        }
    }
}
```

Method checkandadd, given in Listing 7.33, is invoked from method add_operands. This method first checks to see whether the left child of the operator node n is 0. If it is, it builds either a constant leaf node or a variable leaf node, depending on the value removed from the operand queue. The method next checks to see whether the right child of the operator node n is 0. If it is, it builds either a constant node or a variable node, depending on the value removed from the operand queue.

Listing 7.33
Implementation
of Method
Checkandadd

```
void function::checkandadd( node *n )
{
    if ( n -> left == 0 )
    {
        float v = queue[ first++ ];
        if ( v < 100000 || v > 100005 )
        {
            constant *newnode = new constant;
            newnode -> value = v;
            newnode -> left = newnode -> right = 0;
            newnode -> paren = total_paren;
            newnode -> operand = 1;
            n -> left = newnode;
        }
```

```
       else
       {
          variable *newnode = new variable;
          newnode -> index = ( int ) ( v - 100000 );
          newnode -> f = this;
          newnode -> left = newnode -> right = 0;
          newnode -> paren = total_paren;
          newnode -> operand = 1;
          n -> left = newnode;
       }
    }
    if ( n -> right == 0 )
    {
       float v = queue[ first++ ];
       if ( v < 100000 || v > 100005 )
       {
          constant *newnode = new constant;
          newnode -> value = v;
          newnode -> left = newnode -> right = 0;
          newnode -> paren = total_paren;
          newnode -> operand = 1;
          n -> right = newnode;
       }
       else
       {
          variable *newnode = new variable;
          newnode -> index = ( int ) ( v - 100000 );
          newnode -> f = this;
          newnode -> left = newnode -> right = 0;
          newnode -> paren = total_paren;
          newnode -> operand = 1;
          n -> right = newnode;
       }
    }
}
```

We next examine the implementation of the method valid(char* expr), given in Listing 7.34.

In Figure 7.5, we present a finite-state machine model that depicts the syntax of an algebraic expression. Starting in state 0, transitions occur as nonblank symbols are encountered in the string expr. If state 8 is reached before state 10 (not shown in Figure 7.5), the expression is valid. State 10 is an error state. If state 10 is reached, the string expr is invalid.

The method valid declares 10 objects of class state0 and derived classes state1, state2, . . . , state9. Each of these derived classes has an overloaded method, transition, which returns an integer and has a character as its parameter. The transition method for each derived class is based on the finite-state machine model given in Figure 7.5.

The message get_char( ) is sent to object x0. Next a sequence of characters is input until the delimiting character ':' is found. Then one more character is input. The method transition(ch) is sent to object x0. A while loop is entered, testing to

Figure 7.5
Finite-state
machine model
depicting state
transitions in
algebraic
expression.

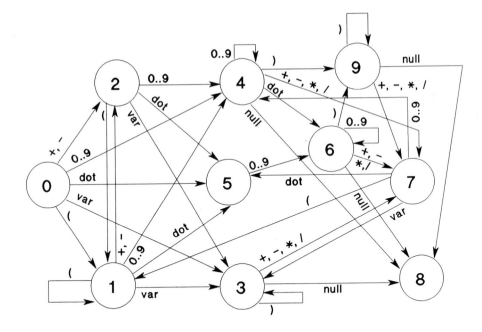

see whether the next state, s, is equal to 8 or equal to 10. As long as the terminating state and error state are not reached, the message transition(ch) is sent to the appropriate object.

Listing 7.34
Implementation
of Method Valid

```
int function::valid( char* expr )
{
    state0 x0;
    state1 x1;
    state2 x2;
    state3 x3;
    state4 x4;
    state5 x5;
    state6 x6;
    state7 x7;
    state9 x9;

    strcpy( expression, expr ); // expression in state.h
    // Scan past the ':' character
    char ch = x0.get_char();
    while ( ch != ':' )
      ch = x0.get_char();
    ch = x0.get_char();
    int s = x0.transition( ch );
    while ( s != 8 && s != 10 )
    {
      if ( s == 1 )
      {
```

```
      ch = x1.get_char();
      s = x1.transition( ch );
   }
   else if ( s == 2 )
   {
      ch = x2.get_char();
      s = x2.transition( ch );
   }
   else if ( s == 3 )
   {
      ch = x3.get_char();
      s = x3.transition( ch );
   }
   else if ( s == 4 )
   {
      ch = x4.get_char();
      s = x4.transition( ch );
   }
   else if ( s == 5 )
   {
      ch = x5.get_char();
      s = x5.transition( ch );
   }
   else if ( s == 6 )
   {
      ch = x6.get_char();
      s = x6.transition( ch );
   }
   else if ( s == 7 )
   {
      ch = x7.get_char();
      s = x7.transition( ch );
   }
   else if ( s == 9 )
   {
      ch = x9.get_char();
      s = x9.transition( ch );
   }
}
if ( s == 10 ) return 0;
else return 1;
}
```

In Listing 7.35, the interface and implementation of class state0 and the derived class state4 are given. The remaining derived classes are presented in Section 7.3.5 along with the full implementation.

The reader should note the static int index declaration in the parent class state0. The storage class static ensures that only one memory location stores a common value of index that is shared by all the subclasses of state0.

Since all the derived classes, state1, . . . , state9, are declared using the public designator, they can all use the parent method get_char( ). Only the method transition is overloaded.

Let us examine state4 in detail. Referring to Figure 7.5, it is evident that a numeral keeps the system in state 4, a left parenthesis brings the system to state

9, an operator symbol brings the system to state 7, a dot brings the system to state 6, and a null terminating character brings the system to state 8. Any other symbol brings the system to state 10.

Before allowing the system to go to state 8, method transition checks to ensure that the cumulative number of parentheses is 0. If not, state 10 is declared.

Listing 7.35
Interface and
Implementation of
Class State0 and
Derived Class4

```
// Finite-state machine class and derived classes
// File state.h

char expression[ 201 ];

const null = 0;

class state0
{  // The abstraction of a state in a finite-state machine
   private:
      static int index;
      // Index location in expression string.
      // This value is common to all state objects.

      static paren_count;
      // Cumulative number of left parentheses minus right parentheses
      // This value is common to all state objects.

   public:
      state0() { index = 0; }

      int get_paren() { return paren_count; }

      void inc_paren() { paren_count++; }
      void dec_paren() { paren_count--; }

      char get_char();

      int transition( unsigned char ch );
      // For a particular set of allowable characters,
      // returns the next state.
};

char state0::get_char()
{
   while ( expression[ index ] == ' ' )
      index++;
   return ( expression[ index++ ] );
}

int state0::transition( unsigned char ch )
{
   if ( ch >= '0' && ch <= '9' ) return 4;
   else if ( ch == '+' || ch == '-' ) return 2;
   else if ( ch == '.' ) return 5;
   else if ( ( ch >= 'A' && ch <= 'Z' ) ||
             ( ch >= 'a' && ch <= 'z' ) )
      return 3;
   else if ( ch == '(' )
   {
      inc_paren();
      return 1;
   }
   else return 10;
}
```

```
class state4 : public state0
{
  public:
    int transition( unsigned char ch )
    {
      if ( ch >= '0' && ch <= '9' ) return 4;
      else if ( ch == ')' && get_paren() > 0 )
      {
        dec_paren();
        return 9;
      }
      else if ( ch == '+' || ch == '-' || ch == '/' || ch == '*' )
        return 7;
      else if ( ch == '.' ) return 6;
      else if ( ch == null && get_paren() == 0 ) return 8;
      else return 10;
    }
};
```

The only class not yet discussed is class symbol_table. The interface and implementation of this class require no discussion because of their simplicity. It is presented in the next section.

7.3.5   Full implementation of function evaluator

Having presented the low-level design details for many of the important methods that implement the function evaluator, we present the complete system here as a convenience to the reader. This is done in Listing 7.36. The thin lines in this listing indicate file boundaries. The code within each dotted line boundary is a separate file.

The code of Listing 7.36 merits careful study. Many of the advanced C++ features introduced in earlier chapters are used in this implementation. The paradigm of object-oriented programming is most clearly demonstrated in the problem decomposition and implementation.

Listing 7.36
Complete
Implementation of
Function Evaluator

```
// Interface of class function
// File function.h

#include "symbol.h"

class node
{
  friend class function;

  protected:
    node *right, *left;
    char info;
    int paren;
    int operand; // 1 if true, 0 if not true
```

Listing 7.36
(continued)

```
        public:
            virtual float eval() { return 0.0; }
    };
    class function
    {
        friend class variable;

        private:
            float queue[ 100 ];
            // Stores operand constants. The values 100,000 ..
            // 100,005 are reserved to indicate a variable.

            node* root;

            symbol_table sym_tab;

            int first, last;

            int total_paren;

            int parenthesis( char ch );

            void add_operator( node *p, node *n, char ch );

            void checkandadd( node *n );

            int precedence( node *op1, char op2 );

            void add_operands( node *n );

            void build_tree( char* s );
            // Constructs an algebraic expression tree from a valid
            // expression. If the expression is invalid, no tree
            // is built.

        public:
            function( char* s ); // Constructor

            ~function(); // Destructor

            int valid( char *expr );
            // Returns 1 if expr is a valid algebraic expression
            // Otherwise returns 0

            void delete_function( node *n = 0, int start = 1 );
            // Call this method with no parameters
            // Deallocates an algebraic expression tree

            float operator ()( float u = 0, float v = 0,
                               float w = 0, float x = 0,
                               float y = 0, float z = 0 );
            // Used to evaluate an object of class function
    };
    class variable : public node
    {
        friend class function;

        private:
            int index; // Index in symbol table
            function* f; //

        public:
            float eval() { return f -> sym_tab.get_value( index ); }
    };
```

```cpp
class constant : public node
{
  friend class function;

  private:
    float value;

  public:
    float eval() { return value; }
};
class plus : public node
{
  public:
    float eval() { return left -> eval() + right -> eval(); }
};
class minus : public node
{
  public:
    float eval() { return left -> eval() - right -> eval(); }
};
class multiply : public node
{
  public:
    float eval() { return left -> eval() * right -> eval(); }
};
class divide : public node
{
  public:
    float eval() { return left -> eval() / right -> eval(); }
};
```

```cpp
// Implementation of class function
// File function.cpp

#include "function.h"
#include "state.h"
#include <stdlib.h>

function::function( char* s ) : sym_tab()
{
  root = 0;
  total_paren = 0;
  first = 0;
  last = 0;
  build_tree( s );
}

function::~function()
{
  delete_function();
}

void function::delete_function( node *n, int start )
{
  node *current;
```

Listing 7.36
(continued)

```
    if ( start )
    {
        current = root;
        start = 0;
        root = 0;
        sym_tab.clear( );
        first = last = 0;
    }
    else
        current = n;
    if ( current != 0 )
    {
        delete_function( current -> left, start );
        delete_function( current -> right, start );
        delete current;
    }
}
int function::parenthesis( char ch )
{
    if ( ch == '(' )
    {
        total_paren++;
        return 1;
    }
    else if ( ch == ')' )
    {
        --total_paren;
        return 1;
    }
    else
        return 0;
}
int function::precedence( node *op1, char op2 )
{
    int flag = 1;
    if ( op1 -> paren < total_paren )
        flag = 0;
    else if ( op1 -> paren > total_paren )
        --op1 -> paren;
    else
    {
        if ( ( op1 -> info == '+' || op1 -> info == '-' ) &&
            ( op2 == '*' || op2 == '/' ) )
            flag = 0;
    }
    return flag;
}
void function::checkandadd( node *n )
{
    if ( n -> left == 0 )
    {
        float v = queue[ first++ ];
        if ( v < 100000 || v > 100005 )
        {
            constant *newnode = new constant;
            newnode -> value = v;
            newnode -> left = newnode -> right = 0;
```

```cpp
            newnode -> paren = total_paren;
            newnode -> operand = 1;
            n -> left = newnode;
        }
        else
        {
            variable *newnode = new variable;
            newnode -> index = ( int ) ( v - 100000 );
            newnode -> f = this;
            newnode -> left = newnode -> right = 0;
            newnode -> paren = total_paren;
            newnode -> operand = 1;
            n -> left = newnode;
        }
    }
    if ( n -> right == 0 )
    {
        float v = queue[ first++ ];
        if ( v < 100000 || v > 100005 )
        {
            constant *newnode = new constant;
            newnode -> value = v;
            newnode -> left = newnode -> right = 0;
            newnode -> paren = total_paren;
            newnode -> operand = 1;
            n -> right = newnode;
        }
        else
        {
            variable *newnode = new variable;
            newnode -> index = ( int ) ( v - 100000 );
            newnode -> f = this;
            newnode -> left = newnode -> right = 0;
            newnode -> paren = total_paren;
            newnode -> operand = 1;
            n -> right = newnode;
        }
    }
}
void function::add_operands( node *n )
{
    if ( root == 0 )
    {
        float v = queue[ first++ ];
        if ( v < 100000 || v > 100005 )
        {
            constant *newnode = new constant;
            newnode -> value = v;
            newnode -> left = newnode -> right = 0;
            newnode -> paren = total_paren;
            newnode -> operand = 1;
            root = newnode;
        }
        else
        {
            variable *newnode = new variable;
            newnode -> index = ( int ) ( v - 100000 );
            newnode -> f = this;
```

Listing 7.36
(continued)

```
            newnode -> left = newnode -> right = 0;
            newnode -> paren = total_paren;
            newnode -> operand = 1;
            root = newnode;
        }
    }
    else
    {
        if ( n != 0 && n -> operand == 0 )
        {
            node *temp = n;

            add_operands( temp -> left );
            checkandadd( temp );
            add_operands( temp -> right );
        }
    }
}

void function::add_operator( node *p, node *n, char ch )
{
    if ( n == 0 )
    {
        switch ( ch )
        {
            case '+' :
                root = new plus;
                root -> info = '+';
                break;
            case '-' :
                root = new minus;
                root -> info = '-';
                break;
            case '*' :
                root = new multiply;
                root -> info = '*';
                break;
            case '/' :
                root = new divide;
                root -> info = '/';
                break;
        }
        root -> paren = total_paren;
        root -> right = root -> left = 0;
        root -> operand = 0;
    }
    else
    {
        node *temp = n;

        if ( !precedence( temp, ch ) )
        {
            if ( temp -> right == 0 )
            {
                switch ( ch )
                {
                    case '+' :
                    {
```

```
            plus *q = new plus;
            q -> info = '+';
            q -> right = q -> left = 0;
            q -> paren = total_paren;
            q -> operand = 0;
            temp -> right = q;
            break;
        }
        case '-' :
        {
            minus *q = new minus;
            q -> info = '-';
            q -> right = q -> left = 0;
            q -> paren = total_paren;
            q -> operand = 0;
            temp -> right = q;
            break;
        }
        case '*' :
        {
            multiply *q = new multiply;
            q -> info = '*';
            q -> right = q -> left = 0;
            q -> paren = total_paren;
            q -> operand = 0;
            temp -> right = q;
            break;
        }
        case '/' :
        {
            divide *q = new divide;
            q -> info = '/';
            temp -> right = q;
            break;
        }
      }
    }
    else
    {
      p = temp;
      add_operator( p, temp -> right, ch );
    }
  }
  else
  {
    if ( p == 0 )
    {
      switch ( ch )
      {
        case '+' :
        {
          plus *r = new plus;
          r -> info = '+';
          r -> paren = total_paren;
          r -> left = temp;
          r -> right = 0;
          r -> operand = 0;
```

Listing 7.36
(continued)

```
            root = r;
            break;
        }
        case '-' :
        {
            minus *r = new minus;
            r -> info = '-';
            r -> paren = total_paren;
            r -> left = temp;
            r -> right = 0;
            r -> operand = 0;
            root = r;
            break;
        }
        case '*' :
        {
            multiply *r = new multiply;
            r -> info = '*';
            r -> paren = total_paren;
            r -> left = temp;
            r -> right = 0;
            r -> operand = 0;
            root = r;
            break;
        }
        case '/' :
        {
            divide *r = new divide;
            r -> info = '/';
            r -> paren = total_paren;
            r -> left = temp;
            r -> right = 0;
            r -> operand = 0;
            root = r;
            break;
        }
    }
}
else
{
    switch ( ch )
    {
        case '+' :
        {
            plus *r = new plus;
            r -> info = '+';
            r -> paren = total_paren;
            r -> left = temp;
            r -> right = 0;
            r -> operand = 0;
            p -> right = r;
            break;
        }
        case '-' :
        {
            minus *r = new minus;
            r -> info = '-';
```

```
                  r -> paren = total_paren;
                  r -> left = temp;
                  r -> right = 0;
                  r -> operand = 0;
                  p -> right = r;
                  break;
                }
                case '*' :
                {
                  multiply *r = new multiply;
                  r -> info = '*';
                  r -> paren = total_paren;
                  r -> left = temp;
                  r -> right = 0;
                  r -> operand = 0;
                  p -> right = r;
                  break;
                }
                case '/' :
                {
                  divide *r = new divide;
                  r -> info = '/';
                  r -> paren = total_paren;
                  r -> left = temp;
                  r -> right = 0;
                  r -> operand = 0;
                  p -> right = r;
                  break;
                }
              }
          }
        }
      }
    }
}

void function::build_tree( char* s )
{
    int var_num; // 0, 1, 2, 3, 4, or 5
    char numeral[ 20 ];
    int numeral_index = 0;

    // Add variables to sym_tab
    int index = 0;
    while ( s[ index ] != ':' )
    {
      if ( s[ index ] >= 'a' && s[ index ] <= 'z' )
        sym_tab.add_variable( s[ index ] );
      index++;
    }
    index++; // Position just past ':' character
    if ( valid( s ) )
    {
      char ch = s[ index ];
      while ( ch != '\0' )
      {
        if ( ch == ' ' )
          ch = s[ ++index ];
```

Listing 7.36
(continued)

```
        else if ( ch >= 'a' && ch <= 'z' ) // variable
        {
            // Determine the index number in symbol table
            var_num = sym_tab.get_index( ch );
            queue[ last++ ] = 100000 + var_num;
            ch = s[ ++index ];
        }
        else if ( parenthesis( ch ) )
            ch = s[ ++index ];
        else if ( ch == '*' || ch == '/' || ch == '+' ||
                ch == '-' )
        {
            add_operator( 0, root, ch );
            ch = s[ ++index ];
        }
        else // Must be the beginning of a numeric literal
        {
            while ( ( s[ index ] >= '0' && s[ index ] <= '9' ) ||
                    s[ index ] == '.' )
              numeral[ numeral_index++ ] = s[ index++ ];
            numeral[ numeral_index ] = '\0';
            numeral_index = 0;
            queue[ last++ ] = atof( numeral );
            ch = s[ index ];
        }
      }
      add_operands( root );
   }
}

float function::operator ()( float u = 0, float v = 0,
                             float w = 0, float x = 0,
                             float y = 0, float z = 0 )
{
  sym_tab.add_value( 0, u );
  sym_tab.add_value( 1, v );
  sym_tab.add_value( 2, w );
  sym_tab.add_value( 3, x );
  sym_tab.add_value( 4, y );
  sym_tab.add_value( 5, z );
  return root -> eval();
}

int function::valid( char* expr )
{
  state0 x0;
  state1 x1;
  state2 x2;
  state3 x3;
  state4 x4;
  state5 x5;
  state6 x6;
  state7 x7;
  state9 x9;

  strcpy( expression, expr ); // expression in state.h
  // Scan past the ':' character
  char ch = x0.get_char();
```

```
   while ( ch != ':' )
      ch = x0.get_char( );
   ch = x0.get_char( );
   int s = x0.transition( ch );
   while ( s != 8 && s != 10 )
   {
      if ( s == 1 )
      {
         ch = x1.get_char( );
         s = x1.transition( ch );
      }
      else if ( s == 2 )
      {
         ch = x2.get_char( );
         s = x2.transition( ch );
      }
      else if ( s == 3 )
      {
         ch = x3.get_char( );
         s = x3.transition( ch );
      }
      else if ( s == 4 )
      {
         ch = x4.get_char( );
         s = x4.transition( ch );
      }
      else if ( s == 5 )
      {
         ch = x5.get_char( );
         s = x5.transition( ch );
      }
      else if ( s == 6 )
      {
         ch = x6.get_char( );
         s = x6.transition( ch );
      }
      else if ( s == 7 )
      {
         ch = x7.get_char( );
         s = x7.transition( ch );
      }
      else if ( s == 9 )
      {
         ch = x9.get_char( );
         s = x9.transition( ch );
      }
   }
   if ( s == 10 ) return 0;
   else return 1;
}
```

```
// Interface to class symbol_table
// File symbol.h

class symbol_table
{
```

Listing 7.36
(continued)

```
        private:
          struct info
          {
            char var_name;
            float var_value;
          };
          info table[ 6 ];
          int table_index;
        public:
          symbol_table();
          void add_value( int index, float r );
          int get_index( char ch );
          void add_variable( char ch );
          float get_value( int index );
          void clear();
};
```

```
// Implementation of class symbol_table
// File symbol.cpp
#include "symbol.h"
symbol_table::symbol_table()
{
   for ( int i = 0; i < 6; i++ )
   {
     table[ i ].var_name = ' ';
     table[ i ].var_value = 0.0;
   }
   table_index = 0;
}
void symbol_table::clear()
{
   for ( int i = 0; i < 6; i++ )
   {
     table[ i ].var_name = ' ';
     table[ i ].var_value = 0.0;
   }
   table_index = 0;
}
void symbol_table::add_value( int index, float r )
{
   table[ index ].var_value = r;
}
int symbol_table::get_index( char ch )
{
   int index = 0;
   while ( table[ index++ ].var_name != ch )
     ;
   return ( index - 1 );
}
void symbol_table::add_variable( char ch )
{
```

```
    if ( table_index < 6 )
      table[ table_index++ ].var_name = ch;
    else
      printf( "\n%cCannot have more than 6 variables",
              '\07' );
}
float symbol_table::get_value( int index )
{
   return table[ index ].var_value;
}
```

```
// Finite-state machine class and derived classes
// File state.h
char expression[ 201 ];

const null = 0;

class state0
{  // The abstraction of a state in a finite-state machine
    private:
      static int index;
      // Index location in expression string.
      // This value is common to all state objects.

      static paren_count;
      // Cumulative number of left parentheses minus right parentheses.
      // This value is common to all state objects.

    public:
      state0() { index = 0; }

      int get_paren() { return paren_count; }

      void inc_paren() { paren_count++; }

      void dec_paren() { paren_count --; }

      char get_char();

      int transition( unsigned char ch );
      // For a particular set of allowable characters,
      // returns the next state.
};
char state0::get_char()
{
   while ( expression[ index ] == ' ' )
      index++;
   return ( expression[ index++ ] );
}
int state0::transition( unsigned char ch )
{
   if ( ch >= '0' && ch <= '9' ) return 4;
   else if ( ch == '+' || ch == '-' ) return 2;
   else if ( ch == '.' ) return 5;
   else if ( ( ch >= 'A' && ch <= 'Z' ) ||
             ( ch >= 'a' && ch <= 'z' ) )
      return 3;
```

Listing 7.36
(continued)

```
            else if ( ch == '(' )
            {
               inc_paren();
               return 1;
            }
            else return 10;
         }
         class state1 : public state0
         {
            public:
              int transition( unsigned char ch )
              {
                if ( ch >= '0' && ch <= '9' ) return 4;
                else if ( ch == '+' || ch == '-' ) return 2;
                else if ( ch == '(' )
                {
                   inc_paren();
                   return 1;
                }
                else if ( ch == '.' ) return 5;
                else if ( ( ch >= 'A' && ch <= 'Z' ) ||
                          ( ch >= 'a' && ch <= 'z' ) ) return 3;
                else return 10;
              }
         };
         class state2 : public state0
         {
            public:
              int transition( unsigned char ch )
              {
                if ( ch >= '0' && ch <= '9' ) return 4;
                else if ( ( ch >= 'A' && ch <= 'Z' ) ||
                          ( ch >= 'a' && ch <= 'z' ) ) return 3;
                else if ( ch == '(' )
                {
                   inc_paren();
                   return 1;
                }
                else if ( ch == '.' ) return 5;
                else return 10;
              }
         };
         class state3 : public state0
         {
            public:
              int transition( unsigned char ch )
              {
                if ( ch == '+' || ch == '-' || ch == '/' || ch == '*' )
                   return 7;
                else if ( ch == ')' && get_paren() > 0 )
                {
                   dec_paren();
                   return 3;
                }
                else if ( ch == null && get_paren() == 0 ) return 8;
                else return 10;
              }
         };
```

```
class state4 : public state0
{

  public:
    int transition( unsigned char ch )
    {

      if ( ch >= '0' && ch <= '9' ) return 4;
      else if ( ch == ')' && get_paren() > 0 )
      {
        dec_paren();
        return 9;
      }
      else if ( ch == '+' || ch == '-' || ch == '/' || ch == '*' )
        return 7;
      else if ( ch == '.' ) return 6;
      else if ( ch == null && get_paren() == 0 ) return 8;
      else return 10;
    }
};
class state5 : public state0
{

  public:
    int transition( unsigned char ch )
    {
      if ( ch >= '0' && ch <= '9' ) return 6;
      else return 10;
    }
};
class state6 : public state0
{

  public:
    int transition( unsigned char ch )
    {
      if ( ch >= '0' && ch <= '9' ) return 6;
      else if ( ch == '+' || ch == '-' || ch == '/' || ch == '*' )
        return 7;
      else if ( ch == ')' )
      {
        dec_paren();
        return 9;
      }
      else if ( ( ch >= 'A' && ch <= 'Z' ) ||
              ( ch >= 'a' && ch <= 'z' ) ) return 7;
      else if ( ch == null && get_paren() == 0 ) return 8;
      else return 10;
    }
};
class state7 : public state0
{

  public:
    int transition( unsigned char ch )
    {
      if ( ch == '(' )
      {
        inc_paren();
        return 1;
      }
```

Listing 7.36
(continued)

```
                              else if ( ( ch >= 'A' && ch <= 'Z' ) ||
                                        ( ch >= 'a' && ch <= 'z' ) ) return 3;
                              else if ( ch >= '0' && ch <= '9' ) return 4;
                              else if ( ch == '.' ) return 5;
                              else return 10;
                    }
          };
          class state9 : public state0
          {
              public:
                int transition( unsigned char ch )
                {
                    if ( ch == '+' || ch == '-' || ch == '/' || ch == '*' )
                      return 7;
                    else if ( ch == ')' )
                    {
                       dec_paren();
                       return 9;
                    }
                    else if ( ch == null && get_paren() == 0 ) return 8;
                    else return 10;
                }
          };
```

Exercises

7.1 Redesign and reimplement the spelling checker of Section 7.1 in detail.

7.2 Redesign and reimplement the bank teller discrete event simulation of Section 7.2 in detail.

7.3 Redesign and reimplement the interactive function evaluator of Section 7.3 in detail.

7.4 Develop a complete case study of your own choice that illustrates the major features of object-oriented programming.

Index

(Page numbers given in **boldface** type indicate a definition; numbers in *italic* indicate a table.)